The Hayocks

Other books by Alex McLatchie:

Mining and Quarrying in Stevenston
Kerelaw House
Last Orders - the History of Pubs and Clubs in Stevenston
Black Friday - the Auchenharvie Pit Disaster
Powderkeg - a Study of the 1913 Strike in Nobel's Factory at Ardeer

The Hayocks

Its History and Development

Alex McLatchie

carn

First Published in Great Britain, 2025.

ISBN – 978 1 911043 29 4

Published by Carn Publishing Ltd.,
Lochnoran House,
Auchinleck,
Ayrshire, KA18 3JW.

www.carnpublishing.com

Printed by Bell & Bain Ltd.,
Glasgow, G46 7UQ.

Contents

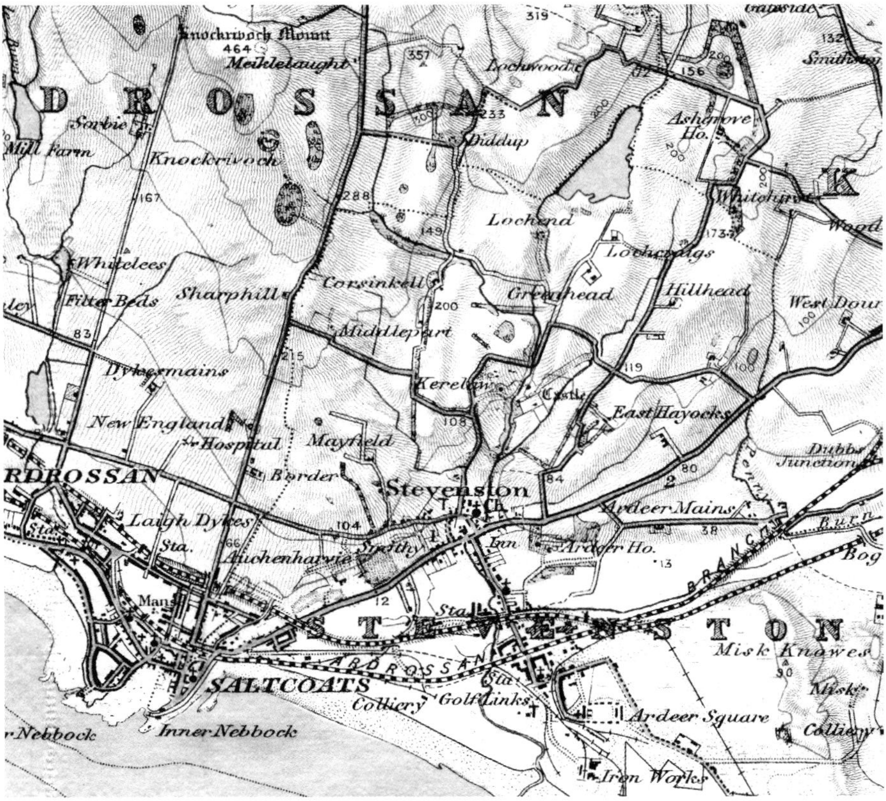

Map 1: Stevenston area from Ordnance Survey One Inch map of 1911.

List of Illustrations

Photographs

Tables

Maps

Sketch Maps

Sketch Plan

Plans

Sketch

Figure

Diagram

Introduction

The naming of the Hayocks is associated with the existence of Hayocks farm. The origins of the names of Ardeer or Stevenston itself, have never been in dispute or caused any controversy. This situation unfortunately does not apply to the term 'Hayocks.' It is generally accepted that the place-name is derived from the Old English (Anglo-Saxon) words 'heah' meaning high and 'ac' meaning oak.[1] This suggests that the name may have originally referred to a high place where oak trees grew. The earliest recorded version of the term 'Haiauches' occurred in the twelfth century and this was later anglicized to Hayocks.

The area under examination has traditionally been simply called the 'Hayocks', and I will adopt this term throughout the study. It never has been labelled a scheme, estate, or neighbourhood.

The principal purpose of this publication is to plug a yawning gap in the availability of local history literature pertaining to the Hayocks and the part it has played in the development of Stevenston. Notable by its absence, is the inclusion of the contribution made by the Hayocks during the past century to the expansion, shape, and character of the town. Prior to the publication of this book in 2025, no coherent, detailed account of the Hayocks and its development had been undertaken, and I hope this account goes some way to redressing the existing imbalance when the history of Stevenston is considered.

When undertaking an in-depth study of a particular area, the initial difficulty lies in the determination of its boundaries. The parameters must be easily recognisable prominent features which collectively provide a simple geometric shape (see Diagram 1). The outline of my Hayocks study area will undoubtedly prove controversial to some readers, as the decision is subjective in nature. I have incorporated the area lying to the north of Castlehill Road and Hillhead Road into the study sector as this landward area has traditionally been considered part of the Hayocks with its own diverse and fascinating history stretching back centuries.

The expansion of Stevenston, caused largely through the development of the Hayocks, was due to the increased demand for housing. The requirement for additional house building in the town was accelerated in the mid-1930s by two factors.

---

1 Mills, A.D. *A Dictionary of British Place-Names.*

Firstly, migration from out-with the area into the town. This movement was instigated by the Nobel's Explosives Company and their rationalisation plans. Nine of their factories, in various parts of the country, were relocated to Ardeer. One of the largest closures occurred in the Falkirk area in 1933 with the demise of detonator production. The workforce was encouraged to move to Stevenston with the promise of long-term employment and modern, subsidised housing. Imperial Chemical Industries (I.C.I.) in conjunction with Ayr County Council started this house building programme in 1935. Within a matter of months, houses were occupied in McGregor Avenue, Wallace Avenue, and the bottom end of Hayocks Road – such was the origin of the Hayocks.

Secondly, internal mobility within the town. One of the largest employers in Stevenston was the Merry and Cunningham owned Stevenston Iron Works located in the Ardeer part of the town, until its liquidation in 1931. It was razed to the ground four years later. Many of its workers were housed in the company-owned Ardeer Square (Auld Square) which consisted of 129 houses. Although these properties were largely derelict, they were not demolished until 1946. This limited redevelopment resulted in the movement of many families to new, lower density, higher quality housing in the Hayocks.

Collecting and recording factual information for those who follow in our footsteps is crucial, if only to allow the next generation to appreciate, and hopefully understand, the myriad social, economic, and political forces which have forged their time and place in history. The research on each topic was comprehensive, but not exhaustive, thereby providing the possibility for more extensive investigative work in the future.

I certainly acknowledge the author to be simply an enthusiastic amateur recorder motivated by a desire to chronicle local historical events. There will be mistakes in this account, as the book is based in part on interviews with a number of knowledgeable individuals, and although every effort was made to corroborate their statements, some discrepancies may surface. If I may not always have recorded the truth, I have not written what I know to be false. Therefore, I would welcome any additions, corrections, or clarifications to the content.

Alex McLatchie
Stevenston

1
The Study Area and Boundaries

The first task in undertaking any study with a spatial aspect is to delineate the boundaries within which the investigation will take place.

The topological map below provides a very simple illustration of my Hayocks study area together with the four selected boundaries.

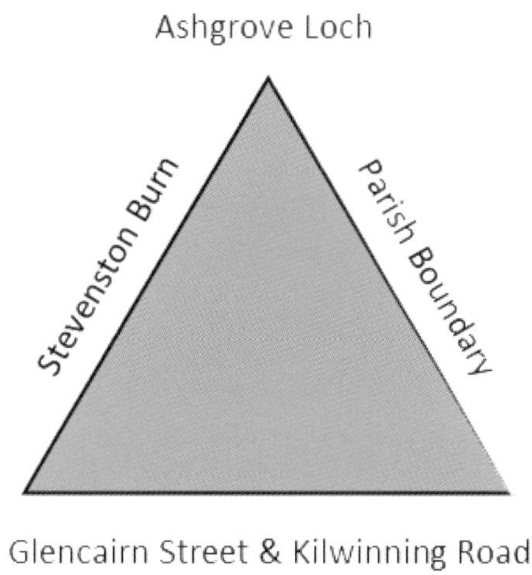

Diagram 1. Topological Map Signifying the Outline of the Hayocks.

I have selected these boundaries for the sake of simplicity. The base of the pyramid is the A738 which incorporates a section of both Glencairn Street and Kilwinning Road. This line separates the northern and southern parts of the town. The western margin of the Hayocks is the Stevenston Burn running from its source in Ashgrove Loch to the tunnels under Glencairn Street. The northern apex is Ashgrove Loch which is included within the study area as the site of a crannog and the northern extremity of the Stevenston parish boundary. The parish boundary 'meanders' its way northwards marking its border with the adjoining Kilwinning parish. Some explanatory detail on each feature would be useful.

Glencairn Street along with Kilwinning Road forms the southern boundary of the Hayocks study area. The street itself – or the by-pass - as it was commonly called, was officially opened for traffic on 20 October

1. Glencairn Street Looking West.

1926. It was the first by-pass road to be built in north Ayrshire and was 1.6 kilometres long and 8.5 metres wide from kerb to kerb (See Photograph 1).

The opening ceremony took place at the point where the new road joined Kilwinning Road. The coloured ribbon was cut, in the presence of a large gathering of guests, by Mr Curtis Gray, the chief official of the Ministry of Transport in Scotland, using a pair of 'souvenir' scissors supplied by Mr John Bannatyne from Irvine, the principal contractor. The formalities were directed by Mr William Gray, County Councillor for West Kilbride, and convenor of the Unemployment Works Committee of the Northern District Committee.

The first vehicle to use the new road was the official car of Mr R. McDonald, District Road Surveyor. The undertaking was financed by the Northern District Committee and the expenditure was supplemented considerably by grants from the Ministry of Transport. The cost of the entire venture expanded due to the necessity to include two expensive culverts under the road. The larger of the two tunnels accommodated the Stevenston Burn, while the other provided a channel for the Quarrel Burn. As a bonus, permission had been granted for the erection of an up-to-date garage where the new road started – opposite the Ardeer Estate gates (See Photograph 2).

After the completion of the official business, the company adjourned to the Kilmeny Hotel in Ardrossan for lunch. Following the meal, Mr William Gray was presented with a silver cigarette box by the contractor and engineer as a souvenir of the occasion. Both Mr R. McDonald, District Road Surveyor, and Mr George McGregor, Ardchoille, Resident

2. Junction of Glencairn Street and Townhead Street with 'Blue Star' Garage.

Engineer, along with Mr John Bannatyne, contractor, were credited with the successful fruition of the scheme. Praise was also directed towards Col. McAlester, Stewarton, Chairman of the District Committee, Mr George Sinclair, Stevenston, Ex-Chairman, and Mr William Gray, West Kilbride, Convenor of the Works Committee, for the keen interest they had voluntarily displayed in the scheme, which as the surveyor had remarked at the luncheon, made great 'in-roads' on their time.

This road building project was conceived with a number of objectives in mind. Firstly, action was needed to relieve the traffic congestion in Main Street, thereby improving road safety for pedestrians. Secondly, meeting the increasing needs of fast-moving motor vehicles, and thirdly, the alleviation of distress caused by unemployment. The first two goals were long-term in nature, whereas the third was a short-term fix to diminish the economic hardship being experienced by many families in the area.

Although the road was widely welcomed by the residents in the town, this viewpoint was not universal. Some ratepayers regarded the other option on the table, namely, the widening of Townhead and Boglemart Streets to be preferable. This action would have resulted in the removal of old dilapidated houses which were a menace to pedestrians owing to the narrowness of the two streets.

The construction of the road also resulted in the loss of some of the most productive agricultural land in the district.

Another complaint involved the subsequent spoilation of an area considered to be a picturesque retreat, namely, the Mill Dam and the ground lying at the side of the High Kirk. The new road cut across this beauty spot, and many locals demanded the inclusion of a covered way beneath the road to preserve what was considered as a 'right of way.'

The building of the by-pass acted as a catalyst for the construction of much needed housing in the shape of Glencairn Street. The street was adjacent to the southern boundary of Kerelaw Estate, and the establishment of the new road in 1926 provided a quicker and more convenient access to the mansion house, and the estate grounds which included the ruins of the castle.

STEVENSTON PARISH BOUNDARY

During the Medieval period, residences which housed lords and other prominent vassals were surrounded by a defined area of jurisdiction and were called 'vills'. Once a vill had been established there was around it a specified area of land which came under the authority of the lord who held the vill. The establishment of parishes was based on the existence of vills. Some vills bore the new proprietors name with the suffix 'ton' affixed. An example would be Stevenston, seen in 'villa Stephani.'

A parish was an area under the jurisdiction of a church and was usually used for administrative purposes. A parish and barony very often encompassed the same area, but there were exceptions. An example of this situation arose some time before the Reformation, c. 1517, when locally,

3. Source of Stevenston Burn within Ashgrove Loch.

the parish and barony were not identical. The barony incorporated the parish boundary, plus the lands of Crosbie in West Kilbride and the lands of Gill and Munnoch in Dalry. Therefore, the barony and parish did not always cover the same area.

Physically many parish boundaries followed watercourses or watersheds, and within the Study Area this boundary stretches from Muirside (National Grid Reference 284428) following the Penny Burn northwards for almost one kilometre before turning towards the north-west, skirting Conns Corner Plantation, before reaching Ashgrove Loch, half-way down its eastern side, near the site of the crannog (NGR 276443).

STEVENSTON BURN

From its source at the south west corner of Ashgrove Loch (NGR 271441 - see Photograph 3), the burn flows in a southerly direction through the Loch Canal. On entering Ardeer Golf Course, the burn meanders in a canalised channel, skirting the eastern edge of the now demolished Lochend farm. The burn is channelled under the A78 by-pass and on re-emerging, hits the confluence with its principal tributary, the Glen Burn. This wider, more prominent watercourse continues southwards through Kerelaw Glen before exiting the Study Area through a tunnel under Glencairn Street where it is joined in the Holm Green by the Quarrel Burn. Throughout its course, several small streams contribute to its discharge, and in its upper course the water quality is good.

2
The Old Estates

HAYOCKS FARM AND HOUSE

This chapter covers the complex backgrounds to Hayocks and Hullerhirst, the two estates entirely within the study area. Two further estates – Kerelaw and Ardeer – also contribute a significant percentage of the land area, but have been omitted because their mansion houses were situated outside my chosen boundaries.

In the sixteenth and seventeenth centuries the main cart-track linking the landward farms to the village of Stevenston and the principal arterial coastal track, ran from Ashgrove southwards by-passing Hillhead and Hayocks farms. These farms along with others in the area, including Castlehill, Hawkhill, and Lochcraigs, were the first sites of human habitation. In all probability, their origins were associated with the presence of the Benedictine order of monks in Kilwinning Abbey. The physical appearance of such early farms is impossible to accurately describe, but turf or clay walls, thatched roofs, and earthen floors formed the basic outline. Only later did stone become a building material.

A few historical documents, as well as old maps, are useful in dating the existence of these local farms. Timothy Pont's map from c. 1600 clearly shows Hilrust (Hullerhirst); nearby Lochwood farm is shown in Herman Moll's 1701 map; Lochend farm in the map produced by Ainslie in 1783; and Hayocks is clearly marked in Roy's *Military Survey* of 1747-1755. Castlehill farm was inhabited by John and Alex Pitcon, John Service, and Allan and Marion Cunninghame in 1560. In the same year, Middle, Over, and Nether Hullerhirst had James Chalmers and John Service Jnr as residents and in 1618, Hew Campbell is noted in Pont's *Cunningham Topographised* as living in Hullerhirst.

The original foundation date for such local farms is impossible to determine, but there is no disputing that they predate the advent of the local mansion houses.

From the 1750s, new wealth from trade, particularly overseas enterprises, resulted in an acceleration in the purchase of estates and in the construction of handsome, classically-detailed houses. The overwhelming majority of such properties had a simple rectangular box shape with hipped roofs and advanced pedimented centres. Most of these country houses included several buildings associated with the production of food, and walled-gardens were de rigueur, for example Kerelaw, Ashgrove, and Hayocks houses. The 'boom-time' for the construction of mansions in Ayrshire covered the second half of the eighteenth century, and a number of local houses fall into this timescale. Kerelaw House – c. 1778; Hullerhirst – c. 1770; Hayocks House – c. 1800; and Ashgrove – pre c. 1775. Seabank was an earlier feature – c. 1708.

The local mansion houses expanded over the years acquiring extensions in keeping with the new styles (for instance Hullerhirst may well have acquired its pediment at a later date), and Hayocks House had several major alterations including the construction of an entire wing on its west side and a single storey extension on its east side.

On examining Map 2, we discover that the term Hayocks covered a surprisingly large number of buildings, but as stated previously, East Hayocks farm existed before Hayocks House.

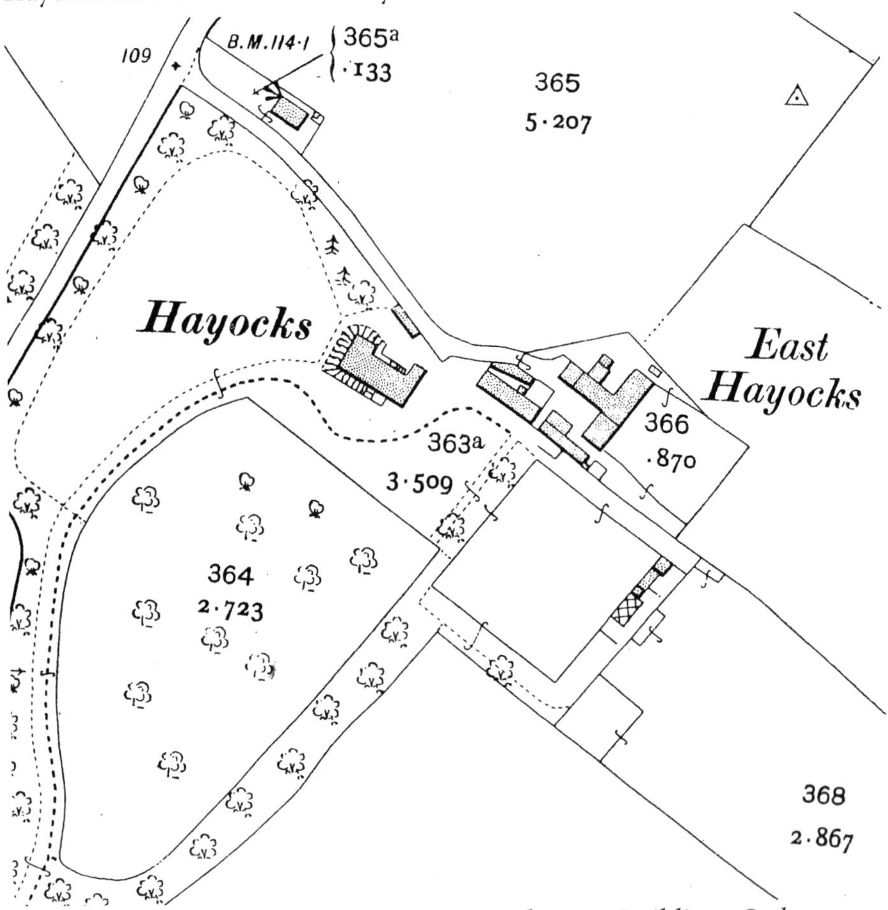

Map 2. Hayocks House and Associated Estate Buildings. Ordnance Survey 1910.

To disentangle the complicated history of the Muir family at Hayocks we need to begin with John Lorimer Muir. This individual was born on the Hayocks estate in 1735 and married Janet Hamilton in 1751. Two of their children were Samuel who was born in 1752 and James four years later in 1756. Subsequently, Samuel married Sibilla (Sybylla) Glen from Kilwinning parish who was five years younger. Their wedding occurred in 1777, the union producing John in 1783 and Janet a year later, as well as Alexander, James, and Jane.

To simplify the situation, the branch of the Muir family who built and owned the mansion house springs from John (born in 1783) who I will label John I. This particular John became a merchant and by the generally accepted construction date of 1810 for the mansion, could possibly have accrued enough wealth to allow him to finance the building of his dream home (possibly with some help from his father, Samuel). The architect of the mansion house remains undocumented.

John I largely remained at Hayocks with his siblings and became a respected landowner with a prominent profile in the local community. He became a Justice of the Peace, and in 1839 was appointed as a Committee Member of the prestigious Ancient Society of Kilwinning Archers.

A pivotal point in the history of the mansion house arose in March 1858 with the death of the unmarried John Muir Esq., aged seventy-five. He died in Hayocks House from paraplegia (injury to the nervous system). John's sister, Mrs Janet Smith, inherited the property, but died a year later. A notice appeared in the *Glasgow Herald* in October 1859 advertising the sale by public roup of the household furniture and plenishing of Hayocks House. In addition to a huge selection of household items which included dining and drawing room tables and chairs, sofas, carpets, piano and stool, silver plated articles, pictures, bedroom furniture, china, crystal, and stoneware, three hundred volumes of books, and kitchen utensils, there was also a small carriage, pony, and harness. Finally, there were milch cows, various farming implements and dairy utensils. The sale was organised by the Trustees of Mrs Smith.

The estate which was 10.5 hectares in size, was sold on 29 February 1860 to Gavin Fullarton of Kerelaw, principally on account of two fields belonging to Hayocks, which lay close to Kerelaw and were separated from the remainder of Hayocks by the road leading to Hullerhirst and Ashgrove.

The mansion house contained a dining room, drawing room, library, four bedrooms, kitchen, servant's room, pantry, and wine cellar; the Offices consisted of stable, coach house, byre, and milk house; while the Garden which extended to 0.2 hectares was enclosed with a substantial stone wall being well-stocked with an excellent assortment of fruit trees and bushes (See Photograph 4). The property was sold by Messrs. Rodger,

4. Showing the One Remaining Wall of Hayocks Old Orchard/Garden.

McInnes, and Macfarlane, Writers in Paisley, for an upset price (reserve price) of £3,000.

Almost immediately, Mr Fullarton attempted to let the property. His wish was granted when Lieutenant Colonel Frederick Neil Edmonstone became the new tenant. This influential and distinguished figure from the well-connected Edmonstone family served in the Bengal Cavalry. He was the son of Sir Charles Edmonstone, Baronet, of Duntreath and Colzium, who although born in Greenwich (in 1764), was the Member of Parliament for Dumbarton. Frederick's mother was Louisa Hotham. Lieutenant Colonel Edmonstone was born on 7 September 1818 and died on 14 August 1865.

On 17 March 1863, Frederick married Henrietta Jane Smith-Neill in Ardeer House. Both Frederick and Henrietta lived in Ardeer House at the time along with other members of the Smith-Neill family. The exact date of their occupation of Hayocks House in unknown, but a report in the *Ardrossan and Saltcoats Herald* dated 15 August 1863 states, 'At Hayocks House, near Stevenston, Gavin Fullarton Esq. of Kerelaw, is making extensive alterations, prior to it being occupied by Col. Edmonstone. The building and joiner work are only in progress, but judging from the plans the old square elevation of the house will be much improved with the addition of extensions at both sides of the building. The extra accommodation will be considerable, resulting in a house with twenty rooms.' The improvements were made from plans supplied by Mr William A. Railton (1820-1902), architect and civil engineer, Kilmarnock. He had been responsible for the erection of several well-known buildings in the locality, including Ardrossan Town Hall in Princes Street in 1858-59. Mr Railton was also extremely helpful to MacGibbon & Ross in measuring and sketching the nearby Kerelaw Doocot (dated 1775).

Unfortunately, Frederick's residency at the renamed 'Hayocks Lodge' was truncated due to his death on 14 August 1865 from heart disease, aged only forty-six years. His widow was still occupying Hayocks Lodge in 1875, but shortly afterwards moved to Corraith House, near Symington. Henrietta, who was the daughter of Lieutenant Colonel William Smith-Neill and Caroline Smith-Neill (nee Spillers), eventually died at Corraith on 28 February 1887, aged 69 years.

After the death of Gavin Fullarton in 1876, Hayocks fell into the ownership of Gavin's great nephew, Captain Fullarton James, Chief Constable of the Northumberland Police Force. After the tenancy of the Lodge was vacated by Henrietta she was replaced by a number of individuals. In 1881, the tenant was a merchant from Glasgow called Robert Knox, with his wife, four daughters and four servants. Ten years later, the tenancy was in the hands of a thirty-one-year-old merchant from Lanark with South American business connections called William Scott. He was still resident in the house in 1895, but by 1898 had been replaced by Mrs Elizabeth Taylor or Grant, widow, and her son George Andrew Grant (he became a Justice of the Peace in May 1900). During the family tenancy, on 18 December 1904, the mansion stables were destroyed by fire causing £500 worth of damage. The Grants occupied the house up until 1912. Following the Grant's occupancy, the tenancy was vacant for a few years.

On 12 March 1919, the house was purchased from James Campbell (who had in February bought the entire Kerelaw Estate from the trustees of the late Gavin Fullarton) by Alexander McGregor – the owner of Ardeer Foundry – for the sum of £3,150. Mr McGregor changed the name of the House to 'Ardchoille.' This is a Gaelic word and was the slogan or the war-cry of the Clan MacGregor, meaning 'high wood', and referred to a secret clan meeting place.

On his purchase of the property, Alexander McGregor was involved in the construction of additional sections and alterations to Ardchoille. These additions were carried out to the designs of Fryers and Penman, a well-known local architectural practice based in Largs. Some of their other activities included the Springvale Infectious Diseases Hospital in Saltcoats in 1899; the Post Office in West Kilbride in 1911; and the enlargement to the house and construction of the West Lodge at Knock Castle, Largs in 1904. Mr McGregor moved into Ardchoille approximately a year after its purchase.

Alexander McGregor was born in 1860 and died on 17 March 1928, aged 68. He purchased the mansion house and some of the fields at Hayocks, extending to 4.7 hectares, from James Campbell on 22 March 1919 for the sum of £3,150. The area in question was bound on the north west and north by the road leading to Hullerhirst. He became a well-known and respected landowner in the town, and participated in many local organisations. In March 1905, Alexander was appointed as a local justice, and this was followed in 1906 with his election onto Stevenston School Board. The following year saw him gain membership of Stevenston Parish Council. Mr McGregor's most prominent position however was as the elected County Councillor for Stevenston and Ardrossan North between December 1922 up to his death in 1928. Although his public and community-based activities were laudable and appreciated, his one historically significant action was to alter the title of his newly acquired Hayocks House or Lodge to Ardchoille.

Mr McGregor's wealth resulted from his ownership of Ardeer Foundry. He was an iron founder and along with his brother, George, who was a cashier, were directors in the company. The business, which was established in 1854, flourished, and on 16 May 1905, incorporated the liquidated Ayrshire Foundry Company Ltd.

On 14 April 1899 it was recorded in the Division of the General Register of Sasines applicable to the County of Ayr, that Patrick Warner agreed a feu contract with the Ayrshire Foundry Company Ltd for a piece of Ardeer Estate measuring 0.3 hectares at the corner of Portland Place and New Street. In August 1906 the company conveyed the plot of land to the Public House Trust (Glasgow District) Ltd for £100, on behalf of a company to be formed and styled the Ayrshire Public House Trust Ltd. The building which resulted from this arrangement became the iconic Ayrshire Houses of Refreshment or Trust Public House.

Alexander (1860-1928) and George (1869-1957) were the sons of George McGregor and Isabella and came from Motherwell. The exact date of their relocation to Stevenston/Saltcoats is unknown, but we have records of George living with his parents in Motherwell in 1891, and being presented with a marble clock and side ornaments by the employees at Ardeer Foundry to mark his marriage. This event occurred in March 1898. This timeline is reinforced by the 1901 Census which places George, his wife, Emily, and daughter, Jane, at 'Gleniffer', Argyll Road, Saltcoats.

Although Alexander only occupied Ardchoille for eight years, there is no suggestion that his brother, George, moved to the house after his death in

1928. In fact, Alexander's widow, Mary Wingfield Lindsay, moved shortly afterwards to South Crescent, Ardrossan, with their daughter. George was resident at 'Red Gables' in Ardrossan in 1937.

Ardchoille was occupied in 1931 by Willam L. McGregor, Alexander's son. The proprietors were the Trustees of the late Alexander McGregor per W. L. McGregor. This situation existed through to 1947 when the property was purchased by Samuel J. Boyd.

In 1955, the foundry was sold to Messrs Brown & Company, having been run (after the retirement of George) by Alexander's youngest son and nephew of George, W. L. McGregor.

Hayocks House/Ardchoille was a two-storey building placed on a raised basement. It had three flat panelled pilasters running the full height of the building, dividing the façade into two unequal sections. Four sash windows decorated the upper floor, and the entire building was lime-washed stucco. The porch was positioned at the top of a flight of steps, and had two Ionic columns. On the right of the main building there was a single storey extension. It had a canted bay window with a parapet above on which was sited a terminal urn finial. The roof was piended and slated, supporting twenty chimneys in three clusters. Whether this addition was constructed in 1863 by Gavin Fullarton or around 1919 by Alexander McGregor is unclear.

Another significant internal modification occurred in 1966 when Scottish & Newcastle Brewers Ltd received approval from the council to carry out alterations. The practising architects were James Houston & Son, Kilbirnie, and W. J. King, Stevenston. At this time the licensee, W. Thornley, described the hotel as 'a large building with separate bedrooms, providing accommodation, meals and facilities for paying guests.'

5. Exhibits the various external features mentioned above. In addition, it shows Hayocks farm steading on the extreme right.

Table 1. List of Owners and Tenants of Ardchoille Hotel 1947-1990.

DATE	PROPRIETOR	TENANT
1947	Samuel J. Boyd	Samuel J. Boyd
1951	Alexander J. Watt	Alexander J. Watt
1960	Robert Paterson	Robert Paterson
1961	A.McEvoy Ltd	----------
1964 - 1990	Scottish & Newcastle Brewers Ltd	1967 – Alex Reid and wife Ellen. 1972-78 – Joe Barraclough. 1978 – Walter Catto (W. Catto (Hotels) Ltd. Manager – Robert Pendleton.
1990	Mr Geeta Singh (C.S. Greyhound Company Ltd).	--------------

Hotel Closed in March 1990.

NOTE - Ardchoille Hotel was listed on 26 February 1980 by Historic Scotland as a Category C Listed Building.

It is helpful to take the other side of the Muir family back to James (born in 1756) – Samuel's younger brother. James married Mary Small from Saltcoats in 1785 and soon afterwards in 1786 John II was born (James was described as a farmer in Hayocks on his son's baptism document). John II married Agnes Muir (this was her maiden name) from Drakemire, Dalry, in September 1816, probably at the Hayocks. Agnes was the only daughter of William Muir of Drakemire and his wife Jean Ker of Auchingree farm, near Beith.

One interesting feature related to James Muir was the fact that he was an antiburgher and member of the Kilwinning Original Secession Church (OSC). In the 1730s there was a growing acceptance of revived patronage whereby the leading landowner of the parish was again influential in the appointment of a new minister. At the same time, an increasing number of people were becoming disaffected towards the Established Church. A minister, the redoubtable Ebineezer Erskine, protested against this increasing trend, and he along with three associates were deposed by the General Assembly in 1740. This date marks the beginning of the Secession. The Secession was strong in Kilwinning, and by the end of the century it was as popular as the established church itself and was a permanent feature. The Kilwinning Secession Congregation quickly became known throughout the country, and they built their first church in 1759.

In 1793, some Stevenston and Saltcoats members disjoined themselves to form a separate group, eventually in 1801 putting up a building in Wellpark Road, Saltcoats. This was known locally for a time as the Pea Doo Kirk. However, the Muir family in Hayocks remained part of the Kilwinning congregation.

With the construction of the mansion house around 1810, the estate was effectively split into two parts. John I became the laird and exhibited his newly found social status through his occupation of his commodious and stately property. The background to his impressive financial acumen is unknown, but as a merchant he was obviously dealing in profitable commodities. This part of the estate was subsequently known as Wester Hayocks to distinguish it from East Hayocks farm.

John II continued to work the farm until his emigration to Canada in 1834. After this date the situation of the farm becomes blurred. The available documentation indicates that two of John II's brothers – Alexander and William – were working East Hayocks farm, certainly between 1850 and 1857. They are recorded as co-owners although Alex was the occupier. By 1861, Alex had retired but continued to occupy the property with his sister Janet Muir and servant Ann McAllister. Two other brothers of John II were James and Samuel and they were actively involved as farming tenants from the early 1840s at the neighbouring Hillhead farm. With the death of Samuel Muir on 21 January 1874, all connection between the Muir family and Hillhead farm disappears. Although resident at Hillhead farm, Samuel somewhere along the line must have inherited East Hayocks farm, as his wife, Janet McAllister, is recorded as being the proprietor of the 'farm, farmhouse, and offices' from 1874 right through to 1901. Census forms and valuation rolls recorded East Hayocks farm as 'farm, farmhouse, and offices,' again indicating the large number of buildings on the estate (See Map 2).

Behind the mansion house was Hayocks farmhouse, which from around 1880 was occupied by Finlay Kerr, a carrier, who traded in the 1870s and 1880s between Stevenston and Ardrossan. In 1901/1902 the farm, farmhouse and offices were owned and occupied by Janet McAllister or Muir (widow) and Ann Muir. A year later, William Muirhead had become the partial owner of the farm along with the heir of the late Samuel Muir. John Kerr was the practising farmer. By 1904, Mr Muirhead had become the sole proprietor and resident of the farm, and he remained in this position until his death at East Hayocks farm in December 1921. His successors were Mary and William Muirhead, but they were in turn replaced in 1925 by David Cleland. The tenants and occupiers were Archibald and James Cleland (tomato houses had been added to the farm lay-out). From this date the farm continued to be operated by the Cleland family up to at least 1960. David (probably the father) died in the 1930s, leaving the two sons to gradually expand the business. By 1943, Archibald and James owned the farm, most of the land, two houses, a tomato house, market garden, and large shed. Archibald Cleland died in 1956, and was buried in Hawkhill Cemetery, but the market garden continued to be operated by his brother, James, and his wife, Jean.

Over the years, a number of buildings on the estate were occupied by employees of the owners. These included coachmen Hugh Newell (1861) and Thomas McDonald (1901- 1905); ploughmen Miller Paton (1861) and Samuel Boyd (1861); gardeners William Kennedy (1901), Thomas Miller (1905-1910), Alex Webster (1922), James Lockerbie (1925 – 1928), John Harvie (1943), John Boyd (1948), and Thomas Clark (1950); groom Alex Coig (1901); chauffeurs Alfred Denny (1910), William Glen (1922- 1925), Alexander Wilson (1928 - 1950), and William Wilson (1943).

The workers listed above, with their particular skills, were considered essential to the smooth running of the estate and lived with their families in some of the smaller properties.

After the death of James on 23 February 1832, John II and Agnes, accompanied by ten of their eleven children, emigrated to Canada (1834). The biographies of two of the grandsons of James Muir and Mary Small[1] state that their grandfather left the estate to his eldest son, John II. John did not want the estate as he had already visited North America and felt there were better opportunities for his family in Canada. The two biographers, Alexander and William Muir, suggest that John II gave the estate to his brothers but on the condition that his eldest son, James (born 28 August 1817) would inherit it from them. This obviously did not occur as James stayed in Canada and inherited his father's lands in Quebec. It is unknown if James gave up his right to inherit or if his uncles reneged on their word. It is distinctly possible that when John II emigrated to Canada in 1834 two of his brothers, Alexander and William took possession of East Hayocks farm. Both were occupying the farm in 1856.

In his youth Alexander Muir (one of the biographers) attended school in Irvine and assisted his father on the farm until he reached the age of thirteen when he left and 'went before the mast.' After he was discharged in London in 1836, he returned home to the Hayocks, but discovered his parents and the other ten children had emigrated to Canada two years previously (two years after the death of John's father). The emigration was possible after John accepted a sum of money from his brothers. On his

1 Adam, Graeme, Mercer. *Prominent Men of Canada*. Canadian Biographical Publishing Company. Toronto 1892.

6. A Simulated Image of Hayocks House from around 1860. Note the absence of the two storey wing on the left side and the single storey wing on the right.

arrival in Canada, John purchased the farm of Howick, fifty kilometres south of Montreal. Both parents died at Howick, John II in 1855 and Agnes in 1871. The seafaring Alex left Greenock for Quebec on the brig Corsair and was reunited with his family six weeks later. He subsequently became a Captain on the Great Lakes and created a boat-building and timber business in conjunction with his brother William in Port Dalhousie in Ontario.

It is surprising to discover that a humble farming family from Hayocks Estate made such a noticeable impact on the business community in Ontario, and are included in a publication which celebrates 'Prominent Men of Canada.'

HULLERHIRST
EARLY HISTORY

Hullerhirst House was the centre of a small estate consisting of little more than one farm, but with the potential for mineral exploitation.

Over the centuries, the name 'Hullerhirst' has had many modifications. On Pont's map of c. 1600 it is called Hilrust (the suffix 'rust' meaning roost). We also encounter the term 'Hilderhurst' and the vernacular 'Hulldruse.' The most recent derivation with the suffix 'Hirst' describes more accurately the site of the House (a barren, unproductive piece of ground, usually a hillock, knoll, or ridge).

The first significant mention of Hullerhirst was carried out by Timothy Pont. This surveyor and cartographer travelled throughout Scotland undertaking ground-breaking work which required determination, perseverance, and no little degree of skill.

The exact date when Pont visited Ayrshire for the mapping of 'Cuninghamia' has never been firmly established, but many experts have concluded the date to be around 1600. It is distinctly possible that he returned to Ayrshire around 1605 to allow him to assemble a list of towns and estates for his topographical account. Research into sixteenth century land owners in North Ayrshire confirms that Pont did stay in Cunningham between 1604 and 1608. Both Stevenston and Kilwinning are marked by symbols in 'Cuninghamia' but are not named.

When Pont visited the parish of Stevenston around 1600, he found it to consist of two parts, Stevenston-Campbell and Stevenston-Cunninghame. The Campbells had for their manor house, Ducathall, which he describes as 'Ye possession of George Campbell of Steeinstone, a pretty dwelling, well planted.'[2] Of this old mansion house there is today no vestige remaining. It seems, however, to have stood on the high ground, above where Ardeer House was sited. The old lands of Ducathall (Dovecothill, or Doucothall) included Hullerhirst, Hayocks, and Castlehill, all situated east of Kerelaw Castle. Sir George Campbell of Loudoun had a charter of the Sheriffship of Ayr from King James II, dated 16 May 1450. It is supposed that the Campbells of Stevenston-Campbell or Ducathall were derived from Hew, a younger son of Sir George.

Hullerhirst Estate was part of Ducathall, but it is imperative to remember that the Campbells of Hullerhirst and the Campbells of Ducathall were separate families.

When Hullerhirst became the residence of the Campbell family is unclear, but the name of Hew Campbell of Hullerhirst, (1575-1630) frequently appears in various pieces of documentation between 1613 and the date of his death in 1630. His name also occurs in the testament of Margaret Cowan of Little Dubbs. This woman was the wife of James Wilson and was living in Little Dubbs in 1603. Hew was also a curator in the testament of Ashinyards in 1613 and 1620, including as a witness in 1618 to the testament of Marion Fleming relict of James Cunynghame (Cunninghame) of Eschinzairdis (Ashgrove).[3] Another of his many duties and responsibilities was in the valuing of the teinds within the Presbytery

2 Pont, Timothy. *Cunningham Topographized.*

3 Paterson, James. *History of the County of Ayr; Genealogical Account of the Families of Ayrshire* Vol 2. Parish of Stevenston p448. 1852.

of Irvine where he was a Sub-Commissioner. J. Robertson claims that Hullerhirst was occupied by the Campbell family up to 1631.[4]

It is distinctly possible that Hew was born at Hullerhirst, but it remains a possibility that his birthplace could have been Loudoun as his father was Sir Hugh Campbell, 1st Lord Campbell of Loudoun. Hew married Jean Cunninghame (1587-1621) of Ashinyards, and the couple had six children. They were George, Janet, Jeane, Margaret, Marie, and James. James later became James of Garnock Campbell. He was born at Hullerhirst in 1605. Margaret Campbell is also mentioned in a record dated 1637.

Sir Robert Cunninghame was Physician to Charles II in Scotland, being appointed shortly after the King's coronation at Scone in 1651. He was also created a Baronet of Nova Scotia in 1673. He was a very wealthy individual and purchased back the Barony of Stevenston from the Earl of Eglinton in 1656, along with the lands of Kilbride and Stewarton. The barony he acquired at this time comprehended the entire parish, including the church lands of Stevenston, Ducathall, Bogend, Ardeer, Hullerhirst, Saltcoats-Campbell and the patronage of the parish church of Stevenston. He died in 1674 and the land passed through the male line to his daughter's cousin, Robert Cunninghame. This Robert was also a physician by profession but took a more active role in the coal and salt industries within the estate.

Robert and his son James were eventually obliged to alienate a greater part of his landed property in Stevenston. Kerelaw was sold to John Hamilton of Grange in 1685; Hullerhirst to William Kelso in 1707; Ducathall and the Lands of Ardeer to the Rev. Patrick Warner in 1708; and the lands of Townhead in Saltcoats, including those on which the town of Saltcoats stood to Lord Eglinton in 1724. It seems Robert retained the twenty-shilling land of Saltcoats-Campbell where he built Seabank House in 1708. He died on 10 July 1715 and was succeeded by his son James who died twenty years later.

THE KELSO FAMILY

The surname Kelso, is one of the earliest recorded names in Britain. There were several branches of the family, the main one being the Kelsos of Kelsoland in Largs.

For many years Hullerhirst was the seat of the Kelso family in Scotland. It was described by James Paterson as 'a handsome, modern, small mansion, occupying a pleasant and commanding situation, about a mile north-east of Stevenston.'[5]

---

4 Robertson, J. *Principal Families in Ayrshire, especially Cunninghame.* 1823. p128.

5 Paterson, James. *History of the County of Ayr; Genealogical Account of the Families of Ayrshire* Vol 2. Parish of Stevenston p448. 1852.

William Kelso sold Kelsoland in Largs to the Brisbanes in 1671. At this time the Kelsos were in serious debt and the Brisbanes, to whom they were related, agreed to pay-off their financial obligations if they acquired Kelsoland. The transaction in 1671 involved Mr James Schaw (Shaw) who on the death of his father-in-law assumed the name of Brisbane. Mr Schaw accordingly became James Brisbane of Brisbane. Around the same time, he disposed of his Bishoptoun estate in Renfrewshire. Subsequently, in 1695, the estate by virtue of a Crown Charter was erected into the barony of Brisbane.

The family home which the Brisbanes acquired in 1671 had been built by the Kelso family in 1636, and after the transaction between the two families in 1671 it is possible that the Kelsos relocated to the Borders.

It is widely publicized that William Kelso I purchased Hullerhirst c. 1707, but his son William II was born at Hullerhirst in 1695. This discrepancy could be explained by the fact that the family initially were tenants in Hullerhirst, becoming the proprietors c. 1707.

William Kelso I who acquired Hullerhirst in 1707 was a shipowner and was probably involved in the coal trade to Ireland. He married Mary Montgomerie of Broomlands, Irvine. Her family also had local shipping interests. William I was born c. 1662 and died in 1742, while Mary's life span lasted from 1664 to 1739.

William I had one son, also William II who married Dorothea Hunter - the fourth daughter of Patrick Hunter 22nd laird of Hunterston - in December 1741. Patrick's brother, Robert, who became the 23rd laird, had shipping contacts in Glasgow.

William II died in 1750 and his wife Dorothea (born in 1720 in West Kilbride) was remarried to Hugh Weir of Kirkhall, Ardrossan. William II and Dorothea had three children – William III who was born in 1745; Mary Kelso, and Patrick Kelso, born 1749. All three children were born at Hullerhirst.

In common with many west of Scotland landowners, William III and his brother Patrick were shipowners. It should be remembered that both brothers would have been less than ten years old on the death of their father, and it seems likely that their 'Uncle Robert' supported the Kelso family and underwrote their careers.

William III and his brother Patrick jointly owned the *Hunterston*, and their connection with the Hunter family and Hunterston would explain the ship's title. It is highly likely, although not documented, that they possessed several other vessels.

The *Hunterston* is listed in the Lloyd's Register in 1776 as being a single-decked brig rated at 110 tons. The vessel was registered in Glasgow and traded between Britain and North Carolina. It is more probable that the ship was built in one of the Greenock yards than on the upper Clyde. However, an alternative explanation is that the vessel was a colonial ship – built in America for trade to Britain. This possibility would fit with her documented trade route. The owners were recorded as 'W. Kelso & Co.' the master of the ship being Patrick Kelso. These facts establish the existence of a business relationship between the two brothers. The business between the two brothers didn't always run smoothly. In fact, between 1775 and 1777 Court of Session records document several legal disputes between the two brothers involving the non-payment of wages.[6] Patrick had been a ship's captain for a number of years. It was recorded that on 5 May 1774, the *Hunterston* (*Hunterstown*) was outbound from Port Roanoke, North Carolina bound for London carrying naval stores and timber. She had sailed from Saltcoats to North America.[7]

While Patrick was involved in the maritime aspects of the business, William ran the coal mine and the limestone quarry at Hullerhirst. He was one of its four tacksmen, and employed about ten miners. He received a quarter of the coal produced, which had been agreed in 1776 as being 10,000 loads at 4¼d per load. The proximity of the coal mine enabled William to build the first draw kiln in the same year, with his initials on the keystone. A mason, John Crauford, was already working for Kelso and may have constructed the kiln.

The *Old Statistical Account* relates: 'Two of the proprietors (Kelso and Hamilton of Grange) have draw kilns which are kept going for a considerable part of the year, to answer the ordinary demand of lime for building, and especially for manure, which is purchased by their own tenants, and by the farmers of the country westward along the shore, where there is none of it.'[8] Hullerhirst was too small to absorb all the lime it produced, although it was used in prodigious quantities on cultivated land. Barrsdyke farm in Cadder was advertised in 1789 as 'lately limed at the rate of 25 carts per acre,' and the tack of William Wilson, Kelso's tenant on Hillhead farm, specified putting '8 chalders of lime' on each acre, about 8.064 tonnes, before ploughing began. Wilson spent £140 sterling on 'the liming and meliorating' of the farm in 1777, when his annual rent was only £42. William Wilson was tacksman at Hillhead Farm in 1777.

As improvements in agriculture became widespread Thomas Tait, tacksman of the limeworks in 1798-99, saw sales double from 7,000 to 14,000 bolls per annum. Some of this was used on the neglected bog lands on the Warner's Ardeer estate.

---

6 NAS CS271/43967 and NAS CS271/43780.

7 North Carolina Port Records.

8 Wodrow, Rev. J. *Old Statistical Account of Scotland* – Vol XII. Parish of Stevenston – 1793.

Lord Eglinton backed the proposed Glasgow, Paisley and Ardrossan Canal from 1800 onwards to overcome his transport difficulties, and export coal and iron to the industries in Glasgow. Engineer John Rennie's 1821 map of its (never completed) route shows the limeworks at Hullerhirst as the only existing one in Stevenston parish, and situated close enough to be able to profit from the canal (See Map 10).

By 1830, Hullerhirst's operation was probably similar to that at nearby Caddell Limeworks, Ardrossan. Farmers from up to 8km away loaded with lime on credit at the works, and paid later by invoice. Some of the workers boarded at a farmhouse with the tacksman, although they ate their meals separately. Hullerhirst quarry, by now inherited by the Hamilton Howe family, had ceased working by late 1837.

Accounts for the building of the new house at Hullerhirst in 1777 show that Kelso was not using his own lime, but took '66 carts of lime from Stevenston at 4d per cart.' The *Old Statistical Account of Scotland* explains, 'Irish limestone is imported at Saltcoats, as ballast, in the coal ships. The lime made of it is whiter than the Scots, and answers better for plaister-work, and for casting of houses and walls.' Kelso used four cartloads of sand and lime 'to cast the house.' Similarly, he used stone from Auchenkist Quarry (1.75km away). Their business interests enabled them to integrate their transport network with the marketing of the limestone and coal they produced. Dublin formed a major export market.

Patrick Kelso married Mary Hamilton on 8 April 1777. She was the third daughter of Robert Hamilton from Saltcoats who had both shipping interests and political influence. Two of Mary's brothers were Alexander (a diplomat and plantation owner), and Robert (a politician and plantation owner). Patrick died in 1791, but had inherited Hullerhirst from his bachelor brother who died suddenly in 1778. It was from 1777 with the marriage of Patrick to Mary that the Hamilton name first appeared in the Kelso's family history. Also, it is worth noting that before this landmark marriage the Kelso family's extensive shipping interests indicated no direct association with the Caribbean trades.

Although William died unexpectedly young in 1778, a number of disputes outstanding with his larger, wealthier colliery neighbours went to law.

In June 1779, a petition by Patrick Warner and Robert Reid Cunninghame proprietors and joint tacksmen of the coal and saltworks of Stevenston was sent to the sheriff depute of Ayrshire concerning three colliers from Stevenston Colliery who had gone to work for Patrick Kelso of Hullerhirst. The colliers were John Smith, James Smith/Bashie and Robert Jamphrad. They were employed to sink a new shaft at Hullerhirst, approximately twelve fathoms deeper than the previous pit, but were widely known as workplace activists and agitators.

The petitioners claimed that the three miners 'left their work without any cause or complaint, deserting their work.' That they 'have gone and entered as shankers to Patrick Kelso of Hullerhirst and his tacksmen to the great detriment and hurt of your Petitioners.'[9]

The three miners claimed they had discharge papers dated 1775, although this was contested. The petitioners requested that Patrick Kelso be provided with a copy of the document and that he be ordained to answer certain relevant questions on the matter.

The case illustrated above, demonstrates the competitive nature of the business operations between these two neighbouring estates. It indicates a strained and possibly fractious working relationship between Patrick Warner and Robert Reid Cunninghame of Stevenston Colliery and Patrick Kelso of Hullerhirst.

Experienced shankers were valuable assets to their employers, and their skills and availability were jealously guarded against the continual interests of competitors. It is therefore not surprising that the defection of these three miners resulted in a petition being conveyed to the sheriff depute of Ayrshire, requesting that Patrick Kelso answer various questions pertaining to his alleged 'hiring' of these men.

Patrick Kelso and Mary Hamilton had three sons – William IV, Robert, and the famous Alexander Hamilton Kelso. A more comprehensive biographical account of Alexander Hamilton Kelso appears in the following chapter.

HAMILTON HOWE FAMILY

At Hullerhirst, the Hamilton name first appears with the marriage of Patrick Kelso to Mary Hamilton. Partick and Mary had six children. The fourth born was Alexander Hamilton Kelso who was born on 13 October 1783 at Hullerhirst. He later, on 24 April 1809, was married to Maria Rosalie, daughter of Edward J. Colbiornsen, a Danish judge. The wedding ceremony took place in Trichinopoly, Madras, India, where he worked for the East India Company. Around the time of his marriage, his maternal uncle Sir Alexander Hamilton died, and Alexander inherited his property. Due to this significant alteration in his material circumstances, Alexander changed his surname to Hamilton. It should be remembered that he married as a Kelso.

When we consider the involvement of the Kelso family in the controversial practice of slavery, the situation is rather convoluted. Although Patrick and William Kelso co-owned several ships in the 1770s, there is no record that

9 Cunninghame of Auchenharvie Collection - CA10/1/19. Ayrshire Archives.

this aspect of their business operations had any direct connection to the West Indies. The situation changes with the arrival of Alexander Hamilton Kelso on the scene. Alexander was Patrick Kelso's second son and nephew of Sir Alexander Hamilton. This last-named gentleman became a wealthy East India merchant and member of Devon's landed gentry where he owned an estate called 'the Retreat.' From his brother, Dr Robert Hamilton, he inherited two plantations on the Caribbean island of Grenada including 'Samaritan Estate,' and 'St Patrick's Estate.' Together his two properties enslaved 140 people.

With the death of Sir Alexander Hamilton in 1809, the major beneficiary was his nephew the Hullerhirst-born Alexander Hamilton Kelso. In his uncle's will he is described as a writer in Madras for the East India Company.

After inheriting the property of his maternal uncle, Alexander Hamilton Kelso changed his name to Alexander Hamilton Hamilton Esq of the Retreat and Hullerhirst (from this date he let Hullerhirst). In addition to securing his uncle's English properties, Alexander also inherited his plantations in Grenada thus becoming a slave master. Moving forward, in 1835 under the terms of emancipation, he received approximately £600,000 (in today's terms) as compensation for the freedom of 140 Grenadian slaves.

It is clearly evident that Alexander Hamilton Hamilton (Kelso) was an active and enthusiastic participant in the slaving principal, using it to forward his social and political ambitions and further progress his upward mobility.

Alexander's elder sister, Ann Kelso, was married to John Howe in 1805. John was a master builder and his son, of the same name, a grocer. In 1841, the family was associated with a property in Titchfield Street, Kilmarnock, but ten years later two other siblings, Jane (born in Stevenston on 19 April 1809), and Alexander Hamilton Howe (born 1813) were resident at Hullerhirst.

The mansion house in 1851 was owned by Alexander Edward Kelso Hamilton who lived at the 'Retreat', Topsham, Devon, with his wife, three of his children, his mother-in-law, four male servants and five female servants. Being an absentee laird, the house was occupied by Miss Jane and Alexander Hamilton Howe (two of the four children of John and Ann Howe, the other two being Jessie and John). From some time prior to 1819 until around 1845 John and Ann lived at Hullerhirst. Ann died around 1840. Earlier in the 1820s, in the House, in addition to John and Ann, was Ann's mother and three servants, Alex and Elizabeth Cameron and William McDonald.

The proprietor, Alexander Edward Kelso Hamilton, was admitted to Trinity, Cambridge, on 10 September 1840. He was the second son of Alexander, formerly of Hullerhirst. He was born in 1822 at the Retreat,

Topsham, Devon and attended private school in Devon, then Harrow. He gained a Bachelor of Arts Degree in 1845. He married Jane Harriet, daughter of Brig-Gen J. T. Lane C.B. in 1853. He died on 25 December 1855.

His son, Alexander, was twenty-two years old when he married Caroline, second daughter of Aylmer Porter Esq, of Southernhay, Exeter, on 11 January 1876. The ceremony took place at St Sidwell's, Exeter, and was carried out by Rev Reginald Barnes, Vicar of Heavitree, assisted by Rev John Lincoln Galton, Rector of St Sidwell's.

Although he was born at Hullerhirst and inherited the house from his father, there is no documented evidence to indicate that Alexander Hamilton Kelso or his wife were ever residents at the house. He continued to live at the 'Retreat', which was located on the outskirts of Topsham in Devon. This property was first recorded as the site which Samuel Buttall from Plymouth bought in 1684 in order to construct a sugar refinery. The next owner was Richard Orme who purchased the building in 1769 and built the present house. His new home which he called the 'Retreat' was completed in 1773. The subsequent proprietor was Sir Alexander Hamilton, whose wealth originated from sugar plantations in Grenada previously owned by his brother Robert. In 1774 Rev John Sweete wrote, 'This is now an excellent house.'[10] The Retreat exists today as a fine Georgian house split into apartments, overlooking the River Exe.

Sir Alexander Hamilton died on 23 June 1809, and sixteen years before his death he submitted a petition to the Diocese of Exeter for licence to construct a seat for himself, his family, and his servants in his local church. He also applied for confirmation of a vault for himself and his family which he had already dug without permission. He was successful on both requests for both a pew and vault.

Twenty years later in June 1813, his successor, Alexander Hamilton Hamilton, petitioned the Diocese for permission to erect a monument to his late uncle and aunt, Sir Alexander Hamilton and Lady Hamilton of the Retreat. Again, his request was successful, and an impressive edifice was erected. Today in Topsham you can enjoy a gentle stroll along the raised riverside walk named the Sir Alex Walk. This walk is presumed to have been laid out by Sir Alexander in 1794 as part of a programme of improvements to the Retreat which he acquired in 1781. It should be noted that Alexander Hamilton Hamilton occupied the Retreat from 1812 to 1851.

After the death of his wife, John Howe lived in the house with his two daughters, Jane (25) and Jessie (15) and a servant, Margaret Hardie.

John died sometime before the marriage of his youngest daughter, Jessie, to Rev George Orr, a minister of the Free Church in Symington,

10 Devon Heritage Centre. DRO 564M/F6/159.

on 15 January 1850. The venue for the wedding was Hullerhirst and it was supervised by Rev Dr Landsborough.

In the following year, Jane had been joined at Hullerhirst by her brother, Alexander, but she was designated as head of the household.

The most prominent and distinguished member of the Howe family was Dr Alexander Hamilton Howe. He was born at Hullerhirst in 1816. His early education consisted of being boarded in Saltcoats with Mr Edward Gibb, parish schoolmaster of Ardrossan. This episode was followed by tuition from Rev Mr Roxburgh from Kilmaurs; and afterwards at Ayr Academy, Glasgow University, Edinburgh University and finally in Paris. His wife Anne Forbes Robertson was born in Edinburgh and it was at this institution that Alexander completed his medical course. After securing his medical qualification he became an Assistant Surgeon (sometime before 1851) attached to the East India Company's Civil Service, although it is highly unlikely that he ever practised. During his time in India, he was a medical officer in charge of C Company of the Third Battalion of the Madras Foot Artillery. This military body was one of the units comprising the Madras Army, which in turn was one of the East India Company Armies. Alexander may well have been involved on the periphery of the First Afghan War (1839 – 1842) attached to the reserve force as he spent approximately ten years in India near the border with Afghanistan.

The date of Alexander's marriage is unknown, and it is possible that he could have been married in India. The 1861 Census inform us that Alexander was married and residing at Hallcraig House, Carluke. This situation could be reinforced by the fact that Alexander's mother-in-law died on 2 July 1858 at Hallcraig. The only two people resident at Hullerhirst during the Census of 1861 were servants Margaret Andrew and Elizabeth Kennedy.

When the Doctor returned to Hullerhirst is unknown, but he was certainly at this location in 1868. We know this fact from his involvement in the General Election campaign of that year.

Dr Howe was a member of the Liberal Party. He campaigned in 1868 election for Mr William Finnie of Newfield. William Finnie was a Scottish lawyer and Liberal Party politician. He was born on 6 November 1827 in Kilmarnock. He was the third son of James Finnie, a merchant in London, Lisbon and Rio de Janeiro. William's mother was Mary Ann Brown. William was educated at Merchiston Castle Academy, Edinburgh, King's College, London and Trinity College, Cambridge.

The Finnie family was involved in the coal industry in the 1860s, and held lands at Galrigs between Newfield and Dundonald. The lands and mansion house of Galrigs was renamed 'Newfield' c. 1723 by Capt. Lawrence Nugent.

William was called to the bar in 1853 but never practised. He was a Justice of the Peace for Ayrshire and married Antoinette Burnard in 1853.

In 1868 the election result for the North Ayrshire constituency, which included Stevenston parish, was as follows:

Candidate	Party	Votes Cast
William Finnie of Newfield	Liberal	1,397
Roger Montgomerie	Conservative	1,322

The very slim majority of 75 votes secured by Mr Finnie was reversed six years later in 1874 when Mr Montgomerie secured 1,563 votes to Mr Finnie's 1,301.

The number of enfranchised individuals in 1868 was greatly restricted, and even in 1883, Stevenston still only had twenty eligible voters.

Alexander was a polymath; excelling in linguistics, and with an enthusiastic approach to both astronomy and botany. He also frequently contributed to the press. He has been described as a 'gifted man, somewhat of a recluse and lover of book-lore.'[11]In 1865 he published a book entitled *A Theoretical Enquiry into the Physical Cause of Epidemic Diseases, accompanied with Tables.* This publication was devoted to proving that epidemics were caused by the effect of the Moon upon the Earth's atmosphere, having an eighteen and a half years' period depending on the revolution of the Moon's nodes. This book was followed in 1866 by another volume called *Reflections on Cholera*. Alexander was a member of the Epidemiological Society, the Royal Asiatic Society, and on 12 January 1883, he was elected a Fellow of the Royal Astronomical Society.

Doctor Alexander Hamilton Howe was possessed of an eccentric character. He gave little consideration to his physical appearance and was observed on a frequent basis to be wearing a shoe on one foot and a boot on the other when attending church. Both the Doctor and his wife Ann Forbes Robertson (died on 6 December 1900) attended the Established Church of Scotland, but he was well known as being sympathetic towards the 'Free Kirk' (Woodside Hall in New Street). His inattention to his mode of dress was a major irritation to his wife, but his dogmatic opinions rendered any meaningful discussion useless. He was also renowned for burning the midnight oil, as astronomy was his pet hobby. He was brusque in his style of conversation, and impetuous, stubborn, and opinionated in his decision-making.

Although a member of the School Board, his personality rendered him a 'loose cannon,' and he regularly disagreed vehemently with other members

11 Wallace, Archibald. *Stevenston Past and Present*. 1902.

of the board, sometimes resulting in lengthy absences from their meetings.

From 1868 until his death in 1895, Dr Howe was permanently based at Hullerhirst. The 1881 Census informs us that he and his wife accommodated two servants in the house, Annie Grayford (domestic cook) and Elizabeth Davidson (house maid). Although only the tenants of the house, the Howe family had a more personal association with the property than the absentee owners. They certainly had a higher profile within the town, actively contributing to a number of organisations and good causes within the local community. These included the distribution of items to the poor of Stevenston in January 1875. The Doctor supplied tea, sugar, and soup, and was joined in this venture by Mrs Edmonstone of Hayocks Lodge and Miss Smith Neill who provided warm clothing. The Smith Neill family had been residents at both Ardeer House and Hayocks House. At this time, Dr Howe was also involved with the School Board, and on 22 December 1876, he was elected chairman at a meeting convened to consider the destitution being experienced by the handloom weavers in the town. The main topic of discussion was whether relief should be given in the form of a gratuity or by providing work. It was agreed to raise, by subscription, a fund to relieve the immediate hardship, and also to provide employment to nearly all the weavers able for outdoor labour in a project to improve the surface of part of New Street. As always, Dr Howe was willing to contribute his expertise in attempting to alleviate the distress being experienced within the community.

In 1897, the social fabric at Hullerhirst was shaken with the announcement that Margaret Anderson Henderson, a domestic servant in the house, had given birth in Paisley to a daughter. The wagging tongues were kept busy with the discovery that the father was the son of a Kilwinning publican.

During the twentieth century, the residency of the house had almost exclusively been monopolised by two unrelated families of Robertsons. This occupancy was not continuous. There were short periods of time when the house echoed to its own private thoughts and dreams.

THE ROBERTSON FAMILY (1901 – 1948)

Alexander Hamilton Howe died on 27 July 1895 (born 25 January 1816) and his gravestone is visible in the High Kirk cemetery (next to the entry to the vault). With the death of his wife, Ann Forbes Robertson, on 6 December 1900 (born 12 December 1815), the occupancy of Hullerhirst passed into the hands of Mr Frederick Lockhart Robertson. In 1901 he became the first Robertson to occupy Hullerhirst as tenant (accompanied by his housekeeper, Annie Atkins). Why he decided to establish an association with this specific property is unclear. The house was advertised for let in the 15 February 1901 copy of the *Ardrossan & Saltcoats Herald*, and was described as having three public rooms, three bedrooms, kitchen, accommodation, and small garden. Ten weeks later, on 3 May, there was a sale of household furniture from Hullerhirst. The public roup was carried out by auctioneer Alex Parker on behalf of agents Gilmour & Christie (Irvine). The furniture and accessories were divided into items from the dining room, library, drawing room, bedrooms, and miscellaneous artefacts. Mahogany tables of differing designs made up the majority of dining room items. The library provided bookcases, chairs, tables, writing desks, and carpets. A walnut piano (by Collard & Collard), mahogany card tables, easy chairs, ottomans, timepieces, rugs, and curtains were pieces from the drawing room. Not surprisingly, the bedrooms provided bedsteads, bedding, and blankets, alongside chests of drawers, wardrobes, dressing tables, and basin-stands and ware. Ancillary objects included a barometer, kitchen furniture and utensils, and a joiner's bench and sundry tools. Who exactly was responsible for the sale is unclear.

The circumstances of the transfer of tenancy of the house after the death of Alexander's widow in 1900 are intriguing. We know that Frederick secured the occupancy immediately after Mrs Howe, and this agreement must have been finalised with the knowledge and permission of the owner, Alexander Kelso Hamilton. However, another factor may well have influenced the destination of the rental agreement. Mrs Howe was the daughter of Alexander Robertson of Hallcraig, and this fact raises the possibility that the transfer was facilitated by an informal family connection. There is no record or documentation to support this supposition, and the situation with the identical surnames may well be purely coincidental. Whatever the background to the transfer, Frederick and his siblings became the tenant/occupiers in 1901 and initiated a family connection with Hullerhirst that lasted almost fifty years. Alexander Robertson of Hallcraig was a Lieutenant Colonel in the East India Company. He in turn was the husband of Ann Robertson Cunninghame (born on 21 September 1784 in Stevenston), with the marriage taking place on 25 July 1810. This meant that Ann was the niece of Robert Cunninghame Esq. of Auchenharvie. When this situation is added to the fact that Dr Alexander Hamilton Howe was the grandnephew of Sir Alexander Hamilton of the Retreat, Devon, it clearly shows the convoluted and inter-related nature of the two principal families associated with Hullerhirst during the nineteenth century.

In the early twentieth century, when Frederick secured the tenancy, the panoramic view from Hullerhirst would have been unrestricted. Looking south, the Ayrshire coast stretched from Irvine Bay to the Heads of Ayr with the Dundonald Hills and Ailsa Craig appearing in bold relief. Immediately to the forefront of the mansion house coming sharply into focus were the well-tended fields of Hawkhill farm. Before the ownership of the Smith family and Robert Montgomerie, it is easy to visualise the distinct profile of John Lockhart following the seasons of the year with his ploughing, sowing, and harvesting.

Beyond the productive acres of Hawkhill, the eye became focused on the golden sand dunes of Ardeer. This wilderness had no agricultural value but was increasingly prominent due to the burgeoning growth of Nobels, whose myriad of chimney stalks were like streaks linking the azure sea and the horizon.

Continuing to look southwards, we had an uninterrupted view of the imposing Hayocks House and the adjoining farm buildings of East Hayocks farm.

A similar vista, slightly to the south-east, pinpointed Castlehill farm, which could be seen nestling on the sloping side of a rocky mound. For many years the farm was under the care of John Smith, and later - from 1880 to the end of the Great War - the guardians of the land were the Barr family. Mention should also be made of Muirside which sits astride the

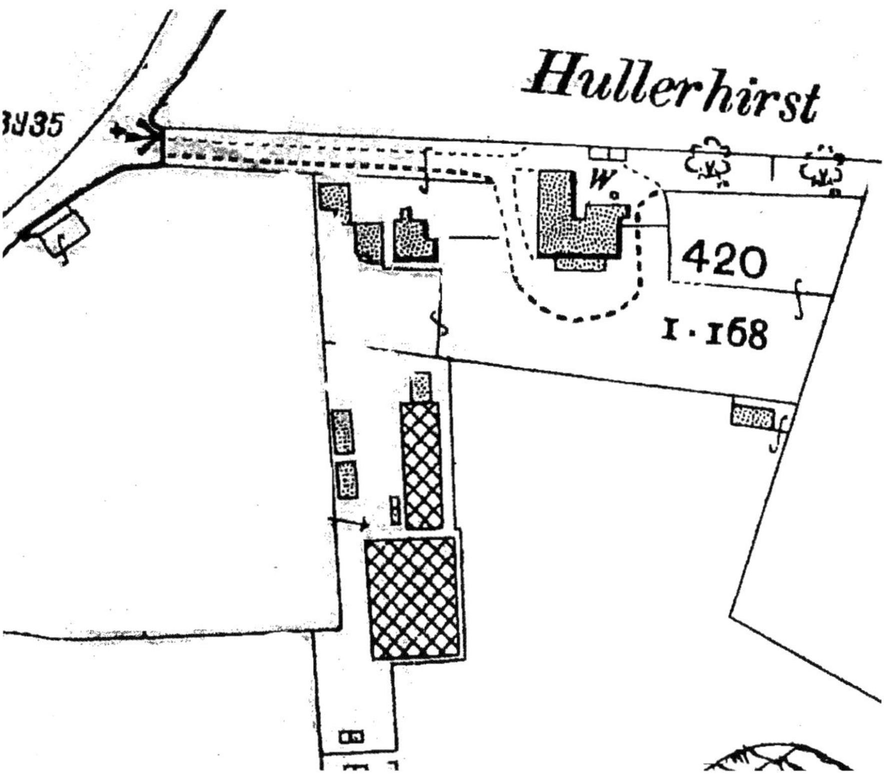

Map 3. Hullerhirst Grounds c. 1910
NOTE – The prominent chequered symbol indicating greenhouses.

parish boundary between Stevenston and Kilwinning.

From the extensive gardens decorating the front of the house the visitor could marvel at the majesty of 'Scotland in Miniature.' The Arran hills provided an impressive back-drop, not only to Hullerhirst, but to the entire parish.

Looking west, on either side of the Greenhead filters of the Irvine and District Water Board, you could discern Lochcraigs and Greenhead farms.

The landscape spectacle from the front upstairs windows of the house would encompass the ruins of Kerelaw Castle and walled orchard. Kerelaw House itself would have largely been obscured by the high and majestic beech trees which sheltered the house on three sides. Finally, the only human feature visible from the rear of the house was the slightly elevated Hillhead farm with its notable farm house dwelling and outhouses.

Early in 1901, Frederick (born circa 1855 in Bonhill) lived at 226 Renfrew Street, Glasgow with his domestic servant, Catherine Fraser. Prior to this date, in 1871, he lived with his family in Greenock. Ten years later he was still living with his parents in Bath Street, Glasgow. Frederick was then a bank clerk. In 1891, still living with his parents in Bath Street, he had progressed to the post of bank agent, and by 1901, he had attained the prestigious position of a fully qualified banker with the Union Bank of Scotland (Ltd) in Great Western Road, Glasgow. This bank was established in 1830 and played a significant role in the financial landscape of the city. When Frederick was an employee, the bank was a notable financial institution heavily involved in supporting the rapidly expanding business and commercial sector. In 1955, the bank merged with the Bank of Scotland.

Being actively involved in such a high-profile occupation carried with it an enhanced position in the social hierarchy. Coming into regular contact with 'men of substance' would have provided Frederick with the possibility of acquiring a prestigious property doubling as a family home and business address. He may well have had conducted business and financial matters with Alexander Hamilton Kelso from whom he rented Hullerhirst between 1901 and 1924.

Not long before his death in October 1925, Frederick became the proprietor of Hullerhirst. His brother, Charles L. Robertson, owned the large greenhouse and store where he grew tomatoes and 'luxury' fruits such as pineapples and nectarines (this being a common pastime adopted by many landowners and landed gentry). These valuable outhouses had been located in the grounds at the front of the House since around 1910 (See Map 3). Charles was born in 1860, unlike his older brother in Edinburgh, and joined Frederick at Hullerhirst around 1905.

In addition to Charles, Frederick had another brother, William Henry Lockhart Robertson, also born in Bonhill. As far as can be ascertained,

William who was a physician and surgeon never lived at Hullerhirst. By entering the medical profession, he was following in the footsteps of his grandfather, John Argyll Robertson (buried in St John's Episcopal Church, Princes Street, Edinburgh, in 1855) and two grand-uncles. One possible explanation for William's absence from Hullerhirst is that he died in Westray, Orkney in 1887 aged only twenty-nine years. His death was caused by typhoid which he contracted from one of his patients.

Retreating back a generation, we find the parents of the six siblings were Frederick Lockhart Robertson (1827-1892) and Elizabeth Mary Hay. The couple were married by Rev Dr Auld in Bonhill on 20 April 1852. Frederick had just taken up his first ministry job in the Church of Scotland in Bonhill Parish Church the previous year. His term of occupancy lasted ten years. He was born on 28 December 1827 in Edinburgh, and after leaving the capital he assumed the role of Assistant Minister in Ayr, residing in Midton Road. This position was followed by postings as minister in Bonhill, Greenock, and finally at St Andrew's Parish Church, Bath Street, Glasgow. He was greatly respected and admired by his congregation at St Andrews and this resulted in the installation of the 'Robertson Memorial Window' within the church. The stained-glass window was commissioned by Mr Andrew Hoggan and Miss Hoggan and was assembled by Mr Stephen Adam. The mosaic presented as the central figure the Apostle Paul preaching at Athens, and bore this inscription:

Erected by loving friends in affectionate remembrance of Frederick Lockhart Robertson, D.D., minister of this parish. Born 28th December

7. Stained-Glass Window within Kilmun Church, Argyll.

1827; died 10th December 1892.

Frederick had become a Doctor of Divinity in 1881, and was affectionately known as the 'Minister of the Saltmarket.' After his funeral service at St Andrew's Parish Church a train departed from St Enoch's Station destined for Kilmun for the interment.

Stephen Adam who was responsible for designing the stained-glass window in St Andrew's Church was also the creator of a stained-glass window in Kilmun Church, Argyll. This particular window reads:

Memory of the Rev. Frederick Lockhart Robertson D.D. Finnartmore died 10th December 1892 and his spouse, Elizabeth Mary Hay died 9th May 1895.

Kilmun Church has now been converted into a visitor centre. It is clearly evident that the minister and Stephen Adam were close friends. This affinity between the two men could well be explained by the fact that Mr Adam was a resident in Bath Street, Glasgow, where he also established his own studio in 1870 at Number 121 (he later died here aged sixty-two). Bath Street was the location of St Andrew's Parish Church where Rev Robertson was the minister. The relationship was probably one of minister and member of his congregation.

We know that Rev Frederick Robertson was a minister in Bonhill from 1851 to 1861 (four of his children were born in the town), and Stephen Adam designed two large-single-light Heritors' Windows for Bonhill Parish Church which were installed in 1880 as a mark of respect for his good friend.

There is a local connection between Mr Adam and Kilwinning. The Rev William Lee Ker was the minister in the Abbey Church in the town from 1866 to his death in May 1902. In the following year, a design by Messrs Stephen Adam & Son for the installation of a window to the late clergyman entitled 'Paul at Athens' was submitted to the congregation and approved.

Stephen Adam (1848-1910) was a Scottish stained-glass designer who became a pioneer in many aspects of his craft. He was born in Bonnington Haugh, Edinburgh, and was educated at Canonmills School. He was apprenticed to Ballantine Brothers in 1861. By 1865 he had joined the studios of Daniel Cottier, and in 1870 established his own stained-glass business in partnership with David Small.

All members of the Robertson family from Frederick Lockhart Robertson D.D. and his wife, Elizabeth Mary Hay, to all six siblings, are mentioned on the family gravestone at Kilmun cemetery in Argyll. On their gravestone is engraved the following detail:

In memory of FREDERICK LOCKHART ROBERTSON D.D. of Finnartmore Kilmun minister of Saint Andrews Parish Church Glasgow, who was born on 28th December 1826 and died on 10th December 1892. The work of righteousness shall be peace, the effect of righteousness quietness and assurance, forever my people shall dwell in a peaceable habitation in sure dwellings and in quiet resting places. Erected by citizens in Glasgow in grateful recognition of his many services to the people. ELIZABETH MARY HAY his wife born 1st August 1825 died 9th May 1895; and of CHARLES LOCKHART ROBERTSON their fourth son died at Hullerhirst on 13th June 1935 and is interred here; ANNIE ELIZABETH LOCKHART ROBERTSON their elder daughter who died at Hullerhirst 23rd April 1941; FLORA DOUGLAS ROBERTSON their younger daughter died 30th April 1948; also in memory of their son WILLIAM HAY ROBERTSON M.B.C.M. died at Westray Orkney 25th August 1887 aged 29; also FRANCIS LOCKHART ROBERTSON who died in Canada 10th September 1887 aged 32; in loving memory of FREDERICK LOCKHART ROBERTSON, their second son who died at Hullerhirst, Stevenston, Ayrshire, 29th October 1925 interred here; (FREDERICK L. LOCKHART ROBERTSON 1925 aged 66) (CHARLES LOCKHART ROBERTSON 1935 aged 74) (ANNIE LOCKHART ROBERTSON 1941 aged 82) (REV F.L. ROBERTSON 1892 aged 65) (FLORA ROBERTSON 1948 aged 85)

8. The Robertson Family Gravestone at Kilmun Cemetery.

(ELIZABETH HAY ROBERTSON 1895 aged 69).

As can be surmised from the gravestone inscription, six members of the family were buried at Kilmun. Only William and Francis were buried elsewhere – in Orkney and Canada respectively (See photograph 8).

None of the family was born at Hullerhirst and none was buried locally, although four of Frederick's children lived and died at the mansion house. The other two sons died at a young age – both in 1887 – well before their brother had taken tenancy of Hullerhirst in 1901.

Although only the offspring of Rev Frederick Lockhart Robertson had any connection with Hullerhirst, we should be aware that his second son, Frederick Charles Lockhart Robertson, who became the tenant of the estate in 1901, was conscious of his obligation to maintain the reputation of the family name within the professional classes in west/central Scotland. The family link to such prominent figures in the artistic, industrial, and political world as Stephen Adam and Sir William Arrol, encouraged him to acquire such a prestigious property (even as a tenant) as Hullerhirst Estate.

The stained-glass window in the Kilmun Visitor Centre commemorating the minister which was designed and donated by Stephen Adam is joined by two large Stephen Adam windows that were donated by the Arrol family. The connection of this high-profile family to Kilmun and Rev Robertson is through Finnartmore House. It would seem Rev Frederick lived near this property, possibly in a cottage. The house itself, in the 1890s, was owned by James Arrol (the brother of Sir William).

Sir William Arrol was a Scottish born civil engineer, bridge builder, innovator in construction methods, as well as politician. Sir William Arrol received his knighthood in 1890 and served as a Liberal Member of Parliament for the South Ayrshire constituency from 1895 until 1906. He lived out his later years at his home, Seafield House in Ayr, where he died on 20 February 1913.

This world-renowned civil engineering company, Sir William Arrol Co. Ltd, had been actively involved in a mining-related project in Stevenston in 1905. The exercise concerned the sinking of two shafts through blown sand to allow the establishment of Ardeer West Pits No. 1 and No. 2 (Shore Pits) at NGR 277402. The loose, wet sand was 27 metres deep overlying the rockhead and this resulted in sinking through 54 metres of unconsolidated material (two shafts of 27 metres) and took eleven months to complete. Mr Robert Main, the General Manager and Director of the Glengarnock Iron & Steel Co. Ltd, realised that the enterprise would be challenging and costly, causing him to acquire the expertise of William Arrol's company.

Frederick's mother, Elizabeth Mary Hay, was born on 1 August 1825 in Dundonald, and spent her early years at Townend House, Symington. Her father was Captain Francis Hay, 34th Regiment of Foot. Her wealthy family apparently owned property at Dornal, near Barrhill. Her association with this estate resulted in a court case in 1926, involving her family.

Going back another two generations we discover a further four physicians in the family, one – John Argyll Robertson, attaining the dizzy heights of Fellow of the Royal College of Surgeons, specialising in eye surgery, and ultimately involved in the establishment of the Eye Dispensary in Edinburgh. Another descendent was Charles Alexander Lockhart Robertson, a psychiatrist, who became a physician in 1856 after studying medicine at Caius College, Cambridge. He worked in various asylums throughout the country, eventually being appointed Inspector for Lunatic Asylums in 1870. Charles died in Exmouth but was buried in London.

It is interesting to note that this family of Robertsons had a connection to Montgreenan House near Kilwinning. Going back to the eighteenth century, Dr Robert Robertson was the eldest son of Alexander Robertson from Eyemouth. When he married, Robert inherited the extensive business interests of his wife's family. The legacy was made conditional upon Robert assuming her name, Glasgow. He became the owner of Mount Greenan and Sans Souci estates in St Vincent, making his fortune from sugar plantations and shipping. Robert Glasgow purchased Montgreenan estate in 1802 and rebuilt the house between the years 1810 and 1817 (in 1971 it was designated an A Listed Building).

One of Robert's brothers was John Argyll Robertson who was the grandfather of Frederick Robertson and his siblings who lived at Hullerhirst. Therefore, the relationship between the Hullerhirst and Montgreenan families was that they were second cousins. Although Dr Robert Glasgow and John Argyll Robertson were brothers, there is no evidence to suggest that John Argyll Robertson directly benefited financially from his brother's participation in the slave trade. John never travelled overseas and was fully committed to promoting his exceptional medical career.

Although Frederick's ancestors were wealthy, well-connected establishment figures, many were undoubtedly talented, gifted individuals. In the faculty of medicine, they were innovators and trailblazers whose endeavours pushed forward the boundaries of scientific knowledge.

Frederick's siblings were completed by two sisters, Annie Lockhart Robertson and Flora Isabella Douglas Robertson. In similar vein to Frederick and Charles, these two sisters never married. When they located to Hullerhirst is a matter of conjecture. It is possible that they accompanied their brother, Charles, around 1905. Virtually nothing is known about the personalities or every-day lives of the family members at Hullerhirst, but in the three-year spell between 1924 and 1926 a series of events impacted on the future ownership and development of the estate. The most defining incident occurred on 29 October 1925 with the death of Frederick at Hullerhirst. The cause of death was heart disease which had been diagnosed a year earlier. Around the same time as the identification of this health problem, the owner of the estate, Alexander Kelso Hamilton, who was still resident at the 'Retreat' in Devon, decided to sell Hullerhirst.

The small residential estate was put up for public auction, within the Faculty Hall, St George's Place, Glasgow, on 27 August 1924. An advert described the lot as 'Hullerhirst Mansion and Ground attached, adjoining Kerelaw and Ashgrove, with a lovely view of the Firth of Clyde.'[12]Although the house could not be described as modern, it was a comfortable family home containing ten apartments with ancillary services. The lands extended to about fifteen hectares, of which thirteen were arable. The reserve price was set at £2,000 but the sale realised £2,660.

Frederick was a retired gentleman of substance who left a personal estate of £12,169 gross (equivalent value today of approximately £7,620,000), and when the house he had rented for almost twenty-five years came on the market he eagerly accepted the opportunity to purchase it. Having to pay well over the reserve price indicates that he had competition in the bidding process, although the eventual procurement price was well within his means. The fact that his brother and two sisters were living with him in the house at the time of the sale, made the acquisition crucial.

After the death of Frederick on 29 October 1925, the ownership of the mansion house, fields, and garden passed jointly to his three siblings, Annie, Flora, and Charles. The latter continued to operate his tomato growing business.

The final element during this period of turmoil related to a court action raised by Annie, Flora, and Charles Robertson on 22 June 1926. At this time all three individuals were still living in Hullerhirst. The hearing was held in the Outer House of the Court of Session and was heard by Lord Moncrieff. The action was raised against Mrs Mary Elizabeth Hay-Boyd or Roberts Hay-Boyd, residing at Townend, near Ayr, and, also, against the trustees acting under the last will and testament of the late Sir William Phipson Beale of Drumlamford, Ayrshire. The case involved his estate of Dornal. The pursuers claimed the entire Dornal estate, but there was a competing claim from the defenders (principally Mrs Hay-Boyd). On the death of her father, Colonel Hay-Boyd in 1905, Dornal was conveyed by his trustees to Frederick Robertson who was a nephew of the deceased. After complicated legal considerations, His Lordship declared that the pursuers had never been the proprietors of Dornal (after the death of Frederick Robertson) and decreed in favour of both defenders.

Such a negative outcome in this high-profile case, must have been a

12 *Scotsman* – 2nd August 1924.

major disappointment to the Robertsons, and almost certainly cemented their continuing presence at Hullerhirst.

Charles Lockhart Robertson died on 13 June 1935 aged seventy-five. His death was registered in Stevenston by his sister, Flora. The two sisters, Annie and Flora were left as proprietors of the estate.

Continuing on with the basic outline of the family history, we learn that the first of the two remaining sisters to meet the grim reaper was Annie who died, as a spinster, on 23 April 1941. She was eighty-two years old, having been born in Bonhill and died at Hullerhirst, leaving a will of £14,459 gross (equivalent today to approximately £920,000). Her probate record was sealed at Llandudno on 31 July 1941 (probate records were relocated to Llandudno during World War Two). Being the incumbent of such a healthy financial reserve would point towards the possession of several property holdings and/or business investments outwith the immediate area.

The youngest of the five siblings was Flora Isabella Douglas Robertson who was born in Greenock in 1862. She died, like Frederick, Charles, and Annie, at Hullerhirst on 30 April 1948, aged eighty-five. The informant on her death certificate was Mr Robert Gray, described as an 'acquaintance.' With the passing of Flora, this grouping of Robertsons disappeared from the Hullerhirst scene after almost half a century. Her probate record was sealed on 2 September in London. This documentation points towards the possibility that she, like her sister, had business interests in the capital.

Annie and Flora continued to be the landowners up until Annie's death in 1941. For the remainder of the war Flora was the sole proprietor, but she delegated the management of the property to a firm of solicitors in Edinburgh named Wallace and Guthrie.

In comparison with their predecessors as tenants, and later, owners of Hullerhirst, the Robertson's influence on local affairs was marginal. The family showed little noticeable interest in the political, commercial, or religious activities in the town.

Shortly after Flora's death, the ownership of the house switched to Mr Robert Gray. The circumstances behind this transfer are obscure and perplexing. We know that this gentleman had acquired the house and land by 1949/50, but a year earlier had been resident at 18 Blacklands Avenue, Kilwinning. It is therefore unclear whether he ever stayed in the house. It is possible that Flora Robertson left the house to Bob Gray who had been the sister's coachman/handyman. He retained ownership of the house until it was purchased by Hugh William Edgar Robertson (known as Edgar) in 1953. This family of Robertsons was not related to the previous incumbents. Bob Gray was a postman in Kilwinning and had two sons, Jim and John. He lived in Dalry Road in the town. When he became an employee of the Post Office is unknown, but it is possible that it overlapped with his ownership of Hullerhirst.

Before selling the house to Edgar Robertson, Mr Gray organised a public sale of antique and modern furniture from the property. This event which was conducted by Robert McTear & Company Ltd, Glasgow, occurred on 19 March 1953 at Hullerhirst, and attracted buyers from all over Scotland and the North of England. The items available for purchase included furniture, bric-a-brac, china, and crystal.

The furniture in particular was in demand and commanded notable interest. Some of the items included a Queen Anne walnut (2ft 3in) bureau-bookcase which sold for £242 (equivalent today to £8,750); a pair of Empire rosewood two-door dwarf display cabinets (3ft 6in) for £10; a suite of six Chippendale mahogany chairs, upholstered in velvet for £72; a pair of oval wall mirrors, in Chippendale-design gilt frames (4ft 6in) for £62; an Empire mahogany oval table for £49. Other pieces included an antique mahogany inlaid glazed two-door bookcase; a Dutch walnut display cabinet, on bombs stand with drawers, and numerous writing desks, tables, chairs, sideboards, and corner cupboards.

The assortment of other articles comprised a pair of Victorian glass lustres which sold for £25 (equivalent today to £875); fine Venetian glass; china, porcelain, crystal, and miscellaneous ornaments: a mahogany inlaid service tray; English and French mantel clocks; oil paintings; water-colours and prints; Persian and eastern rugs; a grandfather clock by W. Keys, Dumbarton, with silvered dial, in antique mahogany inlaid case. There was also a fine selection of valuable books.[13]

13 *Glasgow Herald,* 9th March 1953. Page 12.

9. Hillhead Farm in 2024.

10. Edgar Robertson c. 1920s.

The final sum raised from the sale of such a rare and valuable collection of artefacts was undisclosed, but when added to the acquisition cost of the house and land, must have presented Mr Gray with a substantial sum.

At the time of his death, on 4 May 1963 at Ballochmyle Hospital from cardiac failure aged seventy-four, he was living at 28 Winton Avenue in the town. Surprisingly, on his Death Certificate he is recorded, like his father William, as a joiner journeyman. He was buried in Bridgend Cemetery, Kilwinning.

From 1935 until 1948, we find the fortunes of the two families within the estate, were worlds' apart. The year 1935 was not only significant due to the demise of Charles Robertson but also because it signalled the arrival of Edgar Robertson and his wife at Hillhead farm, a mere 200 metres to the north of the house. During these thirteen years, the two distinct branches of the Robertson clan lived very different but interrelated lives.

THE ROBERTSON FAMILY (1935 – 2022)

Edgar Robertson purchased Hillhead farm in 1935 from the previous owner James Miller who had been the farming proprietor since around 1914.

We know Mr Miller was still the farmer in the early part of 1935 from the fact that his father-in-law, John Hay Steele, who lived at 'Roslyn,' Dynamite Road, Stevenston, died at the farm on 2 February, aged eighty-five. The sale of Hillhead was probably connected to the death of Mr Steel whose son-in-law, Mr Miller, along with his wife Catherine moved into 'Roslyn' and sold the farm. Edgar and his wife Margaret (Peggy) moved from a farm, with low productivity and limited potential, a few miles east of Stewarton, possibly Laigh Clunch. The purchase of this farm had been advised by Edgar's in-laws. Margaret Montgomerie's family already had a Stevenston connection. Her father, Robert, was the tenant and occupier of the nearby Hawkhill farm from around 1898 until the tenancy changed in the 1940s to William Frew, haulage contractor, Station Road, Stevenston. Throughout this period of time, the proprietors of Hawkhill were the Trustees of the late Patrick Warner.

11. John Robertson.

Edgar, whose full name was Hugh William Edgar Robertson, was born on 23 April 1902 at 10 Eglinton Street, Saltcoats, the youngest of a family of ten. His mother, Annabella (Bella) Speir, died on 2 May 1909, aged fifty-one years, in Winton Cottage, Eglinton Street, Saltcoats, and Edgar was probably looked after by his three older sisters until their marriages. The last girl to marry was Jean Robertson in 1919, and she had the longest-lasting legacy with her brother. Annabella had married John Robertson, who was a ham-curer, at the Bog farm, Stevenston, on Boxing Day 1882. Annabella's parents had lived in Dalry but moved to Cowal in the late 1840s where they occupied various farms. Annabella was born at Toward, south of Dunoon, in 1858, but the family

12. The Robertson family taken in 1906/07. The members of the family are as follows:
left to right, back row; Humphrey, Annie, Maggie, Andrew, John Jnr, Jeannie,
front row; John Snr, Edgar, Ella, Annabella, Robert and James.
Ella died as a child, and James died in the First World War in 1915 at Loos.

returned to Ayrshire in the late 1860s and purchased the Bog farm where she was later married.

Edgar himself was married on 9 January 1935 in the Eglinton Arms Hotel, Ardrossan, to Margaret Wilson Montgomerie, a Nursing Sister. She was 29 years old and Edgar was three years older. It was later in the same year that the couple purchased Hillhead farm. The officiating minister at the wedding was Rev John Lindsay Guthrie from the Erskine Church in Kilwinning, and one of the witnesses was George Parker of Meiklelaught farm, Saltcoats (Edgar had lived at this particular farm in the 1920s). At the time of their marriage, both Edgar and Peggy were living at Hawkhill farm, Stevenston, with Robert Montgomerie, the bride's father. Edgar at this time had very little farming knowledge and any expertise possessed by the couple came from Peggy who had lived most of her live at Hawkhill. Their two children were born soon after the move to Hillhead, James in 1936 and Elizabeth the year after.

In 1921, Edgar, then aged nineteen, was living at the family home in 10 Eglinton Street, Saltcoats with his elder brother Robert Speir Robertson (a ham-curer), Robert's Yorkshire-born wife Marion, and his father John (also a ham-curer). Around this particular period, Edgar was employed for a time in a grocer's shop in Duke Street, Glasgow. This situation had been arranged by Edgar's brother, Andrew.

On 26 September 1924 Edgar emigrated to Australia, destined for Sydney. He returned to London from Brisbane on 23 December 1926 on board the *Otranto* which was part of the Orient Steam Navigation Company fleet. On leaving Britain, he submitted his address as 'Winton,' Eglinton Street, Saltcoats, and his occupation as farmer. On his return he was registered as a student at the same Saltcoats address. Soon after his homecoming he resided at Meiklelaught for a while.

As mentioned above, Edgar's father was John Robertson, but after this undisputed fact, the story becomes confusing with several different scenarios.

In some accounts of the early history of this well-known and respected local company of John Robertson & Sons (Hamcurers) Ltd, which latterly operated as Robertson's Fine Foods, based at their factory at 88 Princes Street, Ardrossan, it is stated that the business was founded in 1870 by John Robertson. This storyline is highly implausible. With examination of official documentation, we can deduce that either the year of formation was wrong or the founder was wrongly identified.

The company remained in Robertson ownership for five generations. More recently Iain Robertson was the Managing Director with his son Grant being the Operations Manager. Humphrey Robertson retired in January 2017 after thirty-four years in the business as Sales Director, with his son, Barry, being the Business Development Manager.

John Robertson was born on 23 May 1854 at Woodgreen farm, Kilwinning, to Andrew Robertson and Margaret Gemmell. Andrew, a farmer, was born in 1810 in Stewarton and died in 1859 when John was only five years old. In the reputed year of formation of the company, John had only reached the age of sixteen. His youthfulness, lack of training and necessary experience in the art of ham-curing clearly indicates his inability to create such an enterprise. This assertion is reinforced by the findings in the 1871 Census where John Robertson is recorded as being a grain merchant's clerk, probably with his brother-in-law, Andrew Stevenson, in Main Street, Kilwinning. On the death of Andrew in 1859, his wife and oldest brother, Humphrey continued the business.

By 1881, John was a pork ham-curer with his address being at Woodgreen farm, but he almost certainly boarded in Saltcoats during the working week. The Valuation Rolls from 1885 inform us that John rented premises from his cousin, William Edgar, up to about the turn of the century. William had been brought up on the Robertson farm in Dunlop and was older than John (born 1838). Also involved in earlier ham-curing in Saltcoats was William Craig (born 1845 in Dunlop). Craig's sister married William Edgar. The couple had no children and when William Edgar died, he left significant sums of money to children's charities and the Salvation Army.

The property which John rented was 14 Windmill Street, Saltcoats, and in the flat above the shop he and his wife lived after their marriage in 1882. Their first son, Andrew, was born there in 1883.

By 1905, John had purchased the premises at 14 Windmill Street which he had previously rented from his cousin. He was also the tenant of the curing house (probably the store) at 8 Windmill Street. His business continued to flourish for we have a record of an advertisement posted in the *Ardrossan & Saltcoats Herald,* dated 23 June 1911. The announcement stated:

> John Robertson, Hamcurer
> has opened his New Premises at 14 Windmill Street, Saltcoats, as a Pork Butcher, where he intends to supply the Public with Fresh Pork of Finest Quality and a Few Specialities.

Around this time, John also opened a shop in Stevenston. It was located at 5 New Street. Robert S. Robertson was the tenant in 1935, and the shop was still in existence in 1950.

By 1895, John had become the owner of Winton Cottage, 10 Eglinton Street, Saltcoats (with a family of ten, he eventually bought Abbey Cottage next door to accommodate his brood). His six sons, Andrew, John,

Humphrey, James, Robert, and Edgar followed very different paths through life, but the only individual with any direct connection to Hullerhirst was the youngest, Edgar.

Although several members of John's large family became involved in various capacities within the company (at least one son, Andrew, also became a ham-curer), there is no evidence to support Edgar's direct participation in the ham-curing business. Being the youngest in the family largely removed any overt pressure to become involved in the company. However, it is possible that the significant financial outlay required to purchase Hillhead farm was provided by an increasingly wealthy family. The only tenuous connection between Edgar and the company arises due to the fact that he was named after his father's business partner, William Edgar.

John Robertson's association with Saltcoats, especially Eglinton Street, was duplicated by the presence of his business partner, William Edgar. This gentleman was born on 18 June 1838 in Dunlop. By the age of thirty, he was a grocer and ham-curer (the area around Dunlop and Stewarton was a nucleus for ham-curing). In 1866 he married Agnes Craig, and shortly afterwards moved to Glasgow Street, Ardrossan. But Eglinton Street was acting like a magnet, and in 1881 they had relocated to 15 Eglinton Street. A further move to 27 Eglinton Street occurred sometime before 1891. He was still an active businessman in 1900 when he rented 8 Windmill Street, Saltcoats, and used it as a curing-house. William died in 1919 in Saltcoats, his adopted home.

John Robertson was a well-known and respected business man and establishment figure in Saltcoats with a particular interest in St Cuthbert's Church. He is understood to have been Senior Elder at the time of the opening of the church in 1908. Amazingly, five consecutive generations of his family have become members of this church, many serving as elders. John's youngest daughter, Ella, was one of three children involved in the laying of the memorial stone. For many years within the church there was a system whereby members of the congregation paid a pew rent. This practice has since been discontinued although the pews continue to be numbered, and it appears that as Senior Elder, John chose or was allocated pew number one. Photogrpah 12 shows Edgar next to his father.

With his ever-expanding ham-curing business in the local area, and the enterprise remaining a family concern, it is impossible to arrive at a date which could be considered an inauguration date for the company. However, there is no uncertainty concerning the fact that it became a Limited Company as recently as 1943.

From the available documentation it is highly likely that John Robertson (died 1927) was indeed the founder of this famous local company which bears his name, although the contribution made by William Edgar and William Craig to the initial success of the company should not be underestimated.

Edgar's son, James, was originally based in Hillhead, a farm of approximately thirty-six hectares, and he needed an extra twelve to sixteen hectares of land to make his farming plan feasible. Edgar bought Hullerhirst in 1953 specifically for the ground and not the house. Unfortunately for him, to secure the land holding, he was forced to include the purchase of the house in the transaction. Before his purchase, the house had been unoccupied for a year or so. He attempted to recoup some of his initial financial outlay by leasing the House to a number of individuals for varying periods of time, and he capitalised on the kudos attached to living in such a prestigious property.

Almost immediately after securing the additional ground with the purchase of Hullerhirst, James adopted dual-purpose farming, introducing Simental cross breed cattle to supplement his herd of approximately thirty Ayrshire dairy cows. The resultant quantity of milk was transported to market by road tanker. He cultivated turnips, potatoes, and oats in addition to hay and barley for fodder. Some of the oats were sold to local merchants, and from his two fields of turnips he managed to graze a small number of sheep. It should be noted that his small potato crop was harvested by 'travellers' and largely used by the family. Another visitor to Hillhead in the spring was the mole catcher. A common sight was a line of wire suspended between two trees on which was hung a large number of these small, burrowing mammals, conspicuous by their dark velvety fur and tiny eyes.

Towards the end of the 1950s, James was employing one full-time worker and one part-timer. A typical working day for the part-timer would commence at 7am with the mucking out of the two byres. The dung was transported to the midden by barrow. The other daily task was retrieving pails of water from the bottom of the hill – a distance of around 300 metres – which was then used for cleaning the byres. Other jobs needing attention were then conducted. These included cleaning out the hen-house on wet days, cutting thistles by scythe, plus the cleaning and oiling of the several pieces of machinery which included the old Massey Ferguson tractor, the more modern and powerful Dexter tractor, and the 'Wuffler' which could execute the harvesting, turning, and drying, and bailing. During the harvesting the working day extended to 12-14 hours. James was an inclusive member of the neighbouring farming community, especially at busy times in the calendar, and in the 1960s when Hillhead was 'neighboured' with Castlehill, Lochcraigs and Auchenkist farms for using the threshing mill, he was an active participant. The mobile threshing mill was provided by Robert Borland on an annual basis after the oats crop had been cut. The grain was sold or used as fodder, and the straw used for bedding. There was no heating or running water in any of the outbuildings at Hillhead, the only exception being the milking parlour.

As with many farmers of small farms, James was required to diversify. This strategy necessitated the building of large glasshouses and poultry sheds, the latter being built in 1953 by Richard Maxwell Joiners, Glebe Street, Stevenston. The workmen directly involved in the construction were Bob Leishman (who in 1948 lived in one of the buildings at Hayocks farm), Jimmy Marshall, and Tom Millar. The huts were of a wooden design with asbestos sheet roofing and were sited towards the side/back of the House. After the installation of a heating system in the glasshouses, it became possible to cultivate a selection of exotic fruits including nectarines and pineapples.

Most of the bushes and hedges on the estate were functional 'fence' boundaries without any decorative or commercial function.

Physically, James was about six feet tall, weighing between eleven and a half and twelve stones, was sharp featured and clean-cut. He was more effective, if not accomplished, than his father as a farmer, and his business was only marginally efficient. In his early days he had grand plans to improve the organisation and profitability of the farm, undertaking a course at the Agricultural College where he secured an Ordinary National Certificate (ONC). However, he seems to have lacked the practical skills required to put them into long-term operation. In general terms James tended to be awkward and erratic in his approach to people. This trait was understandable if we consider that James had an irrational dread of failure and fear of falling into poverty. He was a stickler for insurance matters and made full use of the services provided by his solicitor. With his employees he could be blunt, petulant, and rather aloof.

James was a complex character exhibiting several idiosyncrasies in his approach to his business. He regularly frequented the local cattle markets at Kilmarnock, Ayr, and Paisley, and was known to visit some of the more prestigious markets and agricultural shows, such as Smithfield Market in London and the Royal Highland Show in Edinburgh where he kept himself informed of the latest developments and innovations. He was also a member of the Largs Young Farmer's Club which met in the Moorings in the town. He was acquainted with Mr Thomas Donald who owned Kilmarnock market, but as time passed, he more often sold his cattle directly to the local abattoir where Billy Glazebrook was the buyer.

James managed a mixed farm, but bizarrely he never seemed confident or at ease with livestock. Conversely, he had a reputation as an enthusiastic and skilled ploughman, an activity he carried out often wearing a collar and tie and a waistcoat. In summary, James could be described as a rather traditional/conservative farmer.

James Robertson was married in the summer of 1967 in Kilmarnock to a farmer's daughter from Craigie Mains farm near Symington, but the marriage only lasted about fourteen months. His wife's name was Margaret Paton Kilpatrick. After the marriage James, his wife, his mother-in-law, and father -in-law all moved into Hillhead farm, while Edgar and family decanted to Hullerhirst. It is recorded that on the night of the Great Storm which affected the West of Scotland on the night of 14 January and the following morning, Peggy, the wife of Edgar, contacted a local joiner in the middle of the night to request assistance in repairing some damage to the property caused by the hurricane-force winds.

With the death of Flora Robertson in 1948, any female influence in the estate passed into the hands of Peggy Robertson (the daughter of Robert Montgomerie and Jessie Gerrard White of Hawkhill farm). The consensus-of-opinion of those people who had contact with her at Hillhead and Hullerhirst was of a determined, independent woman who was candid and abrupt with strangers. She had a good business brain and was demanding in pursuit of her objectives. Edgar's purchase of Hullerhirst was greatly influenced by her drive and ambition. Peggy could be impatient but was always protective and supportive towards her family. For a considerable part of her life Peggy was employed as a nursing sister.

Elizabeth, like her mother was a nurse, initially practising her nursing skills on various ocean-going liners including firstly the SS *Himalaya*

13. Hullerhirst, 1964.

followed by the more modern SS *Canberra* of the Peninsular & Oriental Steam Navigation Company (P & O Line). On leaving her life on the ocean wave she was employed by the Health Board as a District Nurse. She was a jovial, pleasant, and out-going woman, who when resident at Hillhead was industrious, energetic, and helpful in all aspects of the farm work.

The life-cycles of the four Hillhead/Hullerhirst Robertsons could be summarised in the following manner. Edgar died at Hullerhirst on 7 October 1978, aged seventy-six after a long illness. The funeral service was held in the afternoon of 10 October and carried out by Rev Tom McIntyre, minister of the High Kirk. Funeral arrangements were organised by George Tannahill & Sons. His wife, Margaret Wilson Montgomerie (Peggy), died on 20 September 1991, aged eighty-five. Their son, James Speir Robertson, died at Crosshouse Hospital on 29 January 2016, aged seventy-nine. His funeral service was held, like his fathers' in Stevenston High Kirk. Most recently, on 5 May 2022, Elizabeth, their daughter, died aged eighty-four at Fullarton Care Home, Irvine. Like her brother, the funeral service was held in the High Kirk and was conducted by Rev Scott Cameron. All four members of the family were buried in Hawkhill Cemetery.

Hullerhirst burned down on the evening of Friday 19 August 2022 as a result of wilful fire-raising, and remains today as a roofless shell (See Photograph 14).

From photograph 13 we can see that the building was a late eighteenth

14. Hullerhirst after the disastrous fire of 2022.

century classical house of two storeys, and three bays with a central pediment together with a blind bull's eye and terminal urns. The building was rendered with painted margins. There is an unfortunate 1950's porch in front of the pedimented door-piece. Most of the twelve-pane glazing survives. There is a piended slate roof with symmetrical central stacks, and at the rear is located a low single storey service wing.

HULLERHIRST HOUSE

After Edgar purchased the house and land in 1953, the property lay empty to permit a number of 'improvements' to be carried out. These refinements included the porch. The unsightly porch on the front of the house (See Photo 13) was erected around 1956. The tradesmen concerned in the undertaking were George Maxwell and Matthew Wilson, both joiners, assisted by William Ballantine who laid the brickwork. Mr Ballantine originally worked for John and Matthew McLellan Ltd who had their yard through the close at the top of New Street – No 83 (more recently in the possession of Hugh Frew, lead-worker). McLellan Ltd advertised as Monumental Sculptors, Builders, and Public Works Contractors. However, Mr Ballantine assumed ownership of the business and operated it on a smaller scale. At the time the porch was constructed he ran the business.

Around this time, the house became available for rent, and its availability attracted several tenants on short term lets.

At the entrance to the driveway to the house there was an old stone-built bothy, which in the 1930s and 1940s was used to accommodate farm workers. Specifically, it was sited near the gate piers on the right-hand side of the driveway. At a later date it was utilised for housing calves. Many people will remember this structure, and even when empty, James could not secure permission for its demolition. It eventually disappeared in the 1990s.

The demise of the last remaining mansion house in Stevenston occurred on the evening of 19 August 2022 when it was deliberately set alight. However, serious deterioration had become evident after the death of James Robertson in 2016. Although his sister, Elizabeth, was still alive, she had settled in Hillhead, meaning Hullerhirst was largely unoccupied. With the admission of Elizabeth to a care home in Irvine, the house became a target for repeated acts of vandalism which accelerated and intensified after Elizabeth's death in 2022. It therefore came as no surprise when the final malicious incident resulted in the ruination of the building and its valuable contents. This episode is all the more regrettable when we consider that Hullerhirst was the last remaining mansion house in Stevenston, after the 'disappearance' of Seabank, Ardeer, Kerelaw, and Hayocks Houses.

With the assistance of an acquaintance of James Robertson, I have produced a sketch plan of the house dating from the 1980s (page 60). Although largely accurate, it undoubtedly contains several omissions, especially windows, and incorporates some 'best-guess' features. Hopefully, it does convey the general internal design of the building.

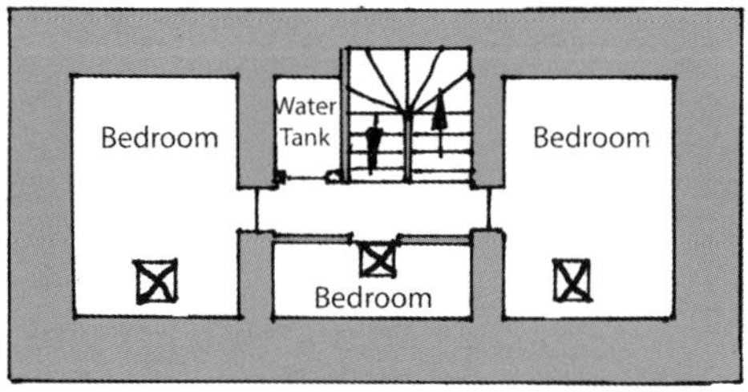

Attic

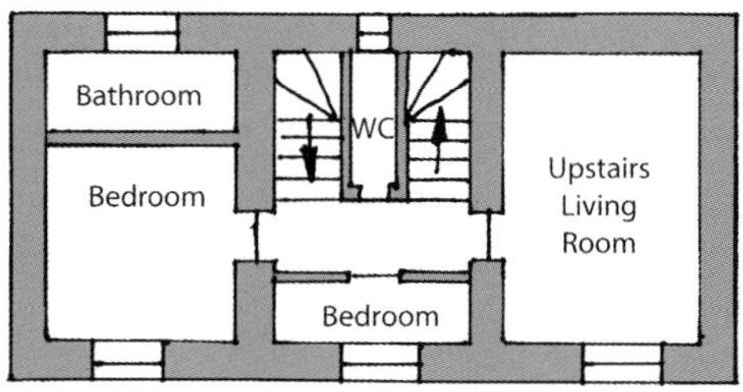

First Floor

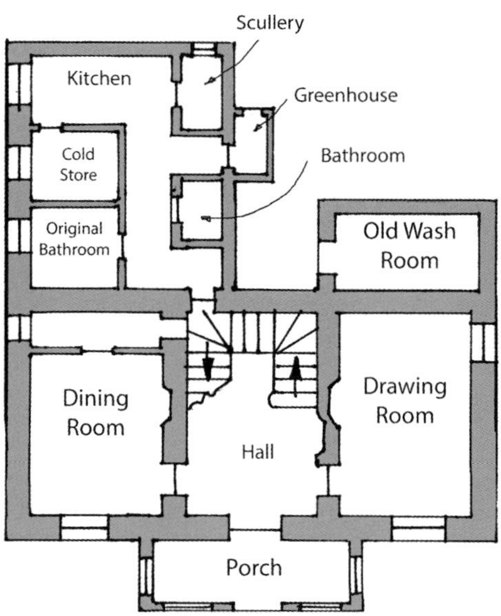

Sketch Plans of Hullerhirst House.

3
Topography and the Evolution of Early Farming

The boundaries of the Hayocks as I have delineated them encompass a large landward area which nowadays lies to the north of the housing zone. Within this rural area the two main land uses over the past three hundred years have been farming and quarrying. These two activities have traditionally been intrinsically linked, for example, the main reason for securing the ownership of Hullerhirst estate in the eighteenth century was the availability of coal and limestone reserves and not the productivity of the land.

My Hayocks study area, lying to the north of Glencairn Street/Kilwinning Road, is almost exclusively on ground above 15 metres. The area slopes gently up to Hullerhirst at 43 metres, culminating in an elevation of 61 metres at Ashgrove. The 15-metre contour line stretches from the ground behind Auchenharvie to the Pennyburn roundabout running parallel to Kilwinning Road. This contour indicates the top of the sea cliff separating the raised beach with its light, sandy soils from the slightly higher inland area overlain by heavier loamy-clay soils.

Another physical difference between the raised beach and higher inland area is the rainfall regime. Table 2 below is a register of the mean monthly rainfall totals in millimetres as recorded at Greenhead Water Works (elevation of 57 metres).

The annual rainfall total of 1,040 mm is approximately 100 -150 mm higher than that received at the coast, and together with the clay nature of the soil explains the existence of pasture as the main land-use in the Hullerhirst area.

Jan	Feb	Mar	Apr	May	Jun
95	83	78	60	65	65

Jul	Aug	Sep	Oct	Nov	Dec	**Year**
83	105	85	98	108	118	**1040**

Table 2. Mean Monthly Rainfall Totals from Greenhead Water Works.

The topography is not uniform with the ground surface moderately undulating in places. Most of the study area is underlain with soils from the Ashgrove Series which belongs to the Ashgrove Association. Consequently, the clay loam soil developed on a deep clay till derived from shales and sandstones from the Carboniferous Limestone Series. Initially, farmers were confronted with soil consisting of a clay texture and plastic consistency rendering the drainage difficult, but over the years this situation has been greatly improved.

Prior to the 1700s, it is almost impossible to describe accurately the appearance of farm buildings, not only locally but nationally in Scotland, as from this period we have neither the records nor surviving buildings to work from.

The oldest standing farmsteads in Scotland are associated with monasteries, and in the landward area of the Hayocks this religious connection is connected to Kilwinning Abbey. The monks who inhabited the Abbey were Tironensian, a branch of the Benedictine order, and since the Tironensians were not particularly proficient or interested in farming, it is likely that most of their lands were rented as farms. Certainly, in the sixteenth century the monks survived through the rents of money, oats, cheese, and poultry, received from their tenant farmers.

Due to the tenuous nature of agriculture, tenants were highly vulnerable to short-term crises such as harvest failures. One example of crop failure occurred in 1782 with the occurrence of a very windy period of westerly winds in August which lasted for a considerable period of time. This stormy weather which damaged the oats crop was followed by a very early and substantial fall of snow which exacerbated the initial crop damage. The yield from the oats crop was drastically diminished resulting in a massive decrease in availability for most tenant farmers. Further trouble arose in 1826 as a result of an extremely hot summer. This episode was afterwards known as 'the year of the short corn and sandy meal.' No rain fell for four months resulting in a crop of dwarf oats and barley which could not be cut, having to be pulled out by the roots.

In the eighteenth century, one of the first figures in the industrial life of Stevenston was the old grain mill (located between the Millhill and Townhead Street) which was possibly built around 1728. It was rebuilt jointly by Alexander Hamilton of Grange (Kerelaw) and Patrick Warner of Ardeer in 1783. Both of these men became joint proprietors, and the tenant farmers from the surrounding area, including the study area, were thirled to the mill and were required to convey their cereals to the mill to ensure its continuing operation (the mill finally closed in April 1935). It is possible, although unlikely, that the Bridgend Mill in Kilwinning received some of the grain harvest. Some repairs were implemented to the machinery in the

Stevenston mill in 1785 and interior alterations were carried out in 1791.

Agriculture in the area remained ineffective until the end of the eighteenth century. During this early period few practical roads existed, making the movement of livestock and produce very difficult. Covering the second half of the eighteenth century the principal diet of the population consisted of oats, milk, and scotch kale. The clayey nature of the soil in the Hayocks area resulted in a scarcity of potatoes and edible root crops such as turnips being cultivated. The local farms such as Lochcraigs, Hillhead, Castlehill, and Lochend were all tenanted with the few landowners receiving over half of all produce. The remaining 40% allowed the farmers a tiny surplus for family consumption and the following year's sowing. The tenant was also obligated to undertake tasks for the landowner such as ploughing and working hay which greatly interfered with work on his own plot.

Tenants were arguably the most important group in the Scottish countryside, as others depended on them for employment and were affected by their prosperity or poverty. The fortunes of the tenantry were equally important to the landowners whose incomes were mainly derived from the rents which they paid. Their poverty has been attributed to insecurity of tenure caused by the prevalence of short leases. This insecurity caused poverty by encouraging low standards of husbandry, as tenants were reluctant to invest labour or capital in improving their holdings if they were likely to be evicted without compensation at the end of a short lease or have their rents raised. When tenants did move to other farms the distances involved were short. Most remained within the same estate.

The farmhouses were mere hovels coated with clay with an open hearth in the middle. The dung was stored at the door. The land was overgrown with rushes and weeds; hedges unkempt; and the few ditches which existed were often blocked and poorly constructed.

The livestock were under-nourished and animal husbandry very basic. Crop rotations were unknown in the outfield which was largely given over to grass, and very restricted in the in-bye with oats, barley and grass comprising a simple rotation.

Moving into the 1800s, George Robertson[1] in 1824 described Hullerhirst as consisting of thirty hectares of good arable land, and the smaller property of Hayocks – perhaps sixteen hectares – as good land. When his favourable description of Grange estate is included, we have a picture of an area of moderate fertility containing a sizeable area of arable land, although pasture remained the principal land-use. Rev Archibald Blair Campbell, minister

1 Robertson, George. *A Genealogical Account of the Principal Families in Ayrshire (Kyle & Cunninghame).* Vol 11. P 251 & 34. Irvine. 1824.

of Abbey Church, Kilwinning,[2] stated that one-third or one-fourth of the land is generally under crop, the rest being pasture. The preponderance of pasture, due to the clay soil which underlies this part of Stevenston parish, explains the relatively high quantity of cheese made in the area, for which a market existed in Glasgow and Paisley.

As the century progressed more modern and effective methods of farming were developed. Improved methods of ploughing were introduced along with fallowing, drilling, turnip cultivation, and a more productive rotation of crops. Tile drainage was introduced (it was introduced into Ayrshire in 1825 by the Duke of Portland), and soil quality was improved by liming. More attention was given to the breeding of horses and cattle, and fences were erected on an extensive scale. Walled gardens or orchards associated with mansion houses became common, as in Hayocks House and Ashgrove House.

In the 1800s Hullerhirst estate was owned by the Kelso Hamilton family, who were absentee lairds, with the House being inhabited by the Hamilton Howes. Neither proprietor nor tenant had any direct association with farming leaving it to the various tenant farmers of Hillhead farm. The influence and impact that the two Robertson families exerted in agricultural terms during the twentieth century was covered in detail in an earlier chapter.

CUSTODIANS OF THE LAND

HILLHEAD FARM

The close-proximity of Hillhead farm to Hullerhirst encourages a coordinated investigation. However, this approach is only valid from 1953 when Edgar Robertson purchased Hullerhirst (he had previously acquired Hillhead in 1935) making him the owner of both properties and most of the surrounding land. From 1953, the farming activities were integrated by Edgar and his son, James.

Before considering the contribution and impact that Edgar and his family had within the estate, it is illuminating to review the chronological history of Hillhead farm with particular emphasis on ownership and tenancy.

Reflecting the situation at the neighbouring mansion house, the earliest owners of Hillhead were the Kelso family – later to become the Hamiltons. James Hamilton was the proprietor in 1822, and Edward Kelso Hamilton (a minor) in 1855. Alexander Kelso Hamilton assumed ownership around 1885. These absentee landlords had their principal family residence at the 'Retreat' in Devon, but they maintained their ownership of Hillhead until

2 Campbell Blair, Archibald. *The Statistical Account of Kilwinning.* 1842.

around 1910 although the day-to-day business was controlled by James Campbell, writer in Saltcoats.

In 1911 the farm changed hands when it was bought by the Reid family. The three family members were Miss Martha Brown Reid, John Owen Reid, and Andrew Reid. This was a farming family, but their ownership was short-lived, terminating after only two years when James Miller, also a practising farmer, purchased the property. After a tenure lasting twenty-two years, Mr Miller sold it to Edgar Robertson in 1935. Edgar and his wife, Peggy, also made the farm their home, and James and Elizabeth were born at Hillhead soon after their occupancy.

In contrast to the limited number of owners of the estate, the situation pertaining to tenancy is very different. Prior to Edgar's purchase of Hillhead in 1935, the farm had been rented by numerous farmers.

The remains of a deserted rural settlement (Little Hillhead) have been identified on Roy's Military Map of 1752-55, but if Little Hillhead was constructed from stone there is no clear geophysical evidence for demolition rubble or building foundations. This point of view reinforces the possibility that Little Hillhead is in fact the present-day Hillhead.

The earliest documented tenant of Little Hillhead was William Wilson in the 1770s, when William and Patrick Kelso were the proprietors. John and Mary Muir occupied Hillhead in 1819. They were joined by James, Alex, and Agnes Paterson, as well as John Bryce. This association between the Muir family and the farm continued through to approximately 1870, with James in 1841, and James and Samuel in 1855. In 1861, both farming brothers James (aged 60) and Samuel (aged 50) were farming thirty-six hectares. They were joined by James's wife, Janet, and three servants: Isabella Kerr (dairymaid), Mary Miller (domestic servant) and Thomas Watt (ploughboy), in addition to two farming labourers. James and Samuel Muir as principal tenants were replaced around 1870 by another farmer named Robert Neilson.

Ten years later the farmhouse was inhabited by James Todd, his wife Janet, and their three sons, Robert, Matthew, and James. As was common in sizeable farms at the time, the Todd family was assisted by three farm servants, and two general servants, Mary Andrew and Sarah Hendry. Mr Todd also employed a dairyman – John Halbert who was accompanied by his wife Helen and their two children, Thomas and Annie.

Between 1888 and 1891, James Todd was replaced by James Barr who farmed the land until succeeded around 1895 by William Smith who also farmed the adjoining farm of Corsankell. Mr Barr's tenancy was terminated when the farm was put up for let. At this time Hillhead extended to about forty-six hectares, significantly larger than its future size. Access to the arable land was set at November 1895, while the farmhouse and grazing became available in May the following year. William Smith employed Thomas McAughtrie, a dairyman, who was accompanied by his wife Mary, and their six children, and he continued with his tenancy up to around 1914 before being replaced by James Miller who also purchased Hillhead.

For a few years duration between 1905 and 1909, a bower by the name of James Ramsay found a home at Hillhead. It is interesting to note that the nearby town of Kilwinning has a long and distinguished history of bow making and archery. This heritage is still celebrated in the town today with the Papingo Shoot and existence of the celebrated Ancient Society of Kilwinning Archers. In the early nineteenth century, a bowery workshop owned by Peter and David Muir existed in the town. These were talented craftsmen in this highly skilled business, and they were treated almost reverentially within the community. Coincidentally, in 1819, a family by the name of Muir were tenants in Hillhead. Kilwinning was also the home of the renowned longbow maker, James Reid.

In addition to providing an income from the agricultural business, Hillhead also possessed mineral reserves. In 1926 Timmis & Company Ltd from Stourbridge were quarrying fireclay from the site. After Timmis, the extraction of this mineral continued under the direction of Peter Spence & Sons Ltd per A. McDougall, c/o W. Kerr (Kilwinning) Ltd.

HAWKHILL

The first documented evidence for the existence of Hawkhill farm occurs in 1841 when it was tenanted by a 40-year-old farmer, John Blair. He was still occupying the farmhouse and working the land twenty years later. In 1861, the farm was thirty-two hectares in size, and Mr Blair employed six labourers and one boy. He inhabited the farmhouse with his wife, Marion (aged forty-two) and young daughter, Margaret. In the same building lived three servants, Mary McDougall (thirty-six), domestic servant, Barbara Campbell (twenty-three), dairymaid, and Joseph Black (eighteen), milkman.

In other buildings at Hawkhill lived John Main, servant, his wife Jane, and son Thomas (seven); Alexander Blair, servant (twenty-seven), his wife Agnes, and sons Alexander and William; James Fleming (seventy) who was a thatcher, his wife Catherine (forty-two) and their son John (fourteen) who was an apprentice cabinet maker.

The farm was part of the extensive Ardeer Estate and was owned by Patrick Warner. At this time, Hawkhill was a mixed farm being sited just above the light, sandy soils of the raised beach. The soil was a loamy, clay, till in nature, allowing oats and fodder crops to be cultivated along with grass for the dairy cattle.

The farmhouse which was recognised as Hawkhill was built sometime prior to 1862. The house formed the west side of a courtyard and was one storey high with an attic. It was rubble built and painted. The margins of the house were also distinctly painted. The house had three bays and a lower one to the north. The west elevation had a central gabled porch, flanking windows and two piended canted dormers. On the east side of the building there was a door with a dated pedimented gable. The roof was slated, and a barn had been constructed on the east side of the steading. Photograph 15 shown below were taken in the late 1950s and clearly mirror the description of the farmhouse and courtyard provided above.

Following Mr Blair, the farm was occupied by John Lockhart who ploughed and sowed the arable land. Exactly when he became the tenant is unclear, but he was certainly the resident in 1879. In this year, John was forty years old and was accompanied by his wife, Annie, their two daughters Lillias and Margaret, and two sons William and Archibald. Within the premises there were also two servants, Agnes Young (general domestic servant) and David McBroom (farm servant).

In Hawkhill Cottage, located within the boundary of the farm, lived the Glover family. This grouping consisted of John, the ploughman father, his wife, Margaret, and sons Robert and John, as well as daughters Jessie, Jeanie and Margaret Ann.

In 1880, the farm was newly tenanted by Hugh Smith. By 1892, Hugh had been joined by his brother, Hamilton Caldwell Smith. Three years later Hugh retired from Hawkhill, through failing health, having occupied the farm for approximately fifteen years. On relocating to Saltcoats he commented that the farm had become unprofitable. He was succeeded by the son of Mr Montgomerie, a farmer from Fairlie Crevoch farm which was located two kilometres north-east of the Girdle Toll, near Cunninghamhead. The new tenant managed to secure a 20% reduction in rent from the proprietor Patrick Warner who was still resident in Torquay, Devon.

The new tenant, Robert Montgomerie, worked the land until approximately 1945 (then aged seventy-eight). During this prolonged period of occupancy not only was he assisted by his wife, Jessie, three daughters and two sons, he also employed a varying number of servants. In 1911, these included Jean McBride, Ellen Stevenson and James Milloy. One of Robert's daughters, Margaret (Peggy), on 9 January 1935 married Edgar Robertson. Later in the same year the couple purchased Hillhead farm.

The nearby Cottage was often inhabited by farm workers (See Table 3 over).

Many of the residents of the cottage were accompanied by their wives and families, living in extremely cramped conditions. Two examples of this situation arose in 1901 and 1911. In the former Mr Colvin, his wife Helen,

Date of Occupancy	Name of Employee	Occupation
1898	Peter Barry	Ploughman
1901	James Colvin	Labourer
1905	Daniel Murchie Jnr	Ploughman
1910	Thomas Kidd	Miner
1911	Susan Kidd	---
1922-1928	Joseph McPhee	Dynamite Worker/ Labourer
1929	John Allan	---
1934	Mrs Margaret Moore	---
1935	John Kane	Ploughman
1937	William Moore	Ploughman
1939	John Kane	Ploughman
1940	John Kane	Ploughman

Table 3. Residents of Hawkhill Cottage.

and their five children, along with a servant, occupied the cottage, and in the latter Mrs Susan Kidd was accompanied by her son and four daughters.

In Scotland at this time, farm servants (stable-lads or dairy-maids) were employed on fixed contracts of six, nine or twelve months. These workers were usually young, single, and peripatetic. Unmarried servants generally boarded in the farmhouse or lived in an outhouse. Married servants resided in cottages on the farm, and these cottages were 'tied' to the landowner's estate. These small buildings were in reality far too small to accommodate the large families of the period. Agricultural labourers were different. They were not tied to fixed contracts.

With the death of Patrick Warner of Ardeer in 1922, the Trustees of P. Warner became the new proprietors. This situation with the trustees as owners and Robert Montgomerie as the tenant continued until the start of the Second World War when Mr Montgomerie was joined by H.M. Secretary of State for the War Department as the joint tenant.

During World War Two, there was a heavy anti-aircraft battery situated in a field immediately to the east of Hawkhill farm. Initially, there were four gun-emplacements sited approximately 150 metres north-east of the farm buildings. Between 1941 and 1945 this number increased to six. In addition, there was an accommodation camp sited to the east of the farm track leading to the main A738 road. The mess room was a large Nissen hut which doubled as a dance hall at the week-ends. South of the emplacements was a GL mat, the site for which was under construction in 1941. This feature was used for radar targeting and tracking.

The battery code was ICI and it was part of the Irvine Gun Defended

15. Aerial View of Hawkhill farm, c. 1960.

Area (GDA). In 1942 it consisted of 4 x 3.7-inch guns with a magazine and command post nearby. A year later the six 3.7-inch guns were supplemented with an EF type radar set.

By 2005, both the farmstead and battery had been demolished and the area is now occupied by a retail park. Hawkhill farm was listed as a Category C building on 26 February 1980, and the circumstances behind its destruction are unclear.

Soon after the end of hostilities in 1945 (around 1948) Hawkhill farm was purchased by a Stevenston haulage contractor called William Frew. Mr Frew was also the occupant of the property, and he later became the owner of the meadow land at Lochend farm. Hawkhill had been previously tenanted by Robert Montgomerie from before 1922.

In 1966, Mr Thomas Frew became the new owner of the farm, a year after the death of his father on 24 November 1965, aged sixty-three. Tom himself died on 10 December 2007 aged seventy-two.

CASTLEHILL

The first documented reference to Castlehill farm occurred in 1560 with John Pitcon, Alex Pitcon, John Service, and Alan and Marian Cunninghame occupying the property. Evidence of mediaeval rural land-use in this area is lacking, but using Corsankell farm as an example, it is possible that some of the other farmsteads – including Castlehill - in the study area have origins dating back to the mediaeval period.

We have records of the ownership of the titles and lands of Castlehill from the early eighteenth century. In 1705, the heirs of Adam Campbell, with the consent of Robert Elphinstone and James Campbell sold threequarters of the property to William Blair. Three years later Mr Blair disposed of Castlehill to Patrick Warner, a minister in Irvine, and his son William Warner. Almost immediately – on 20 August 1708 – it passed into the hands of Alexander Hamilton. There is also evidence that John Glasgow resided at Castlehill in 1705, for we have an account of this gentleman along with Thomas Mitchell of Saltcoats, George Auld of Townhead in Saltcoats, and Robert and James Cunninghame taking out a lease to work coal in the lands of George Heriot's Hospital in Edinburgh.

Moving forward, in 1841, Captain James Patrick of Drumbuie (factor to the Marquis of Hastings) sold Castlehill to Robert Stevenson, a merchant from Saltcoats, for £4,350.

This transaction excluded all rights to the mineral deposits under the property. 'Robert Stevenson shall have no rights to any part of the 200 loads of coal payable yearly during the working of the said coal within the ground of said lands.'[3] These coal deposits were reserved to Patrick Warner of Ardeer.

In the same year, fifty-five year old John Stirrat was farming the thirty-six hectares of Castlehill. Shortly before the death of Mr Stevenson c. 1854, the farm was occupied by John Smith who employed three men. At the time of the census in 1861, living on the farm, there were two sons, John [sixteen years], and James [fourteen] along with two daughters, Elizabeth [eight] and Janet [five]. There were also two dairymaids, Elizabeth Nicol and Ann Barr.

In 1871, Castlehill was put up for auction by the trustees of the late Robert Stevenson – Robert Barr and Alexander Gilmour - and was purchased for the sum of £5,205 by the proprietor of Kerelaw Estate, Gavin Fullarton. Although Gavin died on 28 August 1876 aged eighty-nine, his trustees retained the estate until February 1919 when it was bought by James Campbell for £32,000. Within six weeks, Mr Campbell sold on Castlehill and Hawkhill farms to the Stevenston Co-operative Society Ltd for £2,800.

The Barr family started their long association with Castlehill as tenants around 1880. James farmed the land with his wife, Annabella, plus their daughter, Annabella. There was also his sister, Margaret Barr (also a dairymaid), and three servants, Martha Connel (general servant), John Muir (ploughman) and William Brown (general servant). The previous farmer had been William Vallance.

Sometime between 1891 and 1898, the tenancy was transferred to Robert

3 Disposition by James Patrick in favour of the said Robert Stevenson, merchant in Saltcoats, of lands of Castlehill dated 21st June 1841.

YEAR	PLOUGHMAN
1920	Matt Graham
1922-1923	James Paton
1925	William Crawford
1928	James Currie
1937	David Fell
1940	Robert Turner
1943	James Muir
1947	James Lang
1948	William Kerr

Table 4. List of Ploughmen Working for the Stevenston Co-operative Society.

and Alexander Barr who farmed the land and occupied the farmhouse. Robert was married to Margaret, and had three children, James, Alan, and Margaret. With the purchase of Castlehill by the Stevenston Co-operative in 1919, the Barr family relocated to the Lothians. Dated on the year of their departure were carved on some stonework at the farm the names of Robert's sons, James and Alan.

The new owners – Stevenston Co-operative Society Ltd – employed a farm manager, Peter Reid, who carried out his responsibilities for over twenty years.

Situated a short distance to the east of the farmhouse lies East Castle Hill (also known as Little Hill). It is a prominent flat-topped knoll sited about thirty-three metres above sea level. A small mound has been identified on top of the hill. It is eight paces in diameter and 0.8 metres high, but is not considered an antiquity. It is more likely to be a spoil heap associated with some small-scale quarrying activity. A series of narrow, angular trenches occurring near the perimeter of the knoll are probably the result of First World War military activity.

Castle Hill is located between the farmhouse and Little Hill and is noticeably larger. John Smith in his 1885 publication[4] observed part of a foundation which he concluded was the site of a castle. On the other hand, A. H. Millar[5] surmised that the foundations were simply part of a beacon site.

In his *History of the Counties of Ayr and Wigton*,[6] James Paterson, when referring to Castle Hill, states, 'it is supposed that a castle or fort had existed

4 Smith, John. *Prehistoric Man in Ayrshire*. London. 1895.

5 Millar, A.H. *Castles and Mansions of Ayrshire*. Grimsay Press. 2004.

6 Paterson, James. *History of the County of Ayr; Genealogical Account of the Families of Ayrshire* Vol 2. Parish of Stevenston p. 448. 1852.

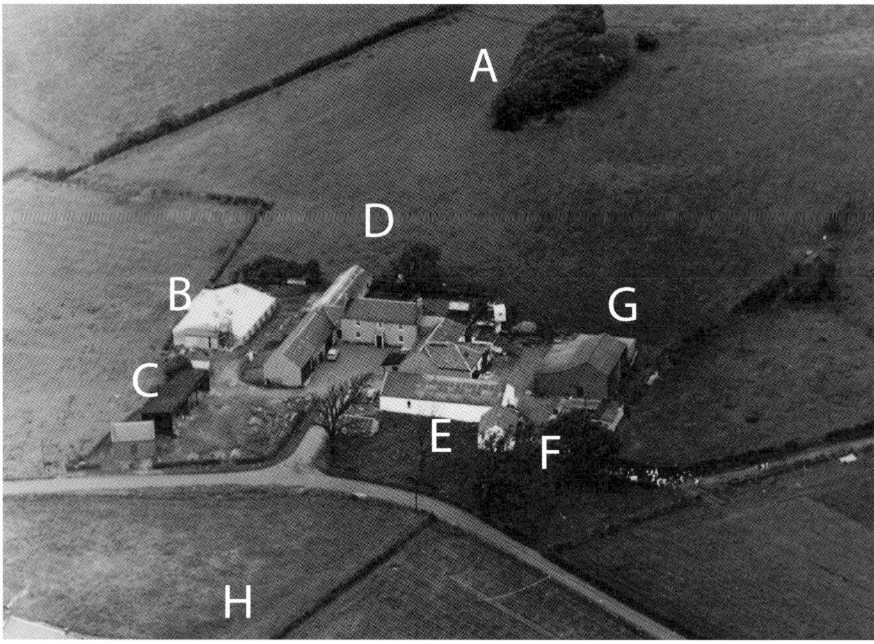

16. Aerial photograph of Castlehill farm from 1964.

A: wood; B: hen house; C: corn shed; D: farmhouse;
E: original byre; F: calf byre; G: hay shed; H: Hawkhill land.

at some early period.'

From the conflicting opinions reached by the three respected historians and authors, it is clear that the nature of the human footprint on both hills is uncertain and open to debate. Fortunately, the geological characteristics are straight forward. Both hills are small vents of basaltic tuff. The rocks are fine-grained, dark-coloured, and intrusive igneous in nature. Rocks of this type can be used in construction or crushed as bottoming, and it is not surprising that this outcrop had been previously quarried on a small scale.

Gavin Reid and his wife Margaret (nee Fife), who came from the Kilbirnie area, purchased the farm in 1949 from the Stevenston Co-operative Society Ltd. This company had their Registered Office in Boglemart Street and had branches in Warner Street, Shore Road, and Bradshaw Street in Saltcoats. The Reids built a dairy byre and hay shed before moving to their new property on 15 May 1950. Gavin and Margaret had four children, two sons, Daniel (born 1945) and Alex (born 1950) along with two daughters. The family moved from Pencot farm which is located near the B707 to the east of Dalry, within Blair Estate. The present Daniel Reid was the fifth generation with that name to be born at Pencot, and the Reids can trace their connection with the Blair Estate back to 1703. Gavin Reid was followed into Pencot by the Stevenson family.

Under the farming regime practised by the Reids, the farm was principally a mixed farm (dairy and oats) with dairying predominating. Most of the herd were pedigree Friesian, some cross bred with Ayrshires. These cattle were often washed down in a small duck-pond situated between the farm buildings and the small quarry. The farm was thirty hectares in extent comprised almost exclusively of grass, with two hectares given over to silage production. Small amounts of turnips and kale were also grown. Between 1950 and 1965, about 1.6 hectares of potatoes were cultivated on the lighter sandy soils. On the instructions of McDowall, Potato Merchants from Ardrossan, the farm grew Second Earlies which were harvested in late August. This arrangement continued the availability of local potatoes after the early Ayrshire potatoes grown along the coast were finished. McDowall's was owned by Robert and Ian Armstrong. Early in his ownership of Castlehill, Gavin Reid kept approximately 200 to 300 hens (this was common practice at the time). By the late 1950s and mid-1960s, the farm also housed about 6,500 battery hens. In 1963, the farm kept around 4,000 hens, the eggs being sold to West Cumberland Farm Egg Packers, Kilmarnock. A further 2,500 hens were added to the operation in 1965, the eggs being sold 'at the door' and to various local retail outlets and milk producers. The egg enterprise diminished from 1978 when it became uneconomic to continue. This situation arose largely from the emergence and subsequent domination of large-scale operators like Lainshaw Farm Eggs from Stewarton, in the local egg producing industry. This company ceased trading as recently as June 2022. The feasibility of the business at Castlehill was further impacted when Anna, one of Gavin's daughters, who was actively involved in the distribution of eggs, left the business having secured employment with the National Farmers Union.

Initially, the accommodation housing the hens was wooden, containing broilers. This building was steadily expanded in size, involving the removal of hedges and other ground alterations, until it was sixty feet long and forty-five feet wide. Towards the end of the 1950s a brick building was erected (sixty feet by twenty feet). Over the years there were on-going alterations to the infrastructure of the egg business with the broilers being housed in cages. The all-important hen slurry store was situated at the gable-end of the building (See Photo 16).

From 1965 due to Gavin Reid's deteriorating health and a shortage of suitable labour, the farm reverted largely to a dairying enterprise. After Mr Reid died on 5 June 1967, the farm was operated by his wife Mrs Margaret Reid and her son, Daniel. In 1977, Daniel became the sole proprietor. It remained within the family possession until 2002 when it was sold, with planning permission, to Mr Robert and Mrs Jeanne Black, who trading under Cabin Developments Ltd extended the residential potential of the site by creating a nine-property development around the original farmhouse. This company became a private, limited company on 1 May 2003.

The isolated building lying across the road from Castlehill was Hawkhill Cottage, a worker's cottage which pre-dated 1950. Fred McCrae, who worked for William Frew of Hawkhill in the early 1950s moved into the cottage when he married. It was extended and then sold to Bill and Ann McVey who had a plasterer's business.

4
Quarrying in Hullerhirst Estate

At this juncture it is appropriate to investigate the impact that quarrying brought to bear on the landward area, especially the Hullerhirst estate.

Aiton[1] has stated that in Ayrshire, lime was used as a fertiliser from about 1730-1740 on the Treesbanks Estate on the outskirts of Kilmarnock, although Pont mentions liming in Stewarton and Dunlop parishes in the early seventeenth century. Strawhorn[2] asserts that 'the Melrose lands at Mauchline were being limed as early as 1528.' No matter when liming started in the county, the limestone was locally quarried on a very small scale and burned in limekilns with coal from accessible seams to generate the sought-after lime, especially on the large farming estates and improved farms. Most sizeable limestone quarries would have their own limekilns where the lime was sold at various prices depending on demand and quality.

North Ayrshire contained the only three economically important limestone beds in the West of Scotland, and within Stevenston parish the most prominent site for limestone quarrying was certainly at Hullerhirst. A simplified borehole section through the Upper Limestone Formation at Hullerhirst (NGR 277431) is shown below in Figure 1.

1 Aiton, W. *The Agriculture of the County of Ayr.* 1811.
2 Strawhorn, J. *Ayrshire: The Story of a County.* AANHS. 1975.

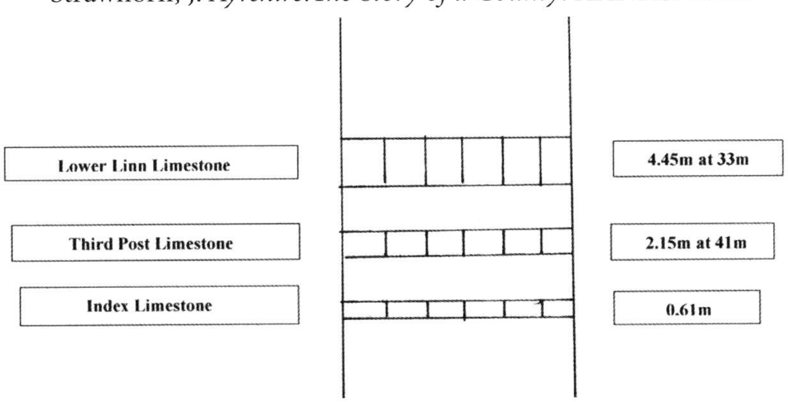

Figure 1. A Simplified Borehole Section through the Upper Limestone Formation at Hullerhirst.

17. The Two Draw Kilns at Hullerhirst - viewed from the south.

This borehole proved three limestones: the Index, Third Post, and Lower Linn Limestones. All three are dark grey and argillaceous. The term 'limestone' is applied to any sedimentary rock consisting essentially of carbonates. The two most important constituents are calcite and dolomite, but small amounts of iron-bearing carbonates may also occur. Limestones can be classified into three major groups: organic; chemical; and detrital or clastic.

Lime in the present context refers to either quicklime (calcium oxide – CaO) or slaked lime (calcium hydroxide – Ca(OH)2). When limestone (calcium carbonate – CaCO3) is burned with coal in a kiln, with the release of carbon dioxide (CO2) it becomes calcium oxide (quicklime).

The Hullerhirst kilns shown above were stone built, and although the quicklime (as a powder) was thoroughly mixed with ash, this did not detract from its usefulness as a fertiliser. Draw kilns – like the ones at Hullerhirst – were usually built into a hillside to allow access at the top, for charging, and at the bottom to permit the recovery of the product. At Hullerhirst, coal as opposed to timber, would be the fuel, as coal was being worked from nearby estates. The coal for the kilns at Hullerhirst was sourced between 1778 and 1791 from the estate itself. In 1782, Grange coal was also used along with supplies from the Misk pits, the Stevenston Colliery pits, the Bartonholm pits, and the nearby Doura pits in Kilwinning.

At Hullerhirst, the kilns were seldom in operation during the winter, the active season ranging from the beginning of June through to August or the

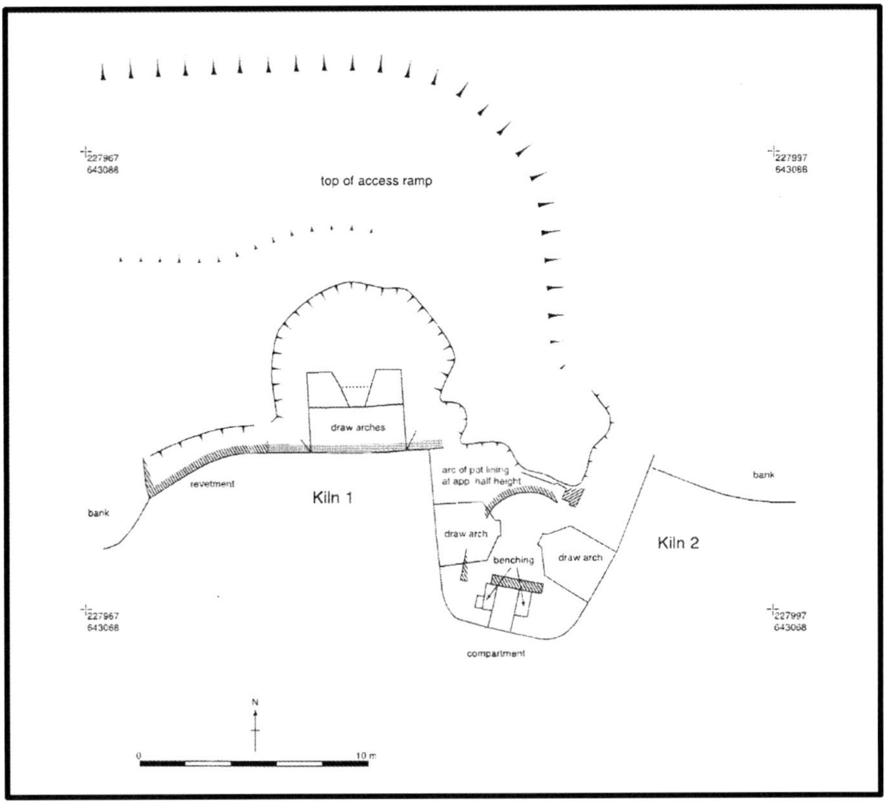

Sketch Map 1. Detailed Plan of the Hullerhirst Kilns.

start of harvesting. It is unknown when the limestone quarries at Hullerhirst were first opened, but on the estate, the largest and earliest of the two kilns had a keystone above the main arch inscribed 'VK 1776.' The property was under the ownership of William Kelso in 1776. In 1707 William Kelso, the grandfather of William and Patrick purchased Hullerhirst estate, and in the 1770s the two grandsons became ship owners. This enabled them to integrate the transport and marketing of lime, limestone, and coal especially to Dublin, which became a major export market. One of the factors which stimulated the interest of William Kelso in securing the Estate was the potential availability of limestone.

In the late eighteenth century and early nineteenth century, the demand for limestone increased for building (mortar and plaster), iron smelting, and especially as an aid in neutralising the naturally occurring acidic, clay soils. Liming reduces soil acidity by raising the pH level, and also breaks down heavy clay soils, making them porous and more workable. Hullerhirst lime was used almost exclusively by the local farming community and by farms on the raised beach to improve soil fertility. Thomas Tait, tacksman at Hullerhirst limeworks around this time, stated that his output of lime doubled within a short period of time from 7,000 bolls per annum to 13,000-14,000 bolls.

Surprisingly, William Kelso did not use his own lime during the construction of the new country house in 1777, instead he used other sources. He probably used Irish limestone which was imported into Saltcoats, as ballast in coal ships. Irish lime was whiter than the local version and was considered better for plaster work and the rendering of houses and walls.

The kilns at Hullerhirst shown above on Map 4 would receive their limestone from the adjoining quarries, but also limestone and coal from Kerelaw Glen which had very old Stoop and Room workings which opened into the glen. It is also possible that limestone came from workings sited approximately 50 metres north of Kerelaw Mains farm. All three sources of limestone came from either the Third Post or Lower Linn Limestone (See figure 11).

With the development and expansion of road and rail transport in the mid-1800s it became cheaper and more convenient to acquire sources of lime from further afield, and local lime-burning activities were abandoned in most places. By 1899, only five quarries and one mine were producing

Map 4. Hullerhirst Quarries and Limekilns, c. 1856.

limestone in Ayrshire. They employed less than 100 workers. In 1937, production was taking place in only four quarries, but by 1944 this number had risen to five.

When the Hullerhirst quarry and limekilns ceased operations is uncertain, but the *New Statistical Account* of the parish (1842) informs us that due to the expiry of the quarry lease, production had stopped by 1837. Before this date, the quarry employed in-excess of eight men, averaged throughout the year. The workers were paid 12s (60p) per week and the quicklime was sold at the kiln at 7p per boll. We are also informed that the limestone quarried in the Grange Estate was for internal estate purposes only. It is also possible that the kilns were abandoned as the demand for lime decreased or a new landowners' lack of interest in exploiting the resource.

In the 8 July 1910 issue of the *Ardrossan and Saltcoats Herald*, the kilns are described as 'old ruins worthy of inspection.' It also added that 'the old limekilns form a comfortable 'doss-house' for homeless wayfarers. 'Camp life has many attractions, and under the shade of the hawthorn the stew pot may be observed simmering.'

In constructing the A78 bypass between 2002 and 2004, the alignment of the road passed very near to the southern end of the bigger quarry. Before their demolition, the remains of the kilns, although ruinous, were inspected and surveyed by archaeologists. They were graded as being of local archaeological importance. It should be noted that the road cutting through the site is at a level which is lower than the floor of the big quarry. Only a small flooded area of quarry face looking towards Castlehill farm now remains.

5
Housing, Retail and Transport Development

At a meeting of the County Council held in the County Hall, Ayr on 29 May 1934, a letter was read from the Department of Health for Scotland regarding houses in Stevenston to provide accommodation for workers being transferred to the town by I.C.I. The department referred to Section 45 (1) (d) of the Housing (Scotland) Act 1925, which enabled the local authority to lease houses erected by them under the act. Such leasing, however, was subject to the consent of the department, who normally were not favourably disposed to give their consent where the houses during the lease were to be exclusively restricted to the employees of a particular employer. They stated clearly that they would not object to the proposal referred to in the letter if the lease provided that any houses that may become vacant and could not be tenanted by the employees of the company would be available for letting to the general population within the county. Accordingly, if the terms of the lease were to embody such a condition and were designed to secure the county council against financial loss, and if the other conditions, restrictions, and stipulations proposed by the council were satisfactory, the department would be prepared to give favourable consideration to any proposals submitted to them. It was agreed to remit to the clerk to continue negotiations with I.C.I.

Two months later, at the beginning of August, I.C.I. informed the council that they were prepared to enter into an agreement, the general terms of which were:

(a) The county council had to build 150 houses and to lease them to I.C.I. for a period of five years at an economic rent, namely: 100 3-apartment houses, £18; 50 4-apartment houses, £23.

(b) I.C.I. were prepared to charge their workers, including sub-tenants, £15-10s for a three-apartment house, and £19 for a four-apartment house (this was later lowered to £18), the balance being met by the company.

(c) In the event of any of the houses not being required by the company during the period of the lease, they were to be let by the county council in the ordinary way. The probable cost of erecting the 150 houses was £51,028. This gave the average actual cost per house of approximately £300.

The council resolved to sanction this expenditure subject to the approval of the Department of Health.

There was some disquiet among a few of the committee members, including Mr Brady representing Irvine. He argued that the whole scheme was financially unsound. He commented that no subsidy was being paid for these houses, and the rents to be charged were not economic rents. He further added that an economic rent would be £23-8s for the three-apartment houses and 29-17s-3d for the four-apartment houses. This meant that the county council were going to subsidize these 150 houses by a sum of over £800. The clerk retorted that the scheme had been approved by the housing committee, and had been sent by the housing committee to the finance committee and that body had also approved the scheme. He also stated that until the Department of Health approved the agreement it could not proceed.

As part of the agreement between I.C.I. and the county council there was an obligation by the council to build forty houses by 1 February 1935. The clerk forcibly stated that unless the arrangement between the two bodies could be finalised immediately, the time-scale needed to erect these properties by February 1935 was impossible to meet. In attempting to further reassure some of the doubters, the clerk emphasised that these houses belonged to the county council and would not be transferred to I.C.I.

The strongest incentive delivered by the company was associated with the substantial increase in employment opportunities in the Stevenston area which would be delivered with the relocation of nine of their factories to Ardeer. The first cluster of forty houses would accommodate key workers from various I.C.I. factories, but many jobs would also become available to local people within a short period of time.

The council were satisfied that rents would be paid punctually and arrears would be minimal, with the difficulty of collecting these rents greatly diminished.

Possibly the principal alteration which arose during the lengthy and complicated negotiations was the extension of the lease period from the original five years to ten, resulting in a termination date of 1945.

The first three street sites in 1935/36 were McGregor Avenue, Wallace Avenue and Hayocks Road. All three were built to link with Glencairn Street and were the first residential areas in what later became known as the 'Hayocks'.

As mentioned above, the residents of these three streets were largely I.C.I. employees. They came largely from Nobel's Westquarter factory which was located at Reddingmuirhead near Falkirk, which closed in 1933. The production of detonators which were originally manufactured at Westquarter (from 1876) was relocated to Ardeer. The highly skilled and experienced workforce at Westquarter were desperately required at

Ardeer and were encouraged to migrate to Stevenston, and assist with the establishment of detonator production at the factory. One way of persuading workers to move was to provide them with newly completed homes. The influx of I.C.I. workers into the town originated not only from the Falkirk area, but from various other Nobel establishments throughout Britain. This was caused by the company's rationalisation plans at the time.

This significant expansion to the residential component of Stevenston in 1935/36 occurred to the north of Glencairn Street and was not universally popular. It exasperated the legitimate concerns of the residents in the central part of the town, but was most vehemently questioned by those living in Ardeer.

There was absolutely no disagreement that Stevenston desperately needed new housing. The 1931 Census showed that there were 1,760 families in Stevenston of whom at August 1930, 329 were living in houses known to be unfit for habitation, a percentage of 18.7 of the total.

As early as September 1933, with the announcement that the county council had agreed, within a span of three years, to build 300 houses in Stevenston, it became apparent that there was little likelihood on any building activity occurring in the Ardeer end of the town. This situation was probably the first example of future discord or friction between the 'tap en' and 'boatem en' of the town.

The reasons for excluding Ardeer from this development were spurious and short-sighted especially when Ardeer Square was earmarked for demolition. The inhabitants were informed that Ardeer was unsuitable for building due to its low-lying situation near the sea. It was claimed that drainage would also be a major difficulty.

The huge potential and possibilities provided by Ardeer to the overall reputation of the town were largely ignored, or at least, placed well down the list of priorities. Its many assets included one of the finest, and safest, stretches of sand on the west coast of Scotland; the existence of a railway station and top-quality golf course. Ardeer also contained most of Stevenston's public works. The inhabitants of Ardeer simply requested the replacement of at least a considerable number of houses due to be demolished by others in the same locality. They were of the opinion that the potential and possibilities of Stevenston as a summer resort could not be fulfilled without further housing development.

The need for a significant expansion of housing in Stevenston was universally acknowledged. The county council preferred to build these homes on a green-field site utilising the pristine rural environment. This approach certainly assisted with the planning process and subsequent cost of the development.

After the flurry of activity in house construction associated with the I.C.I. initiative, the expansion continued. It was recorded in an Ayr County Council meeting dated 26 May 1936 that 160 new houses were to be built, over a period of two years, near the Hayocks Road site. This total constituted the entire number of houses planned for Stevenston parish, thereby excluding any new development elsewhere in the town. The estimated cost was £60,994. The two areas of ground required for the building were acquired from Mr James Campbell of Kerelaw. The first sector was 6.5 hectares in size, the second, 5.0 hectares, and both were scheduled to be completed by early 1939. This initial housing development must have incorporated the area including the bottom part of Hayocks Road and the McGregor Avenue/Wallace Avenue area.

From 28 May 1945, I.C.I. were prepared to transfer these 150 properties back to Ayr County Council due to the expiry of the original deal. The proposition from I.C.I. to offer the houses en masse was rejected by the Council who agreed to accept them as they became vacant, and under certain conditions.

After prolonged and detailed discussions with the county council, I.C.I. consented to extend this arrangement for a further ten years. It is interesting to note that the Stevenston representative on the housing committee, Jimmy Forde, recorded his opposition to such a continuation.

Running in tandem with the situation existing between the county council and I.C.I., it was approved by the county council on 19 December 1944 that another twenty-one temporary houses be constructed in the Hayocks area. The houses were to be accommodated on a 4.4-hectare site which had previously been acquired by the council. It was wholly reserved for residential development, along with a 2.2-hectare site for the construction of a proposed primary school and nursery. Work on the housing started in April 1945. An update presented to the county council stated that all the brickwork had been completed as well as the laying of all drains by 26 June.

Continuing with its policy of forward planning, in May 1945, the council acquired another 4.2-hectare piece of land from James Campbell for the sum of £2,487. Soon afterwards in November 1945, a proposal to construct sixty-nine temporary houses in the area adjoining Hayocks Road received approval from the council. Matching up these house building areas accurately with particular streets is almost impossible, as the council usually described their location simply as a 'Hayocks Road site.' Already in 1946, the council had planned to build 16 houses in open plots in Hayocks Road and Donaldson Avenue. This was clearly a policy to increase housing density, and indicated the existence of a long-term planning strategy.

In the period-of-time prior to 1946 all the house building had been located in a zone west of Hayocks Road in ground purchased in parcels from James Campbell of Kerelaw Estate. In 1946, Ayr County Council became interested in a 40-hectare site lying to the east of Hayocks Road between it and Hawkhill farm. The land was part of the Ardeer Estate and was owned by the Trustees of the late Patrick Warner. They arrived at the conclusion that the site could accommodate approximately 450 houses. It was immediately transparent to the council that the presence of Hawkhill farm was a major obstacle to their long-term plans for the area. The tenant of the farm at this time was Mr William Frew who also ran a haulage contractor's business. To complicate the issue further, Mr Frew purchased the farm in the following year, and he gave no indication of his willingness to sell any of his newly acquired ground. This area eventually comprised a large section of the Hayocks lying east of Hayocks Road.

The accelerated rate of house building in the Hayocks immediately after World War Two involved the following contractors:

Brickwork – James Anderson, Irvine.
Joinery Work – William Reid, Stevenston; David Reid, Stevenston; Norman Gaw, Stevenston; Douglas Peebles, Saltcoats; R. Maxwell, Stevenston.
Glazier Work – George Kirk, Kilmarnock.
Slaters – Douglas Hutchison, Irvine.
Plumbing – James Frew, Stevenston.
Electrical Work – John Jamieson, Saltcoats.
Plaster Work – Robert McCallum, Saltcoats; and William Sinclair, Saltcoats.
Earth Moving Equipment – James Anderson, Irvine.

At the beginning of 1946 the following residential area existed in some shape; McGregor Avenue, completed with approximately 109 houses; Wallace Avenue, completed with approximately 57 houses; Morrison Avenue, with approximately 50 houses; Hayocks Road, with approximately 100 houses; Reid's Avenue, with approximately 40 houses; Donaldson Avenue, with approximately 50 houses; Alexander Avenue, with approximately 30 houses.

Throughout early 1946, Ayr County Council continued to acquire land in various locations within the scheme, not only restricting themselves to the Kerelaw Estate but expanding further north in Hayocks Road. This included a field between Ardchoille House and Hayocks Road.

On the occasion of the Housing Progress Sub-Committee meeting of Ayr County Council on 27 April 1948, it was decided to provide seven sites for the erection of temporary shops at the top of Hayocks Road on a ten-hectare piece of ground to be acquired by the council from Messrs

A. & J. Clelland of East Hayocks farm. This arrangement had previously been approved by the council in March of the previous year, but no formal contract to purchase the land had been concluded.

Owing to the limited restrictions on building which at that time existed, the council decided to solely purchase a small area of 0.2 hectares for the shop sites. Another factor in their decision was that the question of shop sites in general had been delayed over a period of years and was now a priority.

Although temporarily limited, house building in general continued apace, with approximately twelve 'Lindsay' designed homes and sixteen traditional designed houses having been completed by 31 December 1948. The construction method utilised in building Lindsay homes involved a panelised timber frame system. The following month a further four 4-apartment Lindsay houses were completed and occupied in the Kerelaw sector of the expanding scheme.

Due to the scale of house construction and the pace of building required, some of the properties were 'Blackburn' houses. These were first introduced throughout much of Scotland as experimental temporary homes. They were prefabricated houses ('prefabs') which could be erected quickly to satisfy the demand for housing due to an influx of workers. They were designed with a ten-year life span, but many lasted much longer, for example the prefabs in Alexander Avenue.

This on-going rolling approach to house building was demonstrated at the Housing Committee meetings of Ayr County Council attended by Councillor Jimmy Forde. In the January and February meetings of 1949, it was announced that of the sixty-four houses under contract at that time, fifty-two had been completed (forty-six were Lindsay type). The other twelve properties were still in progress. This new housing stock included six 4-apartment, and two 5-apartment houses located in the Kerelaw zone.

Throughout the remainder of 1949, a further twenty-two properties became available for occupation (all located in the Kerelaw sector), and in September 1950, Ayr County Council agreed to additional site preparation for another 14 homes in the same area. An increasingly noticeable trend at this time was the increase in the number of 5-apartment houses. This development points towards an influx of young families.

On 7 June 1949, Mr William W. Small, the council representative for Stevenston and Ardrossan South was elected onto the council housing committee. Shortly after his appointment, at a housing committee meeting of the council held on 6 June 1950, it was noticed that a large number of tenants in Hayocks Road, Donaldson Avenue, Greenhead Avenue, and Reid's Avenue were taking in lodgers and sub-letting parts of their homes. Being the Hayocks, this could only be explained as a new form of community solidarity or entrepreneurial flair.

It is worth noting that the Scottish Special Housing Association Ltd which was founded in 1937, may have been directly involved in this early phase of housing provision, but the SSHA certainly participated in some of the building in the 1950s and 1960s, some examples being Burns Place, Keir Hardie Road, Lesley Place, Wheatley Road, Wheatley Place, a limited number in Hayocks Road (Nos 64 to 78), and Morrison Avenue. Another unusual development occurred in October 1950 when the council agreed to build 6, 4-apartment cottage-type houses at the Hayocks Road site, under the 'Agricultural Workers' Housing Programme 1949/50.' The total cost was £7,839. Cherry & Anderson (digger work and brick work) and Norman Gaw (joinery) both from Stevenston, were heavily involved in the project.

Other supplementary amenities were agreed by the council in 1945 and 1946. These included an application from Mr William Cowan of 35 McGregor Avenue for the let of a piece of ground 13.7x32 metres to be used as an allotment. Also in January 1946, Mr Thomas Meney was granted permission to build a Christian Brethren Gospel Hall adjoining Hayocks Road (in what is now Craigdene Drive). From 1947 onwards this wooden structure became a well-known local feature and was universally called 'Tammy Meney's.' It remains visible to this day, although now in a dilapidated condition.

The motivation behind the process of naming new residential developments is lost in the murky world of council committee meetings. Fortunately, their origins are more transparent as can be seen from the detail below.

The origins or reasons behind the naming of the streets in the Hayocks can be categorised under certain headings.

The following streets were named after local councillors:

a) Morrison Avenue – James Morrison J.P., first Provost of the Burgh of Stevenston from 1952 to 1955. He died on 11 August 1963 (aged 104). He is buried in New Street Cemetery.

b) Alexander Avenue – John Alexander, Parish Councillor (Dec 1913 to Dec 1922) plus (Dec 1928 to Dec 1929) plus County Councillor for Stevenston & Ardrossan South (Dec 1929 to May 1930) plus (May 1931 to May 1933). Lived at Mayville. County Councillor for Stevenston and Ardrossan North (1939 to 1940) plus (1940 to 1941) plus (May 1941 to 1945) plus (May 1945 to 1946). He sat on the Housing Committee of Ayr County Council in January 1945.

c) McGregor Avenue – Alexander McGregor, Ardchoille, was the County Councillor for Stevenston and Ardrossan North between

December 1922 up to his death on 17 March 1928, aged sixty-eight years. He became a Justice of the Peace in March 1905 and Stevenston Parish Councillor in 1907. He was an ironfounder. After his death the same post was held by his son, William L. McGregor, until December 1929.
d) Reid's Avenue – Peter Reid, lived at 29 Boglemart Street. County Councillor for Stevenston and Ardrossan North between December 1913 and December 1922. He was also the District Councillor for Stevenston and Ardrossan North between May 1931 and May 1933.
e) Hamilton Crescent – Thomas C. Hamilton, Glencairn Street. District Councillor for Stevenston and Ardrossan North between May 1941 and May 1946.
f) Forde Crescent – James Forde, J.P. and M.B.E., 11 Millhill Road. County Councillor for Stevenston and Ardrossan North between May 1946 and May 1949. Also, in May 1952. Moved to 33 Greenhead Avenue. Provost 1956-62. Bailie 1952-55. Hon. Treasurer 1963-65. Police Judge 1968. County Representative for the Burgh of Stevenston 1952-66.
g) Clements Place – James Clements J.P., 9 Schoolwell Street. District Councillor for Stevenston and Ardrossan South between May 1946 and May 1949. District Councillor for Stevenston and Ardrossan North between May 1949 and May 1952. Moved to 52 Alexander Avenue. Provost 1962-65. Bailie 1957-61. Hon. Treasurer 1970-74. Police Judge 1969-74. Housing Convener 1956-59. County Representative for Burgh of Stevenston 1958-64. Town Councillor 1952-56.
h) Maxwell Place – Thomas Maxwell, 63 Glencairn Street. District Councillor for Stevenston and Ardrossan North between May 1946 and 1952. Town Councillor 1952-53.
i) Hyslop Road – Thomas H. Hyslop J.P., New Street. District Councillor for Stevenston and Ardrossan South, May 1952. Hon Treasurer 1955-58. Police Judge 1960-66. Housing Convener 1954-56. Town Councillor 1952-55.
j) Lumsden Place – John Lumsden. Bailie between 1958 and 1960. Town Councillor between 1953 and 1958.
k) Gilmour Gardens and Gilmour Wynd – Davidina Gilmour. Town Councillor between 1957 and 1959.

These streets were named after Prominent Biblical/Religious Figures:

a) St James' Place – One of the twelve apostles.
b) St Columba Place – Irish abbot and missionary who was credited

with spreading Christianity to Scotland. His many achievements included founding the abbey on Iona.
c) St John's Place – Jesus' youngest apostle.
d) St Stephen's Place – First martyr for the Christian faith.
e) St Andrew's Place – The first disciple and apostle. The patron saint of Scotland, Greece, and Russia.
f) St Monach's Place – In Pre-Reformation times, Stevenston was one of the parishes where the Benedictine Abbey in Kilwinning held jurisdiction, and St Monach was the Patron and Titular Saint of the church in Stevenston. This Pre-Reformation church was most likely sited where the High Kirk now stands. The memory of St Monach was immortalised in the annual fair held in the town on 30 October. The spectacle was known locally as Sammyneuks Day (it was last held around 1840). Also note-worthy is the aisle in the present High Kirk is entitled St Monach's aisle.

All six place names listed above are cul-de-sacs and constitute a cluster which run into Morrison Avenue, Hyslop Road, and Hamilton Crescent. Only St Monach had any direct relationship with Stevenston.

Another cluster in the same locality commemorates Scotland's national bard, Robert Burns. It consists of Burns Place, Lochlie Place, Mossgiel Place, and Lesley Place. Once again, these four places are all cul-de-sacs. The first is self-explanatory acknowledging the man himself. At the time of the bard, Lochlie, which is situated five kilometres north-west of Mauchline, was a farm extending to fifty-three hectares. It had been rented by William Burnes the father of the poet.

Mossgiel was leased by Robert and his brother Gilbert from Gavin Hamilton. This arrangement for the farm occurred in late 1783, four months before the death of their father.

Lesley Place pays tribute to Lesley Baillie of 'Bonnie Lesley' fame. She was born at Mayville, and was immortalised by Burns who spent a short time with her family as they travelled through Dumfries to England in 1792. The party consisted of Lesley's father, Robert, her sister, Grace (Maria), and Mr Hamilton of Glasgow.

There is no documented evidence that Robert Burns ever visited Stevenston, but the town can rightly claim the distinction of having one of its female residents glorified in verse by our national bard. Such was the prestige attached to this event that in 1952 the motto for the newly created Burgh of Stevenston – 'To spread her conquests farther' was selected from the first verse of the 'Bonnie Lesley' poem.

O saw ye bonnie Lesley
As she gaed o'er the border?

She's gane, like Alexander,
To spread her conquests farther.

Being almost surrounded by farmland, the Hayocks has borrowed a number of street names from local farms. These include Hillhead Road, Castlehill Road, Hawkhill Place, Hawkhill Drive, and Greenhead Avenue. An extension of this rural theme would include Elms Place, Hawthorn Drive and Oakland Drive.

As is common practice in many other settlements, Hayocks has several street names acquired from nearby prominent landmarks. These include Castle Avenue (adjacent to the ruins of Kerelaw Castle); Hayocks Road - the main arterial route running the entire length of the scheme (named after the early access road to Hayocks House and East Hayocks farm); Ashgrove Avenue (recognising the existence of nearby Ashgrove or Ashenyards estate); Kerelaw Avenue (called after the castle and estate); Ardchoille Drive and Ardchoille Lane (the building previously entitled Hayocks House. In 1919, the property was purchased by Alexander McGregor who altered the name to Ardchoille).

Renowned individuals with a national profile also find a space within the fabric of the scheme. Wallace Avenue (celebrating the life and death of William Wallace). He is one of Scotland's greatest national heroes due to his resistance to Edward I. and his involvement in the First War of Scottish Independence. Wheatley Road and Wheatley Place. In this case we have a choice between John Wheatley (1869-1930), a Scottish socialist politician and prominent figure on Red Clydeside, or his nephew, John Thomas (Lord) Wheatley, who was a Labour Party Member of Parliament for Edinburgh East from 1947 to 1954. In 1945, he came a close second behind the sitting M.P., Sir C. MacAndrew (Conservative) in the Westminster election for the Bute and North Ayrshire Constituency which included Stevenston. He is celebrated as the Chairman of the Royal Commission on Local Government in Scotland which was published in September 1969). Due to his involvement in local politics, it is highly likely that the streets were named in his honour.

Another 'weil kent' individual with a national profile and reputation considered worthy of having a street named after him was James Keir Hardie. He was the founder of the Labour Party; a pioneering trade unionist; a campaigner for women's rights; and the first working man to be elected to Parliament. Although born in Legbrannock – a mining village in Lanarkshire – he had a long and meaningful association with Ayrshire. Moving a little closer to home, for a number of years he penned a column in the *Ardrossan and Saltcoats Herald* entitled 'Black Diamonds' under the nom de plume of the 'Trapper.'

The impact of Robert Burns's literary work on Hardie was profound. In 1909, Hardie recorded in the pages of *The Labour Leader*, 'I owe more to Robert Burns than to any other man alive or dead. I had imbibed the liberty-loving spirit and humanitarianism of Burns.' What a coincidence that Burns Place in the Hayocks is located immediately adjacent to Keir Hardie Road. This juxtaposition would have delighted the eminent politician.

Three Scottish islands are commemorated in the development centred around Hawkhill Drive. All three are located off the west coast of the Scottish mainland, they are Skye Place, Barra Place, and Tiree Place. Hawkhill Drive itself was named after Hawkhill farm which in 1948 was purchased by William Frew from the trustees of the late Patrick Warner. The strip of Hawkhill Drive facing the main road was largely the first phase, followed by Skye Place which was partially built ahead of Tiree Place. Several houses in Tiree Place were occupied in January 1995.

Most of the houses in the estate were built by Castleton Homes Ltd, although some in Hawkhill Drive along with Barra Place are McLean Homes. There are also a few 'self-built' homes in Hawkhill Drive.

The one street in the Hayocks which would be instantly recognisable abroad and is not commonly found in other towns is Landsborough Place. The name of this cul-de-sac of sixteen houses situated off Hyslop Road has an international profile.

William Landsborough has an international reputation due to his incredible exploits in Australia. He was born in Stevenston on 21 February 1825, the son of Dr David Landsborough, a clergyman in the town, and was educated in Irvine. William was the first European to traverse Australia from north to south in 1862 after having emigrated to Australia in 1841. He died in 1886 aged sixty-one years in Caloundra, Queensland, and was buried at Toowong Cemetery in Brisbane.

William's father was Rev David Landsborough (1779-1854). In addition to being a man of the cloth, David was also a naturalist and

18. The Reverend David Landsborough.

author. He was ordained on 26 September 1811 to the church in Stevenston. He and his wife, Margaret McLeish, had seven children with three of their four sons – including William – emigrating down under. His remaining son, David, was also a clergyman in Kilmarnock.

Although born in Dalry, Glenkens, Galloway, David spent most of his life in Stevenston, and is in fact buried in the High Kirk Cemetery. In addition to his pastoral duties, he was a major contributor to many other aspects of community life in the town.

I suspect that the small no-through-road was named in memory of the reverend, but it could be argued that the name was chosen as a mark of respect to both David and his internationally renowned son, William.

Campbell Avenue and Cambuskeith Road were built in the mid-to-late 1960s, being similar in design to Mount Pleasant. They were part of the Kerelaw Estate which at that time was owned by James Campbell, the Saltcoats solicitor.

Campbell Avenue celebrates the enormous contribution made by three generations of the Campbell family to the political, administrative, and business life of Stevenston. The family had a very strong bond and affinity with Saltcoats, but their influence on Stevenston must not be underestimated.

The most recent James Campbell to be associated with the solicitor's business in Dockhead Street, Saltcoats, was born in the Bank of Scotland building in 1911. He was intimately tied up with the establishment of Stevenston Burgh which was eventually formed in July 1952. At its inception, Mr Campbell was appointed Interim Town Clerk and Interim Clerk of the Burgh Police Court. During his tenure as Town Clerk of Stevenston, James was involved in all aspects of its administrative function, but his contribution as a legal adviser was particularly valuable.

J. Campbell & Co. had accommodation in 1973 in the Bank of Scotland Buildings at 46 and 73 New Street, plus the Ardeer Branch of Nobel House, in addition to their premises in Saltcoats.

Mr Campbell W.S. M.B.E. died on his 94th birthday on 29 January 2004. Both James and his father, who purchased Kerelaw Estate in 1919, were proud and honoured to have owned the mansion house, and he was immensely saddened and distressed by its demolition in 1971.

It is a distinct possibility that the decision to use the Campbell family name was reinforced by the exploits of Flying Officer Kenneth Campbell during the Second World War, a consequence of which was the award of a Victoria Cross in 1942 for the 'most conspicuous bravery.'

Cambuskeith Road was named after the Cambuskeith branch of the Hamilton clan. The Hamiltons of Grange (Kerelaw) were descended from this branch. There is therefore a historical link between the Hamiltons and

Kerelaw Estate, on which Cambuskeith Road was constructed.

By right, Cambuskeith Road should have been named Hamilton Road, but this possibility was prevented by the existence of Hamilton Crescent. Two streets with identical titles in the same town has not to be encouraged, although a precedent exists in the Hayocks with Hawkhill Drive and Hawkhill Place. The houses in Cambuskeith were occupied from May 1970, following the completion of Campbell Avenue.

Donaldson Avenue was named after Andrew Donaldson who was the Registrar of Births, Deaths, and Marriages in Stevenston in 1935.

Glencairn Street which delineates the southern boundary of the Hayocks (along with Kilwinning Road), strictly speaking is not part of the scheme. Glencairn Gardens which is linked, on the north side, to Glencairn Street is within my study area.

In the past, the Earl of Glencairn was vested as the King's Bailie for the Cunninghame District of Ayrshire. The Glencairns were the Lords of Kerelaw and the naming of the by-pass as Glencairn Street reinforced the connection of the town with Kerelaw.

Etymological studies suggest the reasoning behind the naming of Burnlea Place and Craigdene Drive. The former indicates the presence of a meadow next to a stream, which accurately describes the setting of this side street. Craigdene is more problematical. The prefix 'craig' meaning rocky hill or crag, does not precisely represent the site of Craigdene Drive, although 'dene' being a valley or wooded area is nearer to reality if we accept the wooded area option.

Alternative options covering a miscellaneous group of streets should be considered. Firstly, the small row of houses called Thistle Terrace (allocated in October 1973) could be named after Scotland's national flower or because of its location on ground which adjoined the pavilion of Ardeer Thistle's Ardchoille Football Park. Secondly, there is some debate whether Maxwell Place was named in memory of Councillor Thomas Maxwell (as suggested above) or the Very Reverend Canon Joseph Maxwell, the parish priest in St John's between 1955 and 1975. Thirdly, Hamilton Crescent could commemorate either Councillor Thomas C. Hamilton or the Hamiltons of Grange.

This exercise in investigating the origins of street names in the Hayocks raises several logical questions. For example, there are some peculiar omissions. Why have a 'Wallace' without a 'Bruce' or an absence of anything pertaining to I.C.I. like Nobel or McGowan? There was a noticeable tendency to ignore the Members of Parliament who represented Stevenston, largely because during the house building period these politicians represented the Conservative Party. Individuals like Sir C. G. MacAndrew and Sir Fitzroy Maclean were long-standing MPs. During the same period, the Labour Party dominated the town's representation on Ayr County Council and from 1952, representation on the Town Council. They were hardly likely to commemorate the contribution made by their political adversaries.

Selecting particular years, we can clearly see how the housing in the Hayocks developed and expanded. In the 1935 *North Ayrshire Directory* covering Stevenston, there was no record of any streets existing in the Hayocks. Between 1935 and 1940, we observe the start, and sometimes completion, of the following residential areas: Hayocks Road, McGregor Avenue and Wallace Avenue.

By 1943, the following residential areas were in existence – Hayocks Road, McGregor Avenue, Alexander Avenue, Donaldson Avenue, Morrison Avenue, Reid's Avenue, and Wallace Avenue.

By 1948, in existence were the streets listed above plus, Ashgrove Avenue (t – some temporary 'Blackburn' structures), Burnlea Place (t), Castle Avenue, Elms Place (t), Greenhead Avenue (t), Hawthorn Drive, Kerelaw Avenue (t), and Oakland Drive.

In 1950, there existed the streets listed above plus Ardchoille Drive (t), and Hillhead Road.

Five years later in 1955, there were in existence the streets named above plus, Craigdene Drive, Hyslop Road, Maxwell Place, Forde Crescent (t), and Castlehill Road (1954).

By 1960, there existed the streets listed above plus, Clements Place, Ardchoille Lane, Burns Place, Wheatley Place, Wheatley Road, Hamilton Crescent (1957), Hawkhill Place, Landsborough Place, Keir Hardie Road, Lochlie Place, Mossgiel Place, St Andrew's Place (1957), St Columba Place, St John's Place, St Monach's Place, St Stephen's Place, and Lesley Place.

From this list we can deduce that only a few streets were constructed after 1960. These comprised Campbell Avenue, Cambuskeith Road, Gilmour Wynd, Gilmour Gardens, Morrison Court, St James Place, Glencairn Gardens, and Thistle Terrace.

Morrison Court is interesting as it consists of the only high-rise housing development in the scheme. These flats were originally part of Morrison Avenue and were constructed in the mid-1960s incorporating a 'point block' design. This model involved four apartments on each floor being situated at the corners of the building, giving each flat windows on three sides allowing ample lighting and cross ventilation. Internally there was an absence of corridors which provided greater privacy. Two of the blocks contain fourteen houses, the other two have eight houses each, making a total housing allocation of 44 houses.

The four widely separated structures underwent substantial renovation in 1993 and were allocated their own name: Morrison Court, with its own distinctive numbering sequence. The outcome of this decision resulted in Morrison Avenue losing its even numbers between 90 and 156. Morrison Court contains the only vehicular access to St John's Primary School making it busy at particular times of the day.

Table 5 indicates the residential areas in existence in 1950, the number of homes in each street, and how they have expanded up to the present day. From the total number of seventeen streets, only the ground on which Morrison Avenue was built was not purchased from Mr Campbell of Kerelaw Estate. At a slightly later date we start to see land owned by Patrick Warner of Ardeer and Messrs A. & J. Clelland of East Hayocks farm being purchased by Ayr County Council for the purpose of house building.

Table 5. Street House Numbers 1950 and 2024.

Street Name	Date	Number of Houses
Alexander Avenue	1950	Approx. 55
	2024	59
Ardchoille Drive	1950	3
	2024	6
Ashgrove Avenue	1950	7
	2024	14
Burnlea Place	1950	9
	2024	19
Castle Avenue	1950	14
	2024	14
Donaldson Avenue	1950	70
	2024	70
Elms Place	1950	13
	2024	17
Greenhead Avenue	1950	51
	2024	51
Hawthorn Drive	1950	14
	2024	14
Hayocks Road	1950	Approx. 127
	2024	178
Hillhead Road	1950	7
	2024	13
Kerelaw Avenue	1950	9
	2024	17
McGregor Avenue	1950	109
	2024	109
Morrison Avenue	1950	Approx. 50

	2024	92
Oakland Drive	1950	4
	2024	4
Reid's Avenue	1950	46
	2024	46
Wallace Avenue	1950	57
	2024	57

From Table 5 we can calculate an approximate population for the Hayocks in both 1950 and 2024. Incorporating the number of houses in each of the streets in 1950 and assuming an average occupancy rate of three people, we arrive at a figure of 1,935 individuals. Using the same tenuous technique, a rough figure for the 2024 population would be 4,680. By using only the same seventeen streets in 2024 (from a total of 51) you would assume that the 2024 figure should be higher. This can be explained by the fact that many of the additional streets built between 1950 and 2024 were smaller in size – with the exception of Campbell Avenue, Cambuskeith Road, and Hawkhill.

The size of the streets in the Hayocks range from Hayocks Road which is the longest with 191 houses, down to Oakland Drive and St James Place which are the smallest, with only four homes in each. In 1950, the four houses in Oakland Drive were occupied by Henry Robertson, John Murphy, George Celso, Robert Paterson along with their families.

Ardchoille Lane also has four properties, but is joined by Ardchoille Cottage. The Cottage was owned and occupied by Alexander Wilson in 1963 and three years later the proprietors were Alexander and Mrs Harriet Wilson. By 1968, the sole owner was Mrs Harriet Wilson, followed by James Kirk in 1978.

Several other privately owned properties which were built in the 1930s exist in the scheme. Firstly, at 154 Hayocks Road there is 'Summerlea.' Ownership of this property has changed repeatedly since its construction in the middle to late 1930s. Some of the many proprietors include James Cleland in 1940 – 1950, John Martin in 1959 – 69, William & Mrs Christine Pontin in 1971, and James Keegan in 1978. Sometime after 1965, the path between Forde Crescent and Hayocks Road -which gave entry to an electricity sub-station - closed, and was added to the ground owned by 'Summerlea.' Secondly, there is the 'East Lodge' which in the past was one of two gatehouses to Kerelaw Estate. In 1900, although owned by the Trustees of Gavin Fullarton and tenanted by Mrs Henrietta Betts or Donaldson, it was occupied by a dairymaid named Isabella Lithgow. Twenty-three years later a gardener named David Haddow occupied it. In 1933, George Lennon, a labourer, lived in the property – he was still in the house in 1954. Between 1969 and 1972 it was owned by William Stirling.

The addendums to the names of the various residential areas, for example roads, streets, avenues, courts, lanes, drives, places etc all have specific definitions. An obvious example is the difference between a 'street' and a 'road.' The former has buildings on either side, whereas the latter simply connects two points. It therefore follows that a street is a type of road, but not all roads are streets. Today these designations are considered to be almost synonymous terms. Surprisingly, there are no streets in the Hayocks. On the contrary, both 'avenues' and 'places' are well represented. Avenues are defined as straight roads or streets with trees planted along both sides. At the time of construction Donaldson Avenue, Greenhead Avenue, Reid's Avenue, etc. were on green-field sites and trees must have existed in sizeable quantities. The same logic applies to the term 'place.' These were cul-de-sacs and were built in significant numbers lying off roads and avenues such as Hyslop Road and Morrison Avenue.

Some titles do not mirror reality. For example, Craigdene Drive is not a road that was used to access a private residence, nor was Oakland Drive, but Hawkhill Drive did fulfil that function for Hawkhill farm.

There has been very little housing development in the Hayocks in the past fifty years. Therefore, some of the more modern or fashionable residential names are absent. The only exceptions are the more recently built sites including Glencairn Gardens and Gilmour Wynd.

The five-year period from 1947, when the Local Government Act (Scotland) was passed, to the formation of Stevenston Burgh in 1952, witnessed a continuation of the housing expansion in the Hayocks as organised by Ayr County Council. However, the Local Government Act (Scotland) provided the opportunity for communities such as Stevenston to attain burgh status. The whole procedure was hugely simplified, and the County Councillors and District Councillors representing Stevenston worked tirelessly to achieve the ambition of the townspeople. When burgh status was finally achieved in 1952, the responsibility for housing was shouldered by the new Town Council.

Polling day for the election of Stevenston's first Town Council was 1 July 1952. The returning officer was Sheriff Principal, Mr J. Gordon Thompson. There were twenty-three candidates seeking election, and of the nine successful candidates three had addresses in the Hayocks: Mr James Forde (Senior Bailie) – 33 Greenhead Avenue; Mr James Clements – 52 Alexander Avenue; and Mr Thomas Maxwell – 18 Elms Place.

In the July meeting of the Council, Councillor John McKay Nimmo was appointed Convenor of the Housing Committee. He held this position until 12 January 1953 when he resigned and was replaced by Councillor Thomas Hyslop.

Having acquired responsibility for all housing matters in the town, the council quickly established a framework.

In August 1952, the existing proposal to build twelve new houses at what was later known as Craigdene Drive – wedged between Hayocks Road and Donaldson Avenue – was amended to fourteen properties comprising 3-apartments and housing specifically designed to accommodate elderly citizens. These structures were semi-detached bungalows, the remainder being semi-detached and terraced villas. A year later, a proposition to further increase the allocation of homes for pensioners in Craigdene by two, was accepted. A further imaginative idea was to proceed with the erection of four police houses within this small development. The contractors appointed to construct these houses were as follows: excavator, concrete and brickwork – Cherry & Anderson; glazier and joinery – D. McQ. Reid; plumbing – James Frew & Son; plaster work – Robert McCallum & Son; roofing and roughcasting – J. McGinn & Son; electrical work – James Bonnar; painting – J. Black & Sons.

Mr Cherry of Cherry & Anderson, who were responsible for the brickwork, was summoned to attend a meeting of the Housing Committee to explain the slow progress of the scheme. He explained that due to the variation in housing types within such a small area, the rotation of work which had been adopted, and the difficulties in obtaining suitable tradesmen, the timetable had slipped slightly behind schedule, but the delay would be 'made good.' Finally, he gave an undertaking that the project would be finished by August.

The Town Council were desperate to accelerate their house building programme and at the Housing Committee meeting of the town council held on 16 February 1953, it was announced that Messrs A. & J. Clelland, through their agents Messrs King Sons and Paterson, solicitors, Kilwinning, had agreed to dispose of part of East Hayocks farm to the council at a price to be fixed by the District Valuer. This site amounted to approximately 10 hectares in area and was purchased for £1,750. The owners of the farm requested that the transaction be completed within two months, and that a protective strip adjoining their greenhouses be excluded from the arrangement petitioned by the council. If these two conditions were met the sale of the ten-hectare site could proceed. This was the same area which Ayr County Council had attempted to acquire in 1947. This protracted scenario lasting around six years would eventually result in the construction of a number of streets, including Forde Crescent, Hamilton Crescent, Hyslop Road, Clements Place, Maxwell Place and a number of others. The surveyor reported that only half of the land under negotiations adjoining Hayocks Road could be immediately serviced from the existing sewers and that to service the remaining portion would probably require the construction of a new main sewer to link up with the existing sewers at Hillcrest or Dubbs Road. This led to a situation where the order of house building would be determined by their proximity to the sewer network.

To show their long-term commitment to expanding the urban environment in the Hayocks, the council appointed Mr Harold A. Hammersley, 18 Bridge Street, Dalry, to the post of Rent Collector at a salary of £400 per annum.

At a meeting of the town council convened on 2 March 1953 within the council chambers in New Street, it was intimated that the Department of Health for Scotland had confirmed that planning permission for the use of East Hayocks farm had been granted by the Planning Authority.

In May it was agreed to employ Messrs. Hay & Steel, Architects, Kilmarnock, to have a proper layout plan prepared for the whole of the East Hayocks farm area. This arrangement would speed up the preliminary building work. Hay & Steel were proposed by Councillor Maxwell and seconded by Treasurer Mrs Murdoch. An amendment that Mr Robert Rennie, Architects, Saltcoats be hired was defeated by six votes to three. The completed plan which was presented to the Council on 6 July 1953 included the building of approximately 140 houses, this being the first development of the East Hayocks site. As early as 7 September, the Department of Health agreed in principle to the execution of site preparation work for approximately 120 houses, but agreed to tenders being taken for only 60 houses. As soon as progress had been made on the first 60 houses, the Department would look favourably on a further allocation. The contract price from Blackburn (Dumbarton) Ltd for these 60 houses was £86,471. The homes incorporated 29 3-apartments, and 31 4-apartments. The company pointed out that the price would include the supply and fitment of gas cookers and wash-boilers. Electrical appliances would incur an additional charge of £12 10s per house (this offer was later accepted). It was agreed to invite the Scottish Special Housing Association (SSHA) to contribute a number of homes to the project.

On 21 September, the Burgh Housing Committee received an update on the eighteen houses being constructed in Craigdene Drive. At the same meeting the committee was informed that some of the more established housing areas in the scheme, such as Hayocks Road, were experiencing an increase in changes to the tenancy arrangements. In response to the request from the Council to build additional homes, the SSHA agreed to erect 50 dwellings north of the Stevenston – Kilwinning road, but this was conditional on the Council providing the necessary sewer infrastructure.

In October, the council decided to fix an annual rent of £16 for each of the old person's houses being built in Craigdene Drive, and a month later to arrange a short ceremony to mark the handing over of the first completed house at Craigdene. This took place on 11 December and involved Mr Robert Hunter who became the first tenant. On 16 November 1953, in connection with the development of the East Hayocks farm site, the council agreed to accept the tender of £12,556 from Robert Nixon & Sons (Saltcoats) Ltd for the construction of roads, footpaths and sewers.

In the first meeting of 1954, the council approached the owner of the Ardchoille Hotel to investigate the possibility of securing an access road behind the hotel to permit construction traffic access to the new development site. Subsequently, Mr Alexander Watt agreed to transfer to the council – free of cost – a strip of 0.5 of a hectare on the east side of Hayocks Road, with conditions.

Throughout 1954 and 1955, tenancies continued to be allocated to a number of new properties including those in Craigdene Drive, Castlehill Road, Maxwell Place, Hyslop Road, Clements Place, and Forde Crescent.

The Council was informed on 21 June 1954 that fourteen houses from the first cluster of 60 had been completed at the East Hayocks site. By October this number had increased to 34 and further expanded to 50 by the following January. The full allocation of 60 Blackburn homes was completed by March with two-thirds of the total number being fitted with a heating system by hot-water radiators. At the same time permission had been granted by the Department of Health for the construction of the remaining 60 homes. A month later the council agreed to accept the lowest offer of £73,489 from Lanarkshire Builders Ltd for the contract.

In the meantime, the development of the Ardchoille site continued with the council agreeing to accept a tender from Lanarkshire Builders Ltd of £21,742 for the construction of eighteen houses, but only if the Company agreed to build a further ten houses in the same phase.

The range of local services within the scheme continued to expand with the siting of a bus shelter for A1 Company users in April 1955; the erection of a brick-built sub-station by the South of Scotland Electricity Board at the bottom of Craigdene Drive (the 90 square yards piece of ground was purchased for £5) in October; and a small scale children's play area with equipment costing £616 was agreed for Donaldson Avenue in May 1955.

The agreement between I.C.I. and Ayr County Council for the rent of one hundred 3-apartment and fifty 4-apartment houses, which was mentioned earlier, and was dated 12 November 1937, expired on 15 May 1955. A brief summary of this very important arrangement would be useful. The lease was drawn up in 1934 and provided for the let of 150 houses; one hundred 3-apartments and fifty 4-apartments to the then Nobel's (Explosives) Ltd., by Ayr County Council. The company were given full power to select their sub-tenants. The rents originally fixed were: 3-apartments - £18; 4-apartments - £23 and were payable by the company half yearly each year. It was embodied in the agreement that the rent fixed be an economic proposition on the basis of existing legislation and if there should be any alteration in the legislation which affected the economic rent, the rent should be duly adjusted. The period of this agreement was five years with a provision for its continuation after the expiry of this period. By a Supplemental Agreement dated 30 November 1943, (a) I.C.I. (Explosives) Ltd., took the place of Nobel's (Explosives) Ltd., (b) The rent was increased by £600, viz: £4 per house. By A Minute of Extension dated 29 April 1947, Imperial Chemical Industries Ltd., took the place of I.C.I. (Explosives) Ltd., and the agreement was extended for a period of ten years from 1945. As from 16 May 1952, the Burgh of Stevenston superseded Ayr County Council as the First Party to the Agreement of Lease.

At a Housing Committee meeting of the Burgh held on 9 May 1955, the factor pointed out that a decision was required as to the future rents of these properties. It was resolved that the rents chargeable to the tenants from and after 16 May, be increased to £20 (from £15-10s) for a 3-apartment house and £24 (from £19) for a 4-apartment house.

In addition to the alteration in rents, the termination of this long-lasting agreement resulted in several other changes - an additional burden on the administrative staff and the Housing Collector in view of the responsibility for collection having been transferred to the burgh; the process of accepting existing sub-tenants as tenants of the town council, and the necessity to revise the existing arrangement whereby I.C.I. subsidised the sitting tenants. This final point was the biggest difficulty because the burgh had no statutory authority to subsidise rents in the same way as the I.C.I. and to maintain the status quo it would be necessary to increase the amounts payable by the tenants by the amount by which they were subsidised.

The continuing prominence of housing issues within the town as a whole was illustrated at an electors' meeting held in Ardeer Halls in late April 1960, when the Dean of Guild, Mrs Davidina Gilmour, stated that the 130 houses which were being erected on the sites near Hayocks Road which had previously been temporary prefabs, had all been supplied with sink units and washing machines. These prefabs had reached the end of their stipulated ten-year life-span. She also claimed for Stevenston the distinction of being the first local authority in Scotland to have obtained permission to remove its stock of prefabs (a number were still in existence in Greenhead Ave, Ashgrove Ave, Kerelaw Ave, Hayocks Road, Elms Place, and Burnlea Place in 1955).

Even as early as 1960, there was a growing concern about the absence of a suitable children's playground in the Hayocks. The local politicians explained this situation simply through the difficulty in acquiring a suitable area of ground from the Kerelaw Estate. This state- of-affairs reinforced the concerns of the residents in relation to the high density of housing and relative scarcity of open space in the scheme.

During 1963 houses continued to be constructed and allocated at the Hawkhill site. This convenient label included the extension of Morrison Avenue as well as Lumsden Place. It is very difficult to be precise about the demarcation of the housing zones as designated by both Ayr County Council and Stevenston Burgh. Without the detailed maps used by the planning authorities it is impossible to accurately differentiate between the Hawkhill site, the East Hayocks site, the Ardchoille site, the Hayocks Road site, and the Kerelaw site.

Between December 1961 and January 1963, twenty-four houses built by Atholl Homes Ltd were completed at Morrison Avenue and Lumsden Place, but by June 1963 the contract with Atholl Homes had been terminated by the burgh. This decision had been taken due to the unacceptable delays in completing the contract. Work restarted almost immediately with newly appointed contractors. This large-scale development at the Hawkhill site reached its conclusion by the end of 1964 with the completion of 95 houses. Unusually, all four homes in St James Place were allocated exclusively to Glasgow families. This enlargement of the housing stock was accompanied by the erection of twenty-two lock-up garages at an estimated weekly rent of 9s 6d per garage.

The penultimate large-scale expansion of the housing stock in the Hayocks commenced a few years later with the construction of Campbell Avenue and Cambuskeith Road. This enlargement of the scheme reached its fruition with the completion of Campbell Avenue in the late 1960s and the letting of properties in Cambuskeith from May 1970 onwards.

The most recent sizeable addition to the housing provision within my boundary of the Hayocks is centred on Hawkhill Drive. This development also includes Barra Place, Tiree Place, and Skye Place.

On 27 June 1989, Headway Land submitted an application to Cunninghame District Council through their agent, Valtos Ltd, 140 West George Street, Glasgow, for outline permission for new build housing and the conversion/rehabilitation of existing farm buildings to housing at Hawkhill farm. The proposed number of dwellinghouses was 157 within an area of 6.28 hectares, with an estimated cost of approximately £500,000. This new development would create a gross floorspace of roughly 15,700 square metres. A new vehicular entrance would be required to replace the existing narrow farm access.

Smaller 'green gap' sites within the scheme were also in demand, and Gilmour Wynd and Glencairn Gardens were created. Open space was already being utilised as early as November 1964 when an application by Scottish & Newcastle Brewers Ltd to build private housing on the football

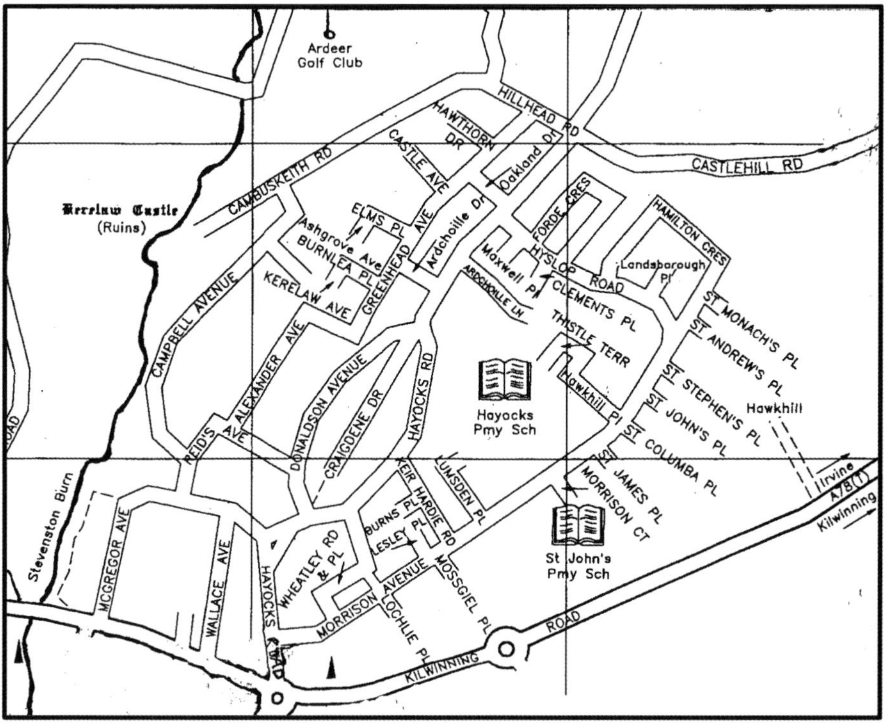

Map 5. Street Plan of the Hayocks c. 1993.

park at Ardchoille used by Ardeer Thistle, was continued for enquiries. It was pointed out that the Thistle had a lease on the area until 1973 and had no intention of giving up their rights. The town council fully supported this position and the application was subsequently rejected.

The farming area and green belt situated to the north of the scheme was also not immune from the interest of developers. An application in August 1974 for permission to utilise about 1.6 hectares of land to the north of the town and immediately west of Greenhead filter station for the erection of sixteen private homes was refused by Ayr County Council. The council pointed out that the proposed development did not accord with the provisions of the approved Development Plan. It also strongly reinforced the notion that there was no special need for housing on this site.

Gap sites within the scheme continue to be developed. At the time of writing, an application for planning permission was submitted to North Ayrshire Council from LMA Architects, Glasgow, on behalf of Nelson Homes (Scotland) Ltd, Coylton, for the erection of twenty-two semi-detached dwellings on the 1.07 hectare site of the former Ardchoille Hotel. This residential development comprised eighteen, two-bedroom two-storey semi-detached houses as well as four, three-bedroom two-storey semi-detached houses. This planning application was received by the council on 24 January 2025.

PROVISION OF RETAIL SERVICES

Even at this early stage of scheme management, the Planning Authority was strict and consistent in its approach to granting permission for retail opportunities. For example, at the January 1949 meeting it was agreed to let a site in Hayocks Road for the sale of fruit and vegetables made by Mr George Scott of Burnbank Street. However, later in the year his application to extend his business to include the sale of 'other foodstuffs' was rejected on the grounds that these items were readily available in two existing outlets in the Hayocks Road shopping cluster. Another example of the stringent controls adopted by the council arose on 5 April when Mr J. McWilliam, 26 Donaldson Avenue, registered his desire to let a piece of ground on which he wished to erect a hut for the purpose of conducting a cycle-hiring business. The County Planning Officer stated his opposition to the plan, commenting that the venture would be more appropriately sited from a shop in the Hayocks Road cluster. Mr McWilliam later withdrew his application. However, some applications were received positively. In September 1950, the council agreed to grant a site to Mr John Murphy for a gent's hairdresser business, and Mr James Morrison for a dairy shop, milk

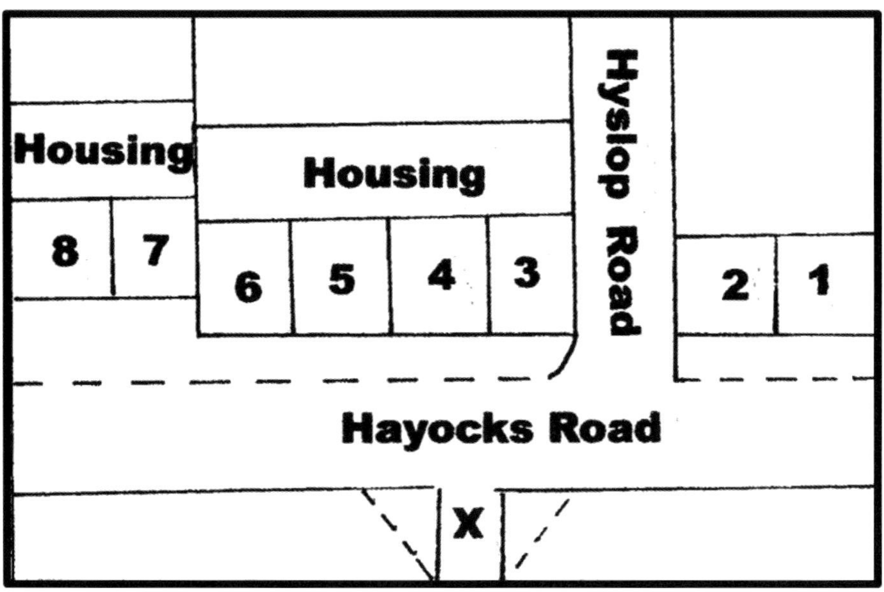

Sketch Map 2. Retail Units at Top of Hayocks Road. c. 1963.

Key. Shops – 1: Stevenston Co-operative. 2: J. M. Winning. 3: Boyd (grocer). 4: Muir (wool shop). 5: Johnny Murphy (barber). 6: Park (baker). 7: Barraclough (grocer). 8: Nellany (bookmaker). X – Oakland Drive.

retail, bakery, and sundries, both at the Hayocks Road cluster.

The provision of retail services within the Hayocks to support a rapidly expanding population of approximately 3,000 people in the 1960s was concentrated at the top end of Hayocks Road and its junction with Hyslop Road. The population of Stevenston town in 1951 was 9,332 and this had increased to 10,270 ten years later. This 9.1% increase in the population size of the town was caused largely by the housing development in the Hayocks. In 1963, there were eight retail units (See Sketch Map 2) at the top of Hayocks Road. These premises are shown in Table 6:

No.	Owners *	Service Provided
132	Stevenston Co-operative Society	Food plus other Services
134	J. M. Winning & Son	Newsagent, Confectioner, Sub Post Office, Tobacconist.
136A	Mrs Phyllis Boyd	General Store - Grocers
138	Andrew Muir	Fabrics – Wool, Thread, etc.
140	John Murphy	Barber
140A	Park Brothers	Bakers
144	Joseph Barraclough	General Store - Grocers
144A	James Nellany	Bookmaker

Table 6. Retail Units at the Top of Hayocks Road in 1963.

*It is important to note that both the Co-operative and J. M. Winning were tenants and not proprietors. These properties were owned by Stevenston Town Council. Also, in a similar theme, Park the bakers were tenants. Their shop was owned by James Gilchrist Ltd from Ayr.

Sometime between 1963 and 1969, Mr Winning purchased his shop, but the Co-op remained tenants.

No.	Owners	Service Provided
132	Kilwinning Co-operative So1ciety	As 1963
134	R. Wishart & W. Gibb	As 1963
136A	Robert & Julie McMullan	As 1963
138	Andrew Muir (Beith) *	As 1963
140	John Boyd **	---
140A	D. McCrossan	---
144	Mrs N. McCutcheon	---
144A	James Nellany	As 1963

Table 7. Retail Units at the Top of Hayocks Road in 1980

As shown in Table 7 overleaf, some of the occupiers were tenants and not owners. For example, the tenant in No. 138 * was Mrs Fay Schlesiger, and in No. 140 ** it was Mrs R. McMullan.

Although the Co-op was still located in No. 132, the operators changed in 1967 from the Stevenston Society to the Kilwinning Society.

No.	Owners	Service Provided
132	Mohammed Arshad	Convenience Store
134	William Fyfe	As 1980
136A	Gurdev Singh	General Store
138	Mrs E. McDonald	---
140	John Boyd	General Store
140A	Parvinder Singh	Shop was Empty
144	Mrs Surinder Singh	---
144A	D. McGuire	Bookmaker (Betting Office)

Table 8. Retail Units at the Top of Hayocks Road in 1990.

The following premises had the following tenants: No. 140 was occupied by Mrs D. McKellar; and No. 144 was occupied by Gurdev Singh.

In addition to this cluster, there were several shops distributed more randomly within the scheme. In particular, the two shops located at the bottom of Keir Hardie Road. Presently, these outlets are occupied by a 'Lifestyle Express' and a fish & chip shop, but their ownership has changed hands on a number of occasions.

These two properties were built in 1970, and the original owners were Aldo Tortolano (fish & chips shop) and Samuel and Lizzie Thomson (general store). Ten years later in 1980, the owners and occupiers were still Aldo, along with Bajhan Singh's convenience store. In 1990, the properties had changed hands again and were operated by Mrs Balvinder Kaur and E. Piacentini. There have also been regular changes in ownership since 1990, but the utilities provided have remained the same.

In 1972/73 Stevenston Town Council built a shop at the southern entry to Campbell Avenue, agreed to sell it to a Mr Stevenson and gave him entry. On 29 August 1977, Mrs Stevenson submitted an application for permission to change the use of the shop into a lounge bar. On 22 November 1977, Cunninghame District Council refused the application on the ground that the proposed development did not include any provision for car parking nor could satisfactory provision be made within the site. Mrs Stevenson appealed to the Secretary of State, and a Public Inquiry was held on 28 September 1978. On 20 February 1979 the Secretary of State supported the Reporter and confirmed that planning permission should be refused.

On 30 April 1979, Mrs Stevenson submitted a new application for change of use and conversion of the vacant shop to form a Lounge Bar with cellar and toilet facilities, and form off-street parking for six cars in an area adjoining and to the south of the shop. The council stated that the land adjoining the shop belonged to them. On 27 November 1979, the council resolved not to sell or lease the adjoining land to the owner of the shop for parking and therefore refused application on the ground that there was no provision for off-street parking within ground which was in the control of the applicant. The building was demolished at a later date.

Another 'legendary' shop was located at No. 2 Hayocks Road across Glencairn Street from the 'Blue Star' garage. The premises have been universally known as 'Pop's' and were owned from around 1935 by Mrs Annie Dow or Paterson or McAlpine. This lady had secured the ground from Major A. L. Warner in 1935 when she lived in Schoolwell Street. From around 1959 the proprietor and tenant was Mr James McAlpine, and he held this position for approximately twenty years. At intervals, other individuals became involved, for example, in 1959 Mr James A. Hosie from Ardrossan who was a monumental sculptor, had leased a small yard and hut adjoining the shop, and in 1980 R. Wishart and W. Gibb had some connection to the business. This couple owned the shop at No. 134 Hayocks Road in the same year. Any development plans Mr McAlpine had for the property were quashed in March 1965 when the Stevenston Burgh Licensing Court refused an application for a provisional certificate in respect of a new public house at the site.

Over the years the building has alternated between a single outlet and a split franchise, and following the modern trend, ownership has fluctuated. In 1963, the property was both a shop and house. One of several proprietors and tenants was Mr Robert Reid in 1990.

By far the largest retail outlet within the Scheme is Hawkhill Retail Park which is built on the site of the former Hawkhill farm. The beginnings of this out-of-town development can be traced back to the early 1990s when Safeway was granted planning permission, on appeal, from the Scottish Office. Chronologically, the following planning permissions were granted: B&Q on 26 September 1995; the other units (units 2, 3, and 4) east of B&Q on 6 June 1996; an amended permission to allow a re-arrangement of the units (essentially, units 3 and 4 could be joined together to make a larger unit) on 2 August 1999. After the year 2000, further permissions were granted to further vary the range of goods that could be sold, and allowed the front of Unit 4 to be used as a drive-through restaurant.

A further extension to the retail site was added when Safeway Stores Plc submitted an application for the enlargement of their existing retail store for additional sales and ancillary floorspace. Another aspect of the application, which was made by Montagu Evans, Edinburgh, on 8 March 2002, involved alterations to the existing petrol filling station.

Any further investigation into the Retail Park must be carried out within the ever changing business machinations which occurred at the time.

On 11 February 2004, shareholders of both the Bradford based William Morrison and Safeway agreed to approve a merger between the two companies. Morrison completed the purchase of Safeway the following month. Soon afterwards, Morrison's first Scottish store opened in Kilmarnock, but it wasn't until November 2005 that Morrison's conversion of the Safeway store in Stevenston was completed.

For most of the history of the Hayocks the only functioning public house was located within the Ardchoille Hotel. The full background to this iconic building, including its previous life as Hayocks House, will be comprehensively covered in a later chapter of the book.

The grocery trade provided some competition to public houses in retailing alcoholic beverages through the institution of the licenced grocer. Table 9 below presents some of the early examples of grocers in the Hayocks who were licence holders:

YEARS	LICENCE HOLDER	ADDRESS of PREMISES
1964-1970	Joseph Barraclough	144 Hayocks Road
1964-1967	Allan McAlpine	2 Hayocks Road
1964-1974	Mrs Phyllis Boyd	136a Hayocks Road
1970-1974	Robert Paterson	2 Hayocks Road
1971-1974	Margaret Monaghan	144 Hayocks Road
1973 ***	David Stevenson	Campbell Avenue

***[This particular scenario is covered in much more detail in the section above].

Table 9. Grocers in the Hayocks who were also Licence Holders.

EARLY TRANSPORT EXPANSION

In consideration of the steadily increasing trend in car ownership in the early 1950s, the burgh had to make provision for garage space. In 1953 there was already a site adjacent to Donaldson Avenue for this purpose, and during the year a further six garages were added to this cluster. So far as garages at individual houses were concerned the Burgh Surveyor recommended that permission to erect these should only be granted in the case of those cottage-type houses where the layout and ground levels would allow a proper run-in, and on the condition that any person being granted permission to erect a garage should be responsible, if required, to reinstate any walls or gateways removed at the termination of his tenancy. The council could also insist on the removal of any garage, on one month's notice, if deemed necessary.

As the Hayocks continued to rapidly expand during the 1930s, 40s and 50s so the demand for a suitable bus service grew. A high percentage of all workers in the scheme were employed by Nobel's/I.C.I. and as the dimensions of the Hayocks increased the clamour for a regular and reliable bus service linking the Hayocks with the 'Dinamite' gained momentum.

In the years prior to the Second World War the workers' buses journeyed only from the top of the Townhead (not the Hayocks) towards the factory. The buses were operated by the Scottish Motor Traction Co. (SMT). These Western SMT buses terminated at George Street and Warner Street where the passengers transferred to trains for the final leg of their journey to the factory. At this time the buses were black and white in colour and did not travel directly to the factory gates. These same vehicles were painted grey during the war, only becoming red after the war ended.

The other prominent bus company operating in the local area during these three decades was the Ayrshire Bus Owners Association (A1 Service Ltd). The Road Traffic Commissioners refused to allocate licenses to the company to permit them to run worker's buses from Townhead to Stevenston Station. Only 'Westerns' could provide this service. The SMT Company was criticised on several occasions for the effectiveness of their service. One such incident arose in October 1953 when the burgh council was confronted by a complaint involving the insufficiency of the arrangements for the bus service after the expiry of certain shifts at the factory. This resulted in the council complaining to the company about

19. A1 Hayocks Bus in Dalry Road, Saltcoats, c. 1963.

their lack of planning and coordination.

A bus service linking the Hayocks with the rest of the town, and operated by A1, was discussed in 1939 but due to the Second World War was held in abeyance until 1946. This was the first functioning bus service geared to the general public in the Hayocks. It started and finished at Parkhouse Garage in Ardrossan taking a circular route through parts of Ardrossan and Saltcoats before coming along the High Road, up McGregor Avenue and down Hayocks Road, through the centre of Stevenston and along the 'Low Road' back into Saltcoats. Photograph 19 shows an A1 Hayocks bus in Dalry Road, Saltcoats around 1963 (note the rear entrance).

The extensive circular bus route within the scheme today came into existence in gradual stages, and the very tight regulation in bus service provision has been relaxed. A further later development was the numbering of buses at the expense of place names. 'New England' and 'Springvale' buses serviced the Hayocks but took different routes through Saltcoats and Ardrossan. This situation very often involved changing buses at Stevenston Cross.

6
Ecclesiastical and Educational

On entering the Hayocks for the first time, a stranger would be confronted by the iconic structure we recognise as St John's R. C. Church. It has been described as 'a striking church, unashamedly of its period.[1] This building, which was opened by the Right Reverend Joseph McGee, Bishop of Galloway, on Thursday 4 July 1963, has a conspicuous, modern design, and conformed with the latest liturgical trends in church building. It was innovative, bold, and futuristic in both its external appearance and internal design.

Two striking features of the church interior are the huge laminated wooden trusses, each weighing two tons, which support the roof. The roof is a spreading inverted V, with a separately roofed clear storey at the apex carrying a fleche. Secondly, there are four exquisitely coloured glass

1 Close, R. & Riches, A. *The Buildings of Scotland : Ayrshire and Arran*. Yale University Press , London 2012.

20. St John's Church in 1963.

windows. These windows depict four Biblical scenes, two on either side of the church. The four themes illustrated in the windows portray 'The Creation,' 'The Fall of Man,' 'The Redemption,' and 'The Resurrection.' There is also a narrow large coloured glass window stretching from top to toe of the south gable end, illustrating St John the Evangelist, the patron saint of the church, and beneath this is the baptistry window.

Another noticeable work of art within the church is the beaten bronze baptismal font which shows a half tree-trunk with a fawn, and a snail near the rim. It was supplied by P. White of Largs.

Structurally, a unique feature of the framework is that only two of the four walls are brick-built (at the gable ends), the sides were assembled using timber between the coloured glass windows. A very real sensation of spaciousness within the church is largely caused by the absence of pillars supporting the roof.

The architect responsible for designing such an impressive building was Mr John B. G. Houston, the son and partner of James Houston who initially became involved in the project in 1958. This well-known business was based at School Wynd, Kilbirnie.

The principal contractors for the new church were:

Builders – Messrs. William McClure & Sons, Irvine.
Joiners – Messrs. A. Reid & Hill, Ltd, Dalry.
Roofing and Roughcasting – J. Simmonds, Saltcoats.
Plumbing – A. McAllister, Saltcoats.
Plasterwork – T. Medine, Dalry.
Coloured Glass – M. Gabriel Loire, Chartres, France.
Painters – T. Lamb & Son, Largs.
Seating – West of Scotland Furniture Co., Beith.
Altars – West of Scotland Furniture Co., Beith.

Undoubtedly one of the most attractive and agreeable internal features of the church are the coloured glass windows. They were designed by the Frenchman, Gabriel Loire (born 21 April 1904 in Pouance, died 27 December 1996 aged ninety-two). Today he is considered one of the best European glassmakers working in the second half of the twentieth century, and the windows within St John's are widely acknowledged as his best work in Ayrshire.

On completing his schooling in Angers in 1926, he went to the Charles Lorin stained glass workshop in Chartres where he worked for ten years. Subsequently, he founded his own stained-glass studio in 1946. He was celebrated for his innovative use of 'slab glass,' a technique involving thicker and stronger glass than traditional stained glass. From a worldwide

21. Cutting the First Sod, Tuesday 6 March 1962, for St John's Church, by Rev. Joseph Maxwell.

portfolio, Loire created a number of windows in Scotland. These included local works such as those located in St Paul's Church, Whiteinch, Glasgow, the Holy Name Church in Oakley, Fife, and Our Lady of Mount Carmel Church in Kilmarnock. This last-named church was also opened in 1963 and the Diocese may have requisitioned the windows for both churches at the same time.

The church has a seating capacity for 420-450 people (500 if the gallery is included) and came with a price tag of approximately £40,000. All expenditure had been cleared by 1967.

After an intensified drive to raise funds by the parishioners in the old chapel-school in Moorpark Road West, the first sod was cut on 6 March 1962 by Rev. Joseph Maxwell, P.P.

The Church building project had been six years in the planning, with Mr Pat Savage being in the position of chairman of the Church Building Committee.

Further progress towards the completion of the project arrived with the laying of the foundation stone. On it is inscribed the following:

This Church is Erected to the Glory of God in Honour of St John the Evangelist.
The Foundation Stone was laid on the 19th September 1962 During the Pontificate of Pope John the XXIII By Joseph Bishop of Galloway.

The Solemn Opening of the church incorporated a Solemn Pontifical High Mass, the celebrant being Joseph McGee D.D. and the preacher was Reverend James Quinn S.J. from Edinburgh, who was a noted Scottish Catholic theologian. The occasion was graced by a capacity congregation of 630 individuals, and while the event was meticulously planned and beautifully executed inside, outside nature bared its teeth, producing a thunderstorm of Biblical proportions.

Assisting Bishop McGee in the solemn celebrations were Rev John Kane, Stevenston-born priest who at this time was on the staff of St Mary's College, Blairs, Kincardineshire; Rev G. Redden, curate of St John's; Rev S. Kennedy, Shortlees, Kilmarnock; the Very Rev Clement Canon McGowan, Largs; Rev M. Littleton, Kilmarnock, and Re. Vincent Walker, Irvine.

The congregation and visiting clergy were welcomed by Rev Joseph N. Maxwell, parish priest of St John's. The oldest parishioners in attendance were Mrs Agnes Hanlon (80), of Craigdene Drive and Mr Michael Leahy (86), son of the parish's first doctor, Dr Edmond Leahy. The first part of the new Compton pipe organ had just been supplied and installed by William Thomson & Sons, Glasgow, and was played by Mr McFarlane, principal teacher of music at St Michael's College, Irvine.

The civic guests at the ceremony and at the reception which followed in the Kilmeny Hotel, Ardrossan, included Provost James Clements accompanied by every member of Stevenston Town Council. Father Maxwell paid tribute to the Town Council for their co-operation and assistance in connection with the site of the new church. He also expressed his appreciation of the assistance provided by many non-Catholics during the intensified drive undertaken to gather funds throughout the previous six years. Provost Clements replied, stating that 'the continuance of church-building in a materialistic and intolerant world augured well for the spiritual well-being of Scotland and Stevenston.' Other speakers included Bishop McGee, Mgr. McQuillan, who had, for six years, been parish priest in Stevenston, and Mr James Houston, jun., the architect from Kilbirnie.

The feu disposition by the landowner, Mr Alfred Lyttleton Warner, to the trustees of the Roman Catholic Diocese of Galloway was dated 20 January 1958. This initial Board of Trustees comprised the Right Reverend (R.R.) Joseph McGhee D.D., Roman Catholic Bishop of Galloway; the R.R. Monsignor Joseph Provost McHardy V.G. M.C., St Margaret's, Ayr; the R.R. Monsignor John Canon McQuillan D.D., St Meddan's, Troon; the R.R. Michael Canon O'Connor, St Mary's, Saltcoats; the Very Reverend John William Canon O'Sullivan, St Andrew's, Dumfries; and the Reverend Joseph Kerr, Girvan.

A stipulation in the transfer document required that building on the site must be instigated within a five-year period. It also granted permission for the erection of a presbytery and hall but excluded access to any mineral deposits. The parcel of land involved in the sale was 0.42 hectares in size and had previously been part of the lands and estate of Ardeer.

A feu disposition dated 5 February 1964 informs us that Allan McAlpine, 4 Castlehill Road, Stevenston, and Robert Paterson, Ardchoille Hotel, Stevenston, being partners and trustees for the firm of Messrs James McAlpine, tobacconist, newsagent, grocer, and general merchants, 2 Hayocks Road, Stevenston, sold a piece of ground approximately 0.8 hectares in size, to the Trustees of the Roman Catholic Diocese of Galloway. This segment of land was adjacent to the church and was purchased for £350.

The initial preference of the church hierarchy for access to the church from Kilwinning Road was not recommended by the planning authority due to its potential impact on traffic flow on the main road. A second option involving a fifteen feet wide road skirting 'Pops' shop onto Hayocks road was also rebuffed. The vehicular entrance which was finally agreed ran parallel to the boundary wall taking in a small section of the monumental sculptor's yard and merging with Hayocks Road. This access is still in use today. It was also agreed to create a walking path into the church grounds from Kilwinning Road running parallel with the side of 'Pop's' shop. A provision for this pedestrian access was finalised in 1990 by Mr Robert Reid, the owner of the shop.

The reason (s) for selecting this particular site to locate the church are unclear. The principal factor in its favour was its centrality. It was much more accessible for its parishioners than the previous chapel school in Moorpark Road West, especially with its proximity to the rapidly expanding Hayocks scheme.

The major physical impediment associated with the site was the poor drainage. The field was in a shallow hollow and frequently became transformed into an area of standing water. Obviously, this difficulty was overcome and the ambitious project continued to completion.

The Chapel House was constructed along with the church, and was enlarged in the 1970s to include a two-storey extension towards the rear.

The plans for the building of a church hall were approved by A. M. Reid, Director of Planning, on 6 September 1985. It is a conventional brick harled structure. This facility replaced a temporary wooden built hall, and was completed in 1987. The building complex consisted of a hall 13 x 10.5 metres, two meeting rooms, toilets, a cloak room, store, and kitchen.

Table 10. Priests in St John's Church, Stevenston, since 1963.

DATES	PARISH PRIESTS	ASSISTANTS	DATES
1955-1975	V. Rev. J. Canon Maxwell*	Rev. G.D. Redden	1961-1964
		Rev. T. Leverage	1964-1968
		Rev. Fr. Kinsler	1968-1972
		Rev. E. Flynn.	1972-1976
1975-1988	Rev T. McGread	Rev. M. Farrington	1976-1981
		Rev. A. Wilson	1981-1986
		Rev. W. McFadden	1986-1989
1988-1997	V. Rev. J. Canon Walls	Rev. M. Chambers	1989-1994
		Rev. D. Conroy	1994-1996
1997-2004	Rev. M. Chambers	Rev. D. Borland	1998-1999
		Rev. S. Sharkey	2000-2001
2004 -	Rev. M. Poland	Rev. B. Mkeri	2020-2022

*Canon Joseph Ninian Maxwell died on 13 March 1976, aged 73.

Items of historical significance continue to be added to the fabric of the church. During the COVID period the sacristy bell, which was used in the original St John's church was re-discovered. Although in a tarnished condition, it was restored to a high standard, and after being mounted on a wooden support, in May 2024, was hung next to the sacristy entrance where it will remain as a tangible link to the old church.

HAYOCKS GOSPEL HALL

Only one other place of worship was based in the Hayocks, and to many residents of a previous generation it was a notable, respected, and enduring element within the community. This idiosyncratic wooden structure was the Hayocks Gospel Hall, universally and affectionately known as 'Tammy Meney's.'

In January 1946, Mr Thomas Meney was granted permission by Ayr County Council to build a Christian Brethren Gospel Hall at the bottom of what was later to become Craigdene Drive. The Chief Planning Officer for the council clearly stipulated that this temporary structure was to be upgraded within a short period of time to a brick building. The passage of time proves that this safeguard was not necessary. For a short period of time before the application was submitted the group of Christians met in the Young Men's Christian Association (YMCA) property in the centre of the town. The history of Tammy Meney's cannot be fully explained and understood without some reference to the Christian (or Open) Brethren movement in Stevenston.

In the mid-1860s, Christians started to meet in small informal groups in selected houses to further their studies of the scriptures. A few years later in response to these activities they decided to form their own independent church, or 'Assembly' based on the following principles: (a) salvation through faith alone (b) baptism by immersion for believers only (c) no clergy or pastors (d) a plurality of unpaid elders to guide the church (e) no association with any denomination or group – total autonomy.

In the late 1870s, the Bridgend School in Alexander Place, which had become vacant, was rented by the group to permit larger gatherings. This opportunity arose due to the fact that a member of the group had been an Assistant Teacher in the old school. The building was renamed the Loan Hall due to its proximity to the town loan (a common grazing area). This property was the rented home of the church until it was purchased by them in 1948.

In 1910, a number of members of the Loan Hall constructed the Bethany Hall in Shore Road in which they instigated a similar, but independent church. This was joined in 1947 by the Hayocks Gospel Hall which was formed by another group of Christians from the Loan Hall who had been holding their assemblies in the YMCA building. It was a widely held view that the rapidly expanding Hayocks scheme badly needed some form of church.

To briefly return to the Loan Hall; it was agreed by the congregation in 1957 that a larger, purpose-built hall was required to permit a wider range of activities. A prominent site for the new structure was chosen near the top of Townhead Street although the name Loan Hall was retained. The new centre of worship opened its doors early in 1958.

In 2004, the congregations in the Loan Hall and Bethany Hall decided to amalgamate and form a new church retaining the principles of the originals. This new entity was entitled the Townhead Christian Fellowship. Christians from the Hayocks Gospel Hall agreed to merge with the Fellowship in November 2008, thus creating one united church very closely reflecting the situation back in 1867.

Tammy Meney's was opened on the afternoon of Saturday 11 January 1947, under the auspices of the Brethren movement (see photo 22). A number of its original membership had previously belonged to the Loan Hall. Four of the original elders at the Hayocks Gospel Hall were Andrew Campbell, George Dunwoodie, Sam Adams, and Thomas Meney. Mr Campbell serving as the secretary and treasurer for a number of years. The opening day celebration was attended by approximately thirty-five adults and a large number of children.

Mr Thomas Meney was a 'larger than life' character and natural leader who held strong religious views. This positive and enthusiastic approach to

22. Opening Day Guests with the Gospel Hall in the Background.

his evangelical beliefs was reinforced by his considerable contribution to charitable causes. This passion was illustrated by his donations of funds to health and medical causes in Africa which included the establishment of the Hayocks Memorial Ward in an African hospital, and the purchase of a large motor vehicle for conversion into a mobile pharmacy and surgical unit, again in Africa. This association with missionary work was a continuing feature during the life-span of the Gospel Hall. A number of missionaries, active and retired, preached at the hall on a regular basis.

Mr Meney was wounded during his army duty in the First World War, and on returning to civilian life was employed in the factory as a general labourer. He married Margaret Brown who was a dynamite worker at Ardeer on 25 August 1920 in Caledonian Road, Stevenston. At the time of his marriage Tommy was living in Boglemart Street. He was born in 1896 and died in 1974, aged 77.

Later in his working life as a foreman, Tommy adopted the roll as a part-time barber in the 'Dinamite' as a means of securing additional funds for his charity work.

The Stevenston Iron Works built by the Glengarnock Iron Company and later owned by Merry & Cunningham Ltd were demolished in 1935. The site was transformed by contractors Shanks & McEwan, and a beach holiday camp was established near the 'Point.' This feature had a short-life span, and with the start of the Second World War, was utilised as a military garrison. A wooden hut which was used as a canteen by the army, and ultimately became Tammy Meney's Hall, was dismantled after the War and the various sections lay in the front garden of Andrew Campbell's home in Hillcrest Drive before completing its journey to Craigdene Drive.

On being reassembled, it had seating accommodation for 160 people and was electrically heated. The location of the Gospel Hall was controlled by the fact that Mr Samuel Adams who was a farmer at the Broom farm provided a slice of one of his fields, free of charge, to facilitate the siting of the hall. He along with Mr Thomas Meney, Mr George Dunwoodie and several others occupied the top table at the official opening.

The afternoon opening conference was split between an hour's praise and prayers and inputs from various guest speakers including Mr Allison, a missionary on leave from West Africa, Messrs Todd and McPike, and the Dickson party from Paisley who provided the singers. A social evening followed the afternoon activities when the Auchinleck Choir furnished the entertainment. The day's proceedings were presided over by Mr Thomas Meney and Mr George Dunwoodie.

The commitment of the congregation to this new venture was amply illustrated by the weekly timetable. In addition to the Sunday School, Bible Class, and Gospel Meeting held every Sunday, activities had also been arranged on Thursdays and Saturdays. The Sunday School was attended by over one hundred children; the annual Sunday School outing was the highlight for the children and included such salubrious destinations as Annbank and Mossblown.

Many individuals have embraced the philosophy and gospel teachings of the Gospel Hall. A few of the more recent elders being Jackie Locke, Roy and Stan Kilpatrick, Arthur Young, and David Wilson.

The final religious service in Tammy Meney's occurred in either October or December 2008, and this was shortly followed by the merger with the Townhead Christian Fellowship. By this time the elders of the Townhead Christian Fellowship decided not to identify with other Christian Brethren groups becoming a completely independent, autonomous evangelical church with no affiliation to any sect or denomination. They therefore do not identify as Brethren. During this period of time when the congregation of Tammy Meney's was considering a merger, they continued to 'spread the word.' This crystallised on 6 January 2007 when the members organised an evening of music and recollection in the Hayocks Community Hall to commemorate the sixtieth anniversary of the Gospel Hall.

When unoccupied, from 2008 through to 2010, the hall suffered several bouts of vandalism, but was eventually transformed into a children's nursery by Linda McNair. The nursery manager spent a year renovating the premises which opened for business in February 2011.

Today the wooden building is in a serious state of disrepair. The roof has collapsed and the interior is exposed to the elements. This is an ignominious conclusion to a project which started in 1946 and ended in 2008. Throughout its long history this innocuous, recycled, wooden building which is squeezed into a tiny plot of ground has been the focal point for community cohesion for many families in the Hayocks and beyond, and its closure and subsequent collapse has left a gap in the provision of locally accessible services which may never be replaced.

EDUCATIONAL

The origin of primary education in the Hayocks can be traced back to December 1944 when the establishment of a primary school and nursery were approved by Ayr County Council on a 2.2 hectare site adjoining Morrison Avenue. This location was later altered slightly to allow the accommodation of a more coherent and integrated housing development. In practice however, Hayocks Primary School did not materialise until 1964.

Building work commenced in June 1962, and by 20 December 1963 the General Purposes Sub-Committee of the Education Committee of Ayr County Council reported that the joinery work was 30% complete; heating 15% complete, and plasterwork 20% done. While the construction work was progressing, the Education Committee started the process of appointing a Head Teacher. On 11 December 1963, the following candidates were invited for interview; George Nisbet, George Robinson, Alexander Weir, Thomas Hamilton, Alexander McKenzie, and James Munn. Resulting from this process, Alexander Weir, George Nisbet, and Alexander McKenzie were selected as a short leet. Subsequently, Mr Weir (from Saltcoats) was appointed as Head Teacher on a clear majority by the committee. Following Mr Weir's tenure, the headteacher's position was occupied by a number of women including Mrs Gaw, Mrs E. McLean, Mrs Moira Crocker, Mrs Maureen Denningberg, Mrs Anne Hunter, and the most recent incumbent Ms Penny McCann.

On 18 March 1964, the Education Committee agreed that in view of the forthcoming transfer of pupils from the primary department of Stevenston High School to the new Hayocks Primary, to transfer Mr White, Depute Head Teacher, and Miss Wilson, Infants' Mistress, from the High School to the new primary.

The school opened on 27 August 1964 with one of its principal objectives being to relieve much of the overcrowding in Stevenston High School. It had a modern design, incorporating many large windows which gave the classrooms an airy, spacious ambience. It is interesting to note that at the beginning of this school term, the total Primary 1 intake in Saltcoats,

Stevenston and Ardrossan was 458. The Stevenston enrolment figures were Stevenston High School – 38; Ardeer Primary School – 28; and the new Hayocks Primary School – 66. At the same time, a significant number of children in P2 to P7 who attended the High School but lived in the Hayocks catchment area, were transferred to their new local school.

Although the school opened at the beginning of the new term, difficulties were immediately experienced. In fact, on 21 August, Stevenston Labour Party sent a letter to the Ayrshire Education Committee expressing concern at the slow rate of progress in the building of the new school. Certain parts of the building had not been completed, but with the full cooperation of the staff, a number of temporary arrangements were successfully implemented. By October, the assembly hall and kitchen were still unfinished (work having only started in June). The necessary precautions required to safe-guard the pupils from the risk of accident had previously been issued by the County Architect. With regards to the failure of the contractors to complete the contract on schedule, Provost James Clements repeatedly raised the issue with the Education Committee of Ayr County Council. The Town Council was informed by the County Clerk, Mr Ivie McCaig, that the decision to open the school at the beginning of the new session although unfinished, would prevent the pupils facing the unsettling experience of first attending one school and then being transferred to another. This explanation met with a mixed reaction from both the town councillors and parents.

St John's Primary School was completed and occupied by 12 September 1973. Prior to this date on 12 April, the superstructure had been completed and the placing of the internal partitions and various site workings were in progress, but the anticipated completion date of July was delayed until August. After the opening, landscaping work continued in the surrounding area. The school was constructed under the same basic plan as that adopted for the nearby St Luke's, St Mark's, and St Anthony's. Surprisingly, the school had no opening ceremony to commemorate the event, and there is no commemorative plaque within the building.

The name for the school was a continuation of the old St John's chapel school in Moorpark Road West which was opened on 2 July 1905. This original place of learning remained open until the new school was opened at Morrison Avenue in 1973.

In the first year of its existence, St John's had a pupil roll marginally exceeding 500, with the space being utilised to capacity with approximately eighteen classrooms. Today the shape of the school is identical to what it was at the time of opening (there have not been any extensions built), although one part of the building has become 'Community Learning and Development' which is no longer under school management.

Shortly after the opening of the new school, it emerged that the Stevenston and Saltcoats town councils had been considering the possibility of utilising Dubbs Quarry as a refuse coup. This open-cast mine was sited across the A78 only 100 metres distant from the school. The matter was raised by Councillor Thomas Murphy who spoke of the anxiety among parents and teachers of St John's Primary School Parent-Teacher Association about the proposal. After extensive consultations within the community, it was agreed to reject the project. Ironically, the open-cast mine lay undisturbed and full of water until it was finally restored and landscaped only a few years ago.

There have been eight headteachers leading the school during its fifty-one-year history. In chronological order they are:

Mrs Elizabeth McArdle (first appointee).
Mrs Anne Monaghan.
Mrs Anne Carmichael.
Mrs Cecelia Dearing.
Mrs Elizabeth Miller.
Mr Kevin Howell.
Mrs Teresa Thornton (acting for a short period of time).
Mrs Karen McAllister (present incumbent).

In keeping with the trend in most schools of this age the pupil roll has fallen, in the case of St John's to between 90 and 100 (there is also an Early Years Class). Today there are twelve available classrooms, but many internal alterations have occurred over the years to include a conference room, photocopying room, and nursery garden. The school library was upgraded in 2023 due to a donation of £1,500 from a past pupil.

The reasons for the declining school population are numerous and complex. The principal cause nationally is undoubtedly demographic. The falling birth rate with its impact on pupil numbers is hardly affected, in an area like Stevenston, by very limited inward migration figures. Local factors must also be incorporated into this intricate web of cause and effect. Council decisions have serious implications when we consider pupil numbers, and one such ramification for St John's was the reduction in student numbers as a direct consequence of the school bus service being discontinued between the school and the Ardeer area.

The school has undertaken many initiatives to ensure its pupils receive a well-rounded educational, cultural, religious, and social experience. The introduction of a Healthy Start Club reflects this caring, inclusive ethos.

St John's has over the years nurtured many talented individuals in the sporting arena. However, more recently, three outstanding and gifted ex-pupils have emerged on the national sporting scene.

Brooke Neely trains both at Irvine Vineburgh Club and Bridgeton in Glasgow where she is a member of the Scotland Elite boxing squad. She has made a meteoric rise within the sport becoming the first Scottish female boxer to win four Great Britain gold medals. The final success of the four by the 18-year-old was in the youth 48kg division. She has also represented Scotland at the GB Junior and Youth Three Nations Championship held at the Ravenscraig Regional Sports Facility in Motherwell in June 2023 where she won gold.

Liam Smith attended St John's Primary from nursery through to Primary Seven. While a pupil at St John's aged six, he played football for TASS and two years later was training with Celtic. In the same year he signed a professional youth contract with Kilmarnock. On leaving St John's, he enrolled at the Grange Academy Scottish Football Performance School in Kilmarnock, and at the age of fourteen, this committed and enthusiastic youth was asked to play with the Kilmarnock reserve squad. With increased exposure within the 'beautiful game,' a number of high profile clubs, including Manchester City, Rangers and Liverpool, noticed his talent and potential. After trials, Liam signed his first professional contract in June 2020 at the age of sixteen with the Manchester club. The winger signed a £200,000 four-year-deal with Pepe Guardiola's giants. After spending a very rewarding three-year spell at the Etihad, Liam signed for Swansea City of the Championship. He was also capped for Scotland at the various age groups from Under 16's onwards. At the time of writing, Liam is on loan from Swansea City to Partick Thistle.

Meredith Reid started her outstanding athletics career while in primary five at St John's when she won the North Ayrshire Cross Country Championship. As a distance runner she excelled, and in her teenage years she attended Glasgow School of Sport where she received specialised coaching. Meredith was quickly selected to represent Scotland at Under 15 and Under 17 levels, participating at various venues throughout Britain. Her aptitude for the sport and capacity for hard work, resulted in her securing an incredible number of Scottish and District titles. At the age of 18 she represented Scotland at Senior level over 3,000 metres in Ireland. This massive achievement was intermingled with triumphs as Scottish U20 Champion in the 3,000m, 5,000m, and 10,000m. Her outstanding talent was recognised in 2022 when she was selected as first reserve for Team Great Britain in the U20 World Cross Country Championship in Australia.

Meredith's trajectory as an outstanding athlete continued when she enrolled as a Law student at Strathclyde University. Here she was granted a 'full blue' in Athletics and Cross Country. This award is the most prestigious sporting achievement presented at university level.

In addition to her prowess on the track, Meredith excelled on the road racing circuit. She finished first female in the 2022 North Ayrshire Athletics Club 10km road race in a time of 36mins 49secs, finishing seventh overall in a mixed field of 264 runners. Even more impressive was running a time of 34min 12secs in the iconic Nigel Barge 10km road race in 2023. This event which is organised by Maryhill Harriers was first run in 1943 and has been won by almost every great Scottish middle-distance athlete. Competing for Inverclyde Athletics Club, she again was the first female finisher, and her time was truly outstanding on this undulating course. In fact, her achievement resulted in Meredith being ranked second in the United Kingdom for the 10km distance for U20s. Finally, returning to the track, her 3,000m indoor performance in the same year gained her the Scottish U20 title and the accolade of ranking first in the UK for the distance.

7
Political History

This section on the history of voting patterns in the Hayocks must by necessity be objective and non-judgemental. The statistics are presented as published by the Returning Officers and are therefore accurate and comprehensive. The detail they contain is both interesting and informative. In addition to the raw data, I have included some other material pertaining to several other aspects of the electoral process such as turnout figures, but a detailed analysis of the political history of the Hayocks is fraught with difficulty and is beyond the scope of this book.

The first District Councillor with a Hayocks address to be elected to Stevenston and Ardrossan North was Michael O'Sullivan. His address was 27 Reid's Avenue and he represented Stevenston Parish on Saltcoats District Council between May 1946 and May 1947. He was followed in 1952, before the burgh election, by James Forde, 33 Greenhead Avenue (as a County Councillor) and James Clements, 52 Alexander Avenue, and Robert McLellan, 113 Hayocks Road (both as District Councillors).

Moving to a more recent time, we can see by examining Table 11 that certain patterns and trends become discernible between the years 1974 and 2003. As a precursor it should be stated that during this period of time each ward in Cunninghame District Council and North Ayrshire Council elected a single councillor by the 'first past the post' electoral system. It is also informative to use some national trends in local government elections as a base line to the situation in Stevenston North. Three points need emphasising: A) The reorganisation of local government in 1974 resulted in a much greater party interest and direct involvement in local elections than was previously the situation; B) Related to point A, from 1974 to 1988 there was an upward trend in the number of candidates, but this tendency should be remembered in the context of many civic minded people being reluctant to seek elected office, due to the costs in time, career prospects and disruption to family life being not inconsiderable; C) The decline in the number of Independent candidates had continued unabated since reorganisation in 1974. The situation in Stevenston North and therefore the Hayocks between 1974 and 1988, mirrors closely these three general observations. In fact, the findings extend well beyond 1988 in some cases up to the present day.

From the first Cunninghame District Council elections held in 1974 stretching through to 2003, the Hayocks has contributed approximately 80% of the voters in the Stevenston North ward. Therefore, the outcome of the elections in Stevenston North will provide a reasonably accurate account of the voting patterns in the Hayocks. However, there may have been discrepancies between the Hayocks vote and other parts of the ward caused, for example by a particular issue restricted to the Mayfield area. Covering the eight elections (excluding by-elections) which occurred in Stevenston North over this period there were no boundary changes of electoral significance. The statistical data emanating from each election is therefore directly comparable. The trends (if any) in various aspects of the electoral process can therefore be examined in Table 11.

It should be noted that 99% of the Stevenston North electorate was located in the residential area north of the High Road, Glencairn Street, and Kilwinning Road between the Tesco Metro and the Pennyburn Roundabout. The northern boundary is the Three Towns By-Pass. There were several anomalies in the landward area north of the by-pass, for example, Hawkhill Cottage was part of Stevenston North while Castlehill and Hillhead farms were included in the adjacent Kilwinning Ward. Mayfield, Lochcraigs, and Middlepart farms were considered part of Stevenston North whereas Lochwood farm was marginally outside.

Table 11. Cunninghame District Council Election Results for STEVENSTON NORTH between 1974 and 1992.

YEAR	ELECT-ORATE	TURN-OUT	RESULT	MAJORITY
1974*	4207	40.6%	Teresa Beattie. Lab. 840 (50.2%)	
			T. Murphy. Ind. 834 (49.8%)	6
1977	4111	45.6%	Ms T. Beattie. Lab. 605 (32.6%)	
			Ms P. Greer. SNP. 604 (32.6%)	
			Ms G Scanlan. Con. 434 (23.4%)	
			R. Stevenson. Lib. 141 (7.6%)	
			J. Logan. SLP. 69 (3.7%)	1
1980	4048	47.2%	Ms T. Beattie. Lab. 1062 (55.5%)	
			Ms J. McMullan. Con. 520 (27.2%)	
			W. Greer. SNP. 325 (17.0%)	542
1984	4087	46.2%	Ms T. Beattie. Lab. 1148 (60.8%)	
			G. Dorrian. Lib/SDP. 493 (26.1%)	
			J. Cownie. Con. 241 (12.8%)	655
1988	3890	48.4%	Ms T. Beattie. Lab. 1293 (68.6%)	
			B. McBlane. SNP. 257 (13.6%)	

			J. McNeil. Con. 207 (11.0%)	
			K. McGilp. Ind. 126 (6.7%)	1036
1992	3611	31.3%	Ms T. Beattie. Lab. 815 (72.0%)	
			K.McGilp. Mod. 314 (27.7%)	501

NOTE: * The newly created Cunninghame District Council (CDC) elections were held on 7 May 1974 and resulted in a council which shadowed until the formation of CDC on 16 May 1975.

Table 12. North Ayrshire Council Election Results for STEVENSTON NORTH, SALTCOATS and STEVENSTON, and STEVENSTON between 1995 and 2022.

YEAR	WARD	NUMBER of SEATS	RESULT
1995**	Stevenston North	1	Allan Munro. Lab.
1999	Stevenston North (Electorate 3548)	1	Allan Munro. Lab. 1170 Majority 593 Kenneth McSkimming SNP 577 Annie Reid Con. 211
2003	Stevenston North (Electorate 3435)	1	Allan Munro Lab. 956 (55.3%) Kenneth McGilp SNP 327 (18.9%) Margaret Walsh Ind. 315 (18.2%) Patricia McPhee Con. 132 (7.6%)
2007***	Saltcoats and Stevenston	4	William Gibson SNP 1629 (22.4%) Ronnie McNicol Ind. 1362 (18.8%) David Munn Lab. 943 (13.0%) Allan Munro Lab. 902 (12.4%) Nan Wallace SNP 691 (9.5%) Sam Taylor Lab.

Year	Ward	Seats	Candidate	Votes
				683 (9.4%)
			Stewart Ferguson Con.	554 (7.6%)
			Margaret Walsh Ind.	496 (6.8%)
2011****	Saltcoats and Stevenston	1	Jim Montgomerie Lab.	
2012	Saltcoats and Stevenston	4	Jim Montgomerie Lab.	1926 (36.2%)
			Willie Gibson SNP	1244 (23.4%)
			Ronnie McNicol Ind.	703 (13.2%)
			Allan Munro Lab.	540 (10.1%)
			Nan Wallace SNP	481 (9.0%)
			David Rocks Con.	193 (3.6%)
			Jimmy Miller ASPP	163 (3.1%)
			Debbie Anderson SocLab	76 (1.4%)
2017*****	Stevenston	3	Davina McTiernan SNP	782 (21.5%)
			John Sweeney Lab.	697 (19.1%)
			Chris Paton SNP	601 (16.5%)
			Jimmy Miller Lab.	579 (15.9%)
			Tom McCammont Con.	573 (15.7%)
			Allan Munro Ind.	172 (4.7%)
			Gerard Pollock Ind.	144 (3.9%)
			David Higgins Ind.	97 (2.7%)
2022	Saltcoats and Stevenston	5	Jean McClung SNP	1908
			Jim Montgomerie Lab.	1822

John Sweeney. Lab.
796
Cameron Inglis Con.
742
Davina McTiernan SNP
666
Ronnie McNicol Ind.
366
David Higgins IndScot.
111
Jimmy Miller Ind.
95

NOTE: Electorate = 16,951; Turnout = 39.6%

NOTE: ** The first election to North Ayrshire Council was held on 6 April 1995 initially operating as a shadow authority alongside the outgoing authority until the new system came into force on 1 April 1996. The new council retained the same electoral boundaries as Cunninghame District Council which existed from 1975 to 1996.

In 1995, Ward 14 (Stevenston North) did not hold an election due to the death of Councillor Theresa Beattie. She died on 20 March 1995 within three weeks of the election for which she was an enrolled candidate. Her death after the close of nominations, meant the April 6 poll was therefore countermanded. The subsequent election which was carried out by Strathclyde Regional Council was won by Allan Munro, the Labour Party candidate.

*** From 2007 when proportional representation was introduced the figures shown indicate the number of First Preference Votes.

**** Jim Montgomerie (Lab) made his first appearance on the political scene when he won the Ward 4 (Saltcoats and Stevenston) by-election held on 25 August 2011. He was successful in securing the one vacant seat caused by the resignation of David Munn the previous Labour councillor.

***** In 2017, the First Preference Vote list was altered after the application of the Election Rules. This process eliminated Chris Paton in favour of Jimmy Miller.

Table 13. Record of Voter Turnout in Areas Covering the Hayocks from 1974 to 2022.

Election Year	Turnout (%)
1974	40.6
1977	45.6
1980	47.2
1984	46.2
1988	48.4
1992	31.3
1999	55.3
2003	50.5
2007	49.5
2011 *	25.4
2012	34.9
2017	39.5
2022	39.6

NOTE: * Election Year 2011 with a noticeably low turnout was a by-election, and traditionally by-elections tend to produce low turnout figures.

Table 14. Percentage Turnout in Contested Wards in the Four Ayrshire Districts for 1992.

Ayrshire Districts	Percentage Turnout
Cunninghame	39.6
Kilmarnock and Loudoun	45.4
Kyle and Carrick	48.6
Cumnock and Doon Valley	42.7

The average national figure for turnouts in Scottish Districts in 1992 was 41.4%. The figures in Table 14 clearly show that of the four Ayrshire Districts, only Cunninghame District fell below the national average for voter turnout in local government elections held in this year. Since 1992, this trend of active participation in local elections within the four Districts has largely continued, although the actual figures have fluctuated. The picture is further complicated by the reduction of the four Districts into three Council Areas (North, East and South Ayrshire).

With the reorganisation of the local government boundaries, and the disappearance of the Stevenston North ward after the 2003 election, voter turnout started to dip (evident from Table 13). There also seems to be a loose correlation between the number of candidates standing for election in a ward and the turnout figures.

In Stevenston North ward, the electorate ranged over the years (1974 to 2003) from 4207 to 3435. The lowest figure belongs to the year 2003, and this trend was one reason for the reorganisation of local government boundaries which came into existence in 2007.

The North Ayrshire Council election in 2007 was held on 3 May. This election was the first one using eight new wards created as a result of the Local Governance (Scotland) Act 2004. It adopted the Single Transferable Vote system form of proportional representation. The new wards replaced the thirty single-member wards which used the first past the post system of election. The Hayocks was incorporated into the new ward of Saltcoats and Stevenston. This alteration in the ward boundaries rendered comparisons with pre 2007 elections results almost meaningless. It also meant that the Hayocks vote was incorporated into the larger Saltcoats and Stevenston ward, making its voting outcome more difficult to discern.

Several alterations in the electoral process took place in 2017. This election used ten wards which were created as a result of the Fifth Statutory Review of Electoral Arrangements. The Hayocks voters were included in the Stevenston ward. It used the Single Transferable Vote system, a form of proportional representation in which multiple candidates are elected in each ward and voters rank these candidates in order of preference.

The most recent local council election occurred in 2022, again utilising the Single Transferable Vote system, but the Saltcoats and Stevenston ward was reintroduced and included the Hayocks.

The number of rejected ballot papers has traditionally been low in local council elections, but this changed with the introduction of the proportional representation system of voting. In the most recent election in 2022 the number of spoiled ballot papers in Ward 5, which included the Hayocks, totalled 202. In most cases, the spoiling of ballot papers was not malicious and was caused by an inability to fully understand the voting procedure.

Psephology is an inexact science. The factors influencing the electoral preferences of individual voters are numerous, complex, and variable. In local elections less importance is attached to Party allegiance and more to the characteristics and personal qualities of each candidate. Representing an established political party with its organisational framework certainly helps in raising the profile of a candidate, but a previous record of community service; a local address; being a member of a well-respected and 'weil-kent local family, are all positive electoral attributes in local elections. It is also factually correct to state that a local, hard-working, visible, and accessible councillor with Party endorsement is difficult to replace.

Certain individuals who have served the Hayocks with distinction through their longevity in the political scene are listed below:

> James Morrison and James Patrick – County Councillors and District Councillors who represented Stevenston & Ardrossan North.
> James Forde, James (Jimmy) Clements and Thomas Hyslop – County and District Councillors as well as Town Councillors.
> Archie Lambie – Town Councillor and Strathclyde Region Councillor.
> Allan Munro – Stevenston North Councillor and Saltcoats and Stevenston Councillor.
> Theresa Beattie – Town Councillor and Stevenston North Councillor.

From the last few years of the town council through the entire duration of Cunninghame District Council one figure maintained a reputation for her devotion to public service.

From the beginning of her formal participation in local politics with her election to Stevenston Town Council in 1973, Theresa Beattie showed the temperament, determination and aptitude which would characterise her long and distinguished service to Stevenston. She entered the political arena in the final days of the Town Council having been elected along with Matt Smith and Matilda Lewis in 1973. Within a year she stood for election to the newly created Cunninghame District Council. Theresa was chosen to contest the ward of Stevenston North, going head-to-head at the ballot box with Thomas Murphy who had been a Town Councillor from 1966 to 1974 and a past Housing Convener. Theresa stood on a Labour Party ticket against her better known and respected Independent opponent. Mrs Beattie prevailed in an extremely close encounter with a majority of six votes (See Table 11). If her first encounter with the electorate of Stevenston North – including the Hayocks – was nerve shattering, the outcome of her second experience in 1977 was received with incredulity. The five-sided contest resulted (after several recounts) in Theresa emerging victorious with a majority of a single vote over her nearest rival Ms P. Greer (SNP) from Kilwinning, both women securing 32.6% of the vote. The commonly voiced opinion in political circles that 'every single vote counts' was certainly vindicated in this contest. Within two minutes of the polling station being closed John Beattie – the husband of Theresa – delivered a Labour supporter by car to the venue. His action resulted in his wife being re-elected in Stevenston North with the smallest majority in Scotland. Surprisingly, an equal share of the votes cast would have resulted in the contest being decided by the toss of a coin.

Having established her credentials as a woman of integrity, strong principle, and quiet dignity and an inspirational, and highly motivated politician, her contact with the ballot box became a less stressful experience. Her four subsequent elections resulted in fluctuating but comfortable majorities (See Table 11). Within the local Labour Party, she was recognised as an electoral asset, and when this was combined with her growing reputation as a gifted, conscientious, and forward-thinking councillor, Theresa quickly gained a prominent local profile. Amongst many other posts, she was Convener of Cunninghame District Council from 1984 to 1988, and Leader of the Labour group on two occasions, from 1977 to 1980 and from 1992 until her death in 1995.

In Stevenston North (including the Hayocks), Mrs Beattie's paramount objectives were the provision of services and jobs for local people. She was an enthusiastic advocate for leisure facilities, especially for young people, and identified the political system as a means of progress for her constituents. Unusually, she was trusted and admired by adherents of every political view.

Permeating her entire political career was a desire to encourage more women to engage in the political scene, and she herself served on a wide range of local government organisations including board membership of Irvine Development Corporation.

Mrs Beattie was an experienced and hardened politician who learned how to win without resorting to confrontation. After the 1984 election, Theresa became the new council convener after a three-cornered fight for the job. She defeated opponents Tom Dickie and Jim Clements with a comfortable majority. She also instigated a reshuffle aimed at providing the younger members of the council with a taste of responsibility. It would be naïve to think that this major reshuffle was welcomed by all councillors, but Mrs Beattie had the authority and legitimacy to carry it out.

In addition to the first Cunninghame District Council elections held in 1974 there were also elections for Strathclyde Regional Council. This regional authority had responsibility for education, social work, police, fire, sewage, strategic planning, roads, and transport. The Hayocks was incorporated into electoral area 90 – Kilwinning and Stevenston (there being 103 electoral areas in total, electing that number of regional councillors). The first election for Kilwinning and Stevenston resulted in Mr Ronald Carson (Lab) gaining 55% of the vote and a majority of 729 votes. Mr Carson, who was the Chairman of the Ayrshire & Arran Health Board came from Beith, but after interview was selected to contest Area 90 for the Labour Party. Thereafter, in the five subsequent elections - 1978 to 1994, Archie Lambie (Lab) represented Kilwinning and Stevenston on the

Regional Council. He surprisingly doubled the Labour majority in 1978. Although Archie was a Glaswegian through-and-through he was also a Hayocks man, staying in Forde Crescent for a number of years.

The transition from the Burgh to C.D.C. and S.R.C. was not without its trials and tribulations. A minute from the Town Council dated 2 September 1974 states that the council were prepared to let C.D.C. know their agenda, but without accepting that C.D.C. had any control over their projects. Mr R. Carson, who had been chosen to represent Kilwinning and Stevenston in the approaching S.R.C. election, was however in constant contact the Town Council regarding various administrative issues. From the final Burgh meeting on 21 April 1975 it was agreed to arrange a farewell dinner/ dance for all staff and employees.

On gaining election to Cunninghame District Council in 1974, Theresa Beattie quickly formed the opinion that this particular District Council could survive, and in fact, flourish as a unitary authority. She was confident in her own judgement and worked tirelessly for its creation. Theresa saw change as a challenge, and she was the driving force behind the fight to create the new council. Her grit and determination were rewarded when the Secretary of State for Scotland from 1990-1995, Ian Lang, gave the go-ahead for the new North Ayrshire Council based on the existing Cunninghame borders. Her stance on local government re-organisation was not universally popular within the council, and a few months before the 1995 election Fullarton councillor David O'Neill along with five other councillors defied the group line and challenged Mrs Beattie's authority on the matter. It is a pity that Mrs Beattie died within three weeks of the first election to North Ayrshire Council, for which she was a candidate, and did not witness the formation of the authority she had laboured so hard to establish.

On a personal level, Theresa Garvey was born on 21 November 1923 at 4 Alexander Place, Stevenston. Her father, Thomas, was a coal merchant in the town, and her mother, Joan (nee Livingston). At the time of her marriage to John Beattie on 5 March 1946 in Ardeer Church, she was a hospital nurse living at Stonefield Road, Blantyre. John lived locally in Reid's Avenue, having been born on 14 April 1923 in 23 Limekiln Road. After leaving nursing, Theresa attained the position of Social Work Manager, at the same time maintaining her support for the Salvation Army and continual involvement with young people. After leaving the Royal Navy, John worked in the factory, and he and Theresa had two daughters, Lilian and Elaine. John died in 1982, aged 59 years.

Mrs Beattie lived in Townhead Street for many years and her name is commemorated in Stevenston through Beattie Court, the Hayocks Community Hall, and the Beattie Memorial Library. Her fellow Stevenston councillor for many years, Sam Gooding (Stevenston South), described Theresa as a 'tower of strength, a person for the people, tolerant, with a deep respect for political opponents.'[1]

1 *Irvine Herald*. 14th April 1995.

8
Sporting Activities

ARCHERY

For a period-of-time, in excess of four centuries, up until the middle of the seventeenth century, landowners and noblemen throughout Scotland, by royal decree, were required to parade their armed retainers at regular intervals for a show of weapons and exhibition of military prowess. These wapenschaws tested the skill of the archers as they attempted to dislodge a model of a parrot, called a papingo, from the top of a tower or high tree, and were held every Sunday after church services. These events were largely considered to be a form of amusement and not nearly as important as the serious business of butt shooting. However, there was a serious side to papingo shooting, as aiming at an elevated target, such as defenders atop a castle wall, was considered an essential skill.

With the advent of firearms as a more potent weapon in the seventeenth century, interest in archery diminished. Only in a few areas around the country did archery retain its appeal. One such location was Kilwinning and its immediate surroundings.

The Ancient Society of Kilwinning Archers was formed in 1483 and is still in existence, although not with a continuous history. Its early formation date makes it the oldest archery organisation in Britain and probably in the world. It is widely acknowledged that the Kilwinning papingo shoot was first contested in 1488, but the earliest existing record of a meeting of the Kilwinning archers is dated 4 September 1688.

Where the papingo was placed for the contests during the first hundred years of the Kilwinning Society of Archers is unknown, but from the latter part of the sixteenth century it was placed on top of the remaining tower of the ruined Kilwinning Abbey (the abbey was destroyed in 1561). The tower was demolished by lightning in 1821 and since the present abbey clock tower was erected on the site in 1822 the papingo has been placed there for every contest.

Whoever was the first to 'ding doon' the papingo received the accolade of being the captain of the archers for the following year. In the early years of the society the winner's prize was a multi-coloured Persian taffeta, but after many years the award was changed to a piece of silver, to be purchased by the captain demitting office. This development ended the classless status

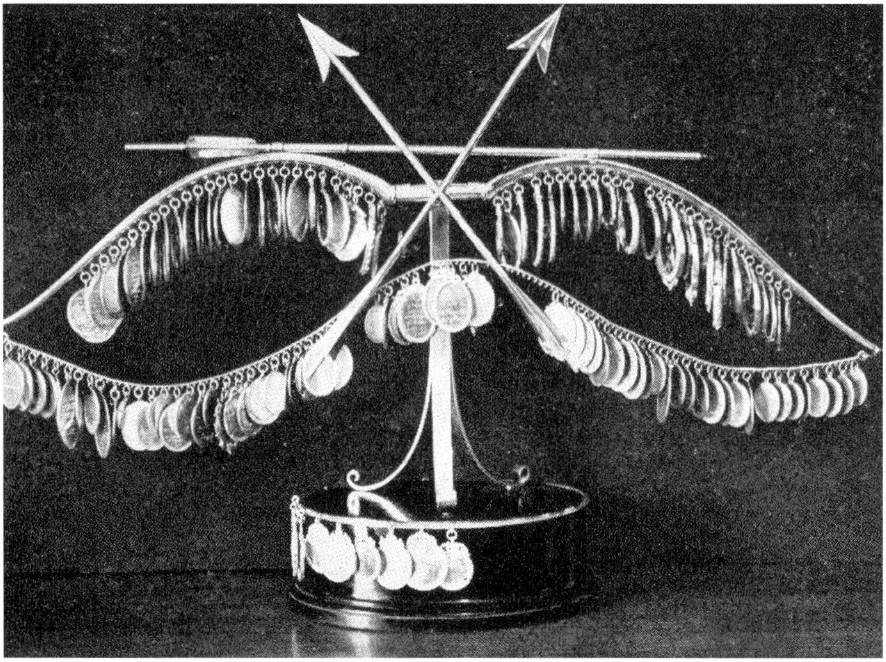

23. The Silver Arrow Trophy.

of the society as only the wealthier members could afford the piece of silver. The elitist characteristic of the society was confirmed before the end of the eighteenth century in its decision to introduce three contests annually on the day of the papingo shoot – one each for the 'boys,' the 'merchants and tradesmen,' and the 'gentlemen.' However, only the 'gentlemen' (landowners and wealthy establishment figures) were eligible to shoot for the papingo trophy. Many of the wealthy participants regarded the organisation as a means of increasing their social status, a medium which encouraged networking and opportunities to 'press the flesh.' This aspect was considerably more important than serious competition.

This class distinction within the organisation emphasised social divisions and resulted in a loss of enthusiasm and popularity for archery with ordinary working people.

The Silver Arrow Trophy (See Photo 23) for the winner of the Papingo shoot was presented to the Society by David Muir in 1724, and in fact he was the first winner of the trophy.

As intimated above, many of the members of the society and participants in the papingo shoot were affluent proprietors of local estates. They lived in imposing country houses exuding wealth, social status, authority, and power. Within our study area these included Hullerhirst, Hayocks, Kerelaw (Grange), and Ashgrove. In Stevenston we must also include Seabank and Ardeer. During the eighteenth and nineteenth centuries when the local estates were owned by wealthy, influential families residing – with the exception of a few absentee landlords – in their country houses, archery was a popular pastime and vehicle for mixing with like-minded men. In the Stevenston area the principal organisation catering for the advancement of archery was the Ancient Society of Kilwinning Archers.

The minutes of the Society record the following information with reference to a number of local landowning families.

The earliest mention of recreation involving a bow and arrow at Hullerhirst was on 19 May 1774 when we are informed that the 'Antient prize of Papingo was gained by William Kelso Esq of Hilderhist at Kilwinning.' On the reverse of his medal (no. 47) which was added to the Papingo Trophy was a stylised coat of arms and the Latin motto 'ubique aut nusquam' – 'everywhere or nowhere.' The competition could have been won by either the father or son as both were called William. Four years later on 5 June 1778, Patrick (the brother of the son William) competed for the medal without success.

Moving to the small Hayocks estate, there is recorded from the annual meeting of the society in 1839 that John Muir Esq. of Hayocks along with another six gentlemen were appointed as committee members for the ensuing twelve months.

The Muir or Mure family had a close connection with the society over the years. In fact, it was David Mure who presented the Silver Arrow to the society in 1724. In the local area, Muir, as a surname, over a long period of time, has been very common. To unravel the possible relationships between the different branches of the Muir family would be a tortuous exercise in detective work. However, we possess some indisputable data indicating that John Muir was resident in West Hayocks in 1837. He was still there in 1857 and was described as a merchant and Justice of the Peace.

The Muirs who resided at Hayocks House must not be confused with their Kilwinning namesakes. For many years, Kilwinning had not only been a hub for archery as a form of social recreation, but as a centre for bow-making. One of its brightest lights was Peter Muir who was the youngest of ten children of William Muir, carpenter and bow-maker. Peter became proficient with a bow at an early age and was apprenticed to his father at his bowyery workshop in Kilwinning. His uncle, David Muir, seems to have greatly influenced his development and style, for in 1829 Peter was offered employment in Edinburgh by the Royal Company of Archers, the Queen's bodyguard in Scotland. Muir's bows displayed a number of features indicative of his desire to develop a distinct Scottish style.

Peter Muir was also an excellent archer, winning the Grand National Meeting championship medal in 1845, 1847, and 1863. However, he never forgot his roots in Kilwinning and in 1864 he featured on the medal list

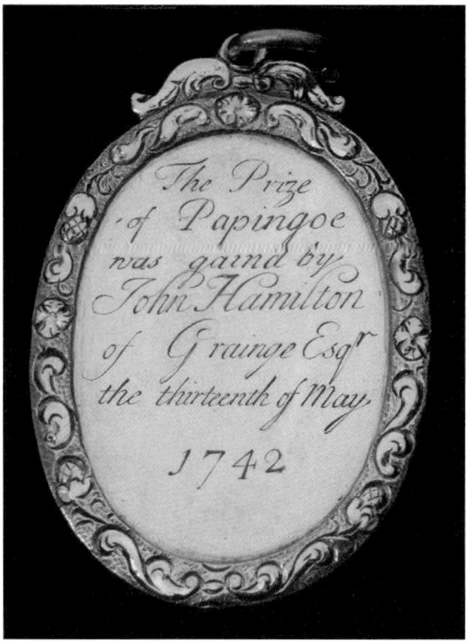

24. The Papingo Prize Medal won by John Hamilton of Grange.

for the Papingo shoot. He returned the year later, listed as 'Peter Muir Esq. of Edinburgh,' and gained the prize of a silver fork and knife.

Kilwinning was also the home of a number of other bowyers, one of the most prominent being James Reid who was renowned as a longbow maker.

To complicate the issue further, Hillhead farm in Hullerhirst Estate was tenanted by a family of Muirs between 1815 and approximately 1870, but it seems unlikely they were involved in archery or bowyery. However, around 1907, Hillhead was occupied by a bower named James Ramsay.

Concerning the Grange Estate, on 20 May 1736, the Prize of Papingo was gained by Walter Hamilton for his thirteen year old brother, John. John himself won the Papingo in 1742 (See Photo 24). He was the older brother of Alexander Hamilton who, being the youngest of three brothers and therefore not expecting to inherit much of the family estate, had travelled to the Caribbean to seek his fortune. His son, also Alexander Hamilton, who was the nephew of John Hamilton of Grange the medal winner, became the first Secretary of the United States Treasury, and one of the founding fathers of the U.S. A. In 1740, Walter gained the Papingo prize on behalf of Robert Kerr Esq., Director of the Chancellery. In addition to John and Walter, a first cousin, also called Alexander, has a medal on the silver arrow. He won the competition in 1778. On the reverse of his medal is a stylised oak tree, which is the crest of the Hamilton family, and underneath it in a scroll is the Latin motto 'viridis et fructifera' – 'flourishing and fruit bearing.' This particular Alexander built Kerelaw House in 1787 and laid the foundation stone of the new Eglinton Castle in 1797 on behalf of the 12th Earl of Eglinton. He was still active in the Society in 1794, as on 17 July it is recorded that he acted as President at their anniversary meeting.

Although any in-depth investigation into the relationships between the local landowners and the recreational and social aspects of archery in the eighteenth and nineteenth centuries is beyond the scope of this book, we know that due to the proximity of Kilwinning as a centre for bowyery and the existence of the Ancient Society of Kilwinning Archers, a number of estate-owning families had long established associations with the sport.

In this respect, the Stevenston estates of Hullerhirst, Hayocks, Kerelaw (Grange), Ardeer, and Auchenharvie (Seabank), all had some attachment to the sport.

FOOTBALL

ARDEER THISTLE

In season 1959-1960, the most successful Junior football team in Ayrshire was Ardeer Thistle whose home venue was Ardchoille Park. They reached the semi-final of the Scottish Junior Cup; they won the Ayrshire Cup, the League Cup, the Western League North Section and the championship decider for the 'Daily Record' Cup. They also played in the final of the Irvine and District Cup and in the semi-final of the Vernon Trophy. This outstanding achievement was all the more notable when we realise that the team had to compete in a congested end to the season, playing four ties between Monday and Saturday in one week. Their domination of the Western League North Section can be demonstrated by examining the League Table below.

	P	W	L	D	F	A	Pts
Irvine Meadow XI	21	13	4	4	69	40	30
Kilwinning Rangers	21	13	6	2	73	41	28
ARDEER THISTLE	15	12	0	3	64	30	27
Winton Rovers	19	12	6	1	52	37	25
Ardeer Recreation	20	9	6	5	40	35	23
Troon Juniors	20	7	6	7	34	36	21
Largs Thistle	21	9	9	3	51	57	21
Dalry Thistle	20	8	8	4	54	44	20

The table indicates the positions of the top eight clubs from a complete quota of fifteen teams. This was the situation existing on 5 March 1960 with roughly threequarters of the season completed. The very healthy position of the 'Thistle' is clearly evident. Also noteworthy is the fact that Stevenston had two junior clubs at this time. The Thistle played at Ardchoille, while the Rec was based at the Ardeer Recreation Ground. Between 1928 and 1952 the club was in abeyance (having formed in 1900) and it wasn't until 1954 that their new home at Ardchoille was suitable for purpose. It was sited below and immediately in front of the hotel.

As always in football, the league competition is the 'bread and butter' for all clubs. However, the Scottish Junior Cup remains the Holy Grail, and the Thistle had never reached this pinnacle of achievement in their sixty-year history.

On 5 March 1960, the Thistle welcomed Shettleston to the 'choille in

25. Opening of Ardchoille Park 1953 by Provost Morrison and Willie Mann.

the sixth round of the national competition. The fixture was always going to be a difficult task for the home team as their opponents were beaten finalists in 1959. It was pointed out by many pundits that having reached the final, only to be narrowly beaten by Irvine Meadow, had given Shettleston experience of the big occasion which the Thistle did not possess. Many Thistle men countered this opinion by stating that during this season the Thistle had played 31 games without defeat, having scored 135 goals for 52 against – a remarkable record.

Ardeer had ground advantage and a massive home support which certainly increased their confidence. Their park had been located in front of the hotel since 1952 and the bedrock of their followers came from the Hayocks (Ardeer Recreation tended to attract their support from the centre of the town and Ardeer).

The two protagonists were not strangers to each other in this competition as they met in the fourth round in Stevenston in January 1956. A huge crowd – providing a gate return of £180 – inspired the Thistle to victory by the narrow margin of 3-2. It is interesting to note that three of the 1960 Thistle team – Bishop, Brannan and Murray – played against Shettleston in 1956.

In the week before the game, club officials with the assistance of many willing hands, laid dozens of sleepers to increase the holding capacity of the terracing as they expected from 8,000 to 10,000 spectators. This event generated the largest gathering of people in the history of the Hayocks. The official attendance was 8,868 spectators which accrued gate money of £404. The actual crowd inside the ground exceeded this figure as a number of boys and youth had 'sneaked-in' through expertly prepared and cleverly camouflaged entry points in the external fence. In the scheme, the estimates of the crowd grew daily. During the following week, on reading the match

26. Ardchoille Park during the Scottish Cup Quarter-Final between the Thistle and Shettleston.

report which contained the attendance figure, one weil kent worthy – while partaking of a small refreshment in a local hostelry – was heard to proclaim 'there wis mair than that behin the goals.'

The playing surface was in a shallow bowl which during the winter months made the surface heavy and sticky. On the day of the quarter-final, however, the pitch was in excellent condition, and when combined with the acceptable overhead conditions resulted in a fine spectacle. The spectators occupied every vantage point, even gathering in front of the press box. On entering this cauldron, the Thistle team received a tumultuous reception, as did the Shettleston players from their large travelling support. With both teams at full strength the game kicked-off before a boisterous, animated but well-behaved crowd.

In only the second minute, Brannan scored for the Thistle after a lightning counter-attack. The visitors were soon threatening the Thistle goal in search of an equaliser, and O'Brien came close with a strike which hit the upright. Thomson was kept busy but was defending stoutly. As Shettleston settled, Bishop was called upon to make a good double save from O'Brien and Quinn, with Mulholland also heading inches wide. As half time approached, Bishop dived to save on the goal line from a Davis effort. The game was now developing a pattern with Shettleston retaining much of the ball but Ardeer looking increasingly dangerous with their quick and incisive counter attacks. The half time score was Ardeer Thistle, 1; Shettleston, 0. The second half opened with the visitors pressurising the Thistle defence. However, as the game progressed Ardeer were steadily gaining the ascendency, and they got their reward with a second goal after fourteen minutes of the second half. Duffy set-up Templeton who was clinical in his finishing. As the half wore on, the Thistle got their third goal, again from a very sharp Templeton. Approaching the ninety-minute mark Mulholland notched up a consolation goal for the Glasgow club which was almost immediately neutralised by a fine goal from Reilly. The final result was Ardeer Thistle, 4; Shettleston, 1.

Over the ninety minutes, Ardeer were the better team; the opposition being outplayed in almost every position. This result maintained the Thistle's incredible unbeaten record. The teams were – Ardeer Thistle: Bishop; Sweeney and Thomson; Hood, Andrew and Murray; Templeton, Brannan, Duffy, McLeod and Reilly. Shettleston – Brown; Reid and Murray; Sinclair, Bell and Duncanson; Carlyle, Mulholland, O'Brien, Davis and Quinn. The referee was Mr E. R. Hall from Dunfermline.

Ardeer marching proudly and confidently into the semi-finals of the National Trophy for the first time in their history was the end result of this match. However, the very positive impact on the community in the Hayocks was longer-lasting. Stevenston very rarely made the national headlines in a sporting context, and the mention of the Hayocks was unprecedented. The national coverage of the event generated a genuine source of satisfaction within the community.

A successful Junior football team requires a hard-working, well-organised committee and Ardeer were fortunate in possessing a determined group of local enthusiasts. The manager was Alex Kelso; the 'sponge man' was Danny Higgins; and the committee consisted of Willie Peddie, Alan McAlpine, Alan Tomley, Tom Dickie, and S. Burns, while the women's committee included Margaret Marshall, Annie Robertson, Kate Paterson, Jeanette Wright, and Mrs Scott.

In the other quarter-final match, Greenock Juniors defeated Johnstone Burgh 3 – 1, clearing the way for a semi-final clash with Ardeer at Firhill Park on 30 April.

Conditions in Glasgow were ideal for the most important game in the history of the Thistle, and the teams were at full strength – Murray the Thistle left-half having passed a late fitness test. Ardeer opened the scoring in the twelfth minute when Hogg, in attempting to clear a cross, sliced the ball into his own net. This scoreline was against the run of play as the Thistle defence had been under pressure and looked decidedly shaky. The goal however jagged the Thistle into action and six minutes later they doubled their lead when Reilly received a pass from McLeod and strode past his brother, at right-back for Greenock, and smashed the ball into the net. The third Ardeer goal came curtesy of McLeod in the twenty-fifth minute. Unfortunately, in the run up to the goal Murray received a serious injury which required him to leave the pitch for the remainder of the first half (there were no substitutes permitted in Scottish football in 1960). Greenock took full advantage of their superiority in numbers to cut the deficit to two goals when McKellar released an unstoppable twenty-yard thunderbolt five minutes before half-time. Half-time score, Ardeer Thistle, 3 Greenock Juniors, 1.

Murray resumed in the second-half in the outside-left position but it was immediately apparent that he was going to be virtually a passenger. Further tragedy struck Ardeer when Brannan had to leave the pitch after receiving the full impact of a shot in the face. Not surprisingly, with Brannan still in the pavilion, Greenock reduced the leeway with a twenty-five yard 'bobby-dazzler' from Stewart. The equaliser arrived with fifteen minutes remaining. Final-result, Ardeer Thistle, 3 Greenock Juniors, 3.

While Ardeer were extremely unfortunate in respect of injuries which undoubtedly changed the complexion of the second half, Greenock played the more attractive football and deserved a draw. The teams were; Ardeer –

Bishop

Sweeney Thomson

Hood Andrew Murray

Templeton Brannan Duffy McLeod Reilly

The Greenock line-up was; McGinlay; Reilly and Hogg; Stewart, Buchanan and Brabender, Gibson, McCartney, McKellar, Samuel and Winter.

Referee – J. R. P. Gordon from Newport.

This team became so famous that the young supporters could rhyme off the players in a far more proficient fashion than their twelve times table.

The replay was won 2 – 0 by Greenock, but in controversial circumstances. Greenock's first goal was deemed to have crossed the goal line by referee Gordon, to the consternation of the Thistle players and supporters. The second turning point involved a stone-wall penalty claim by Ardeer which was disregarded by Mr Gordon.

There was little doubt that Greenock were the better team over the ninety minutes, but the Thistle were very unfortunate in the two crucial decisions that went against them. This result ended Ardeer's pursuit of the Holy Grail for another season, but in this season, they continued to dominate Ayrshire football collecting almost every trophy available to them. They brought distinction to Stevenston and especially the Hayocks, and the happenings in this season continue to be debated and discussed in reverential tones by some of our more senior citizens.

To reinforce the belief that the Thistle were an exceptional side, it should be stated that at the end of the season the team was dismantled. They lost the services of at least four players to senior clubs. Matt Thomson was capped for Junior Scotland and signed for Motherwell (he was later awarded the M.B.E. for services to industry); Sandy Hood left for Hamilton Accies; McLeod for Dundee United, and Reilly – 'a versatile teenage player' - signed for Celtic. Tommy Duffy remains in the Guinness Book of Records for his extraordinary feat of scoring 97 goals in 62 matches in the 1959-60 season. As a postscript, Greenock Juniors were beaten 3 – 1 by St Andrews United in the final at Hampden Park before a crowd of 34,603.

Ardeer continued to be an integral part of the Hayocks community until they left the 'choille in 1973 to begin a new chapter in their history at the Ardeer Recreation ground.

ARDEER ROVERS

Remaining in the football theme, another memorable achievement occurred in 2005 when Ardeer Rovers won the British Energy Ayrshire Challenge Amateur Cup. The significance of the victory lay in the fact that the team was 'hame-knitted,' and played their home fixtures at Ardchoille Park. The facilities at the 'choille' were spartan. Initially the Rovers changed in the old pigeon hut, a part of which had been converted by the addition of a few showers. The team then moved to an adjoining concrete unit, which succumbed to a malicious fire. Finally, they acquired a port-a-cabin at the rear of the Community Centre.

The date was Saturday 16 April 2005. The venue Rugby Park, Kilmarnock. The occasion the Ayrshire Amateur Cup Final between Ardeer Rovers and Newmilns Vesuvius. The team had reached the final by eliminating Ayr (7-0), Beith (5-2), Logan Ams (6-1), Hurlford (2-1 A.E.T.), and Crosshouse Waverley (3-2).

The Rovers switched their usual black and red strips to a light blue outfit sponsored by 'Scottish Leader,' for the final. On the big day, the team had a light training session in the morning at the Auchenhavie Astro-Turf, followed by a light lunch at Potters. The team took an enthusiastic and boisterous support to Rugby Park, and after their monumental achievement returned to Potters with the trophy for a 'small refreshment.'

Ardeer made history by reaching the British Energy Ayrshire Cup Final for the first time after coming back from behind to edge out their local rivals, Crosshouse, in a cliffhanger of a last-four tie at Blair Park, Hurlford. The Rovers were awarded a penalty by referee H. Howie in 10 minutes after Lee Currie was upended by Gary Clelland. Mark Kelly expertly netted the spot-kick. Crosshouse levelled 10 minutes later through Ryan McCall. The Waverley were the better team in the first half, but with John O'Hare in excellent form, the score remained 1-1 at the interval. In 65 minutes, Crosshouse took the lead through Ricky Carswell, but Ardeer drew level when Kelly played in David Monaghan to knock the ball over the line from barely a yard. With 15 minutes remaining Rovers secured victory when 'Bully' Webster outstripped the Waverley defence to shoot home from 15 yards. In the 80th minute Rovers were reduced to ten men when Craig Higgins was red-carded for a last man challenge, but held firm to record a famous and unexpected victory.

The result in the final was a surprise with Newmilns starting as firm favourites, having beaten the Rovers 5-0 in a league match in late February. They were later to be crowned comfortable winners of the Lindsay Fencing Premier Division (26 points above Ardeer).

The Final was a closely contested encounter with the battling qualities and phenomenal team spirit of Ardeer proving vital. They were never overawed and at times out-fought and out-thought their opponents, in the end richly deserving their triumph.

The first half was reasonably even with play swinging from end to end. In 25 minutes, Rovers were awarded a free-kick 25 yards from goal following a foul on Mark Kelly. Graham floated in the set-piece to Fletcher to smash the ball past the despairing Steven Quinn from 12 yards. Throughout the first 45 minutes O'Hare exhibited a save pair of hands, but the game was all square in 60 minutes when John Mason outjumped the Rovers defence to head home from 12 yards. Late in the tie, Billy Gilmour's rasping drive from 10 yards rocketed off the bar. Both teams were visibly tiring, and the game went into extra-time where there were few clear-cut chances.

The lottery of penalties was won by Ardeer (3-1). Alex Webster missed the first penalty, but the other three were successfully converted by D. Monaghan, R. McKinney, and S. Fletcher. However, goalkeeper John O'Hare was the man-of-the-match with three saves from the penalty spot. The match was evenly balanced and fiercely competitive resulting in the referee, Mr Greg Aitken, bookings three Ardeer players – J. Lyndsey, K. Fitzpatrick, and B. Gilmour. The starting eleven on cup final day were:

O'Hare
Higgins Lindsay
Adams
Fitzpatrick
Graham Gilmour Webster Monaghan
Kelly Fletcher

27. Celebrations After the Cup Success. From left to right – Mark Kelly, Billy Gilmour, Kenny Fitzpatrick, John O'Hare, Dougie Graham, John McMillan (coach), and Ross McKinney.

The substitutes were Harvey, Currie, Frew, McKinney, and Byrne. Harvey was brought on in the first half to replace an injured Fitzpatrick, while Currie and McKinney made second half appearances.

All of these players stayed in the Three Towns, with the exception of Lee Currie, from Kilwinning, with ten living in Stevenston. This was the first time in their history that Ardeer Rovers had landed the showpiece domestic trophy. Manager John McMillan was also a Hayocks man.

Although Alex (Bully) Webster was captain and lifted the Cup, Billy Gilmour played for the Ayrshire Amateur Select in the National Inter-District Trophy.

Having been promoted from Division 1 the previous season, Ardeer were adapting to life in the Premier League. By the New Year they had accumulated 12 points from 8 games giving them a position of sixth in a league of twelve teams. They maintained this relative position and finished mid-table in the league. Their top scorers were D. Graham, C. Daniel, and M. Kelly, each finding the net on nine occasions.

The Rovers' fantastic achievement in Season 2004-05 is all the more outstanding when we consider all the players were local (a number residing in the Hayocks). To capture the Ayrshire Cup immediately after gaining promotion was also very unusual. To find possible reasons for their success we have to examine the development of the club over the years prior to 2004-05.

In season 2002-2003, although playing in Division 1, Ardeer had a successful season. The team reached the fifth round of the Scottish Cup before being knocked out by Balearie in a very close encounter. They were narrowly beaten 2-1 A.E.T. by Maybole in the final of the Donsport Trophy. Having finished second in the league, they were beaten 4-2 by the Dirrans in the League play-off final. Seven of the pool of players in the Donsport Final were also on the team sheet in the Ayrshire Cup winning side two years later. The team also reached the semi-final of the James Scott Trophy but were beaten 4-1 by Largs. During this season the top scorers were Mark Kelly and S. Fletcher each with 24 goals.

Ardeer's very impressive showing in the second half of season 2002-2003 was followed up by an incredible start to season 2003-2004. The team won eleven consecutive league matches before losing 1-2 to Winlinton Wolves on 7 February. Their cup results were less impressive, being eliminated from the Ayrshire Cup by Fenwick; the James Scott Memorial Trophy by Knockentiber; the Donsport Trophy by Minishant; the West of Scotland Cup by Orchard Park Mount; and the Scottish Cup by Glenmavis – all before mid-November. The Rovers were declared Division 1 league winners on Saturday 15 May 2004, one point in front of Craigie. The First Division Championship decider a week later, resulted in a resounding 3-0 victory for Ardeer over Cumnock.

These two positive and encouraging seasons leading up to 2004-2005 laid the foundations for the cup achievement. The team selection was gaining consistency, and playing in the Premier League provided the necessary experience required to compete with the 'big boys.'

The season following their cup success started with the Rovers suffering a 1-5 thrashing to Mossblown at Ardchoille Park. This result was an omen of things to come. Coach John McMillan lost the nucleus of his team to competitors like Newmilns, Clark Drive, Crosshouse Waverley, Knockentiber, and Hurlford Thistle. They won only a few league and cup games and were increasingly on the end of embarrassing defeats. The number of players attending training diminished; turn-over of players increased; and the number available to the manager for selection diminished. One positive feature was the continuing goal-scoring exploits of both D. Monaghan and C. Daniel.

This highly successful period in the history of the club ended in season 2005-2006 when the Rovers were relegated from the Premier League, accruing only six points from twenty-two games. The significance of the Ayrshire Cup victory during the previous season was brought into focus by the fact that Newmilns Vesuvius reached the semi-final of the Scottish Amateur Cup (beaten by Falkirk Ams) in season 2005-2006 and also won a very close Premier League title.

It must be remembered that an achievement of this magnitude can

28. Ardeer Rovers at Rugby Park with the British Energy Ayrshire Cup.

only be realised due to the vital and unselfish contribution of a number of 'back room boys'. In the cup-winning year Ian Foote was the secretary; Colin Frew was treasurer; Jamie McCrae was president; John McMillan was coach and sponge-man; and finally, two indispensable committee members were Alan Bridges and Stuart Irvine. Any income which was needed for the purchase of equipment and travel expenses was acquired through various fund-raising activities involving a number of enthusiastic and committed individuals. These included Craig Mochan of Potters, plus the players themselves.

9
Other Remaining Land-uses

HAWKHILL CEMETERY

One of the earliest non-agricultural land-uses within the Hayocks study area was Hawkhill Cemetery (only predated by the Greenhead Water Filter Works).

In December 1926, a petition was presented by Stevenston Parish Council to the Sheriff of Ayrshire at Kilmarnock under the powers conferred by the Burial Grounds (Scotland) Act 1855. The petition requested the court to appoint a time from and after which the plot or area of ground measuring two hectares lying on the north-west of the public road leading from Stevenston to Kilwinning, and being part of the lands of Hawkhill farm could become an optional extra to the existing burial ground in New Street. The expansion of this graveyard was restricted by its surroundings and was approaching its intended capacity. It should be noted that cremation in the 1930s was very rare. The parish council also asked the court to sanction the exclusive right of burial within this area to the council. Thirdly, they wished the right to construct a chapel, vault or any other building related to burials, along with gravestone monuments.

The prices for lairs or grave spaces ranged from £1 15s to £3 10s depending on the location within the cemetery. An additional charge of 5 shillings for all lairs where the intending purchaser was not a ratepayer and not resident in the parish.

The schedule of interment fees depended again on the location of the grave within the cemetery, and the age of the deceased. Bizarrely, an extra charge was levied for coffins made from elm, ash, and oak, in addition to Sunday interments.

Although the above preparations were made in December 1926, the cemetery itself did not start fulfilling its function until 1930 (it was recorded in the 1928 Valuation Roll). This makes it a relatively modern burial ground which today contains over 2,000 grey, red, and black granite headstones along with a number of terrazzo and marble memorials. Most of the larger, more imposing stones are sited in the older sections of the cemetery.

In 1931, a scheme for widening the main road from Stevenston to Kilwinning was started, and the boundary of the new road was made uniform with the frontage of the cemetery. This front wall was constructed of old red sandstone which was railed at a later date. There are four imposing old red sandstone pillars at the entrance. Other additions were the harled lodge on the right side of the entrance which was built prior to 1937, along with a little waiting room of brick with wooden windows and a hipped tiled roof. This more modern construction dates from sometime after 1962.

A number of gravestones commemorate those men who fought and died in continental Europe during the First World War. In all probability many of those retrospective inscriptions commemorating the sacrifice made by a son would be added on the death of a parent.

Some of the First World War fatalities include Stephen Buchanan Hill who was reported missing in France on 28 August 1917; Gunner David Niven Gilmour R.F.A. who fell in action in France on 29 August 1918, aged 22. One stone is dedicated to two young brothers, Robert and Duncan Murray, who 'fell in the Great War 1914 – 18.' In addition to France, other theatres of war included the Dardanelles. Most of the epitaphs simply state 'fell in action.'

The Second World War also took a heavy toll on members of the armed forces. There are over thirty gravestones dedicated to the memory of soldiers, sailors and airmen from Stevenston who were killed in action between 1939 and 1945. Some of the locations recorded on these memorials include Germany, Italy, Belgium, Burma, and the Middle East. One soldier, Thomas (Gary) Johnston was the recipient of the Military Cross and the Belgian Croix de Guerre. Another stone records:

> F/SGT. PILOT
> Hugh Howie Craig R.A.F.V.R.
> Killed in Action
> 27th January. 1944 Aged 25
> Interred at Heerstrasse, Germany.

The original necessity and impetus for the construction of the Hayocks was to provide homes for Nobel Explosives Company workers being relocated to Stevenston from other Nobel facilities in the Central Belt. It is a reflection of the dangerous nature of the work at Ardeer that Hawkhill Cemetery has a significant number of graves directly attributable to fatal accidents at the 'Dinamite.' One tragedy which occurred on 27 January 1938 resulted in the deaths of six workers. The graves of four of the deceased men are situated in a cluster in Section A of the cemetery. These four victims were Alexander Stewart Cameron (aged 59), Frederick Smith (aged 41), James McLelland (aged 28), and Joseph Hamilton (aged 59).

In the following year, on 28 September 1939, a further explosion resulted in the deaths of a number of workers. Due to Britain declaring war on Germany on 3 September 1939, this explosion occurred during wartime and due to the sensitive nature of the manufacture of explosives at Ardeer, the details of this incident, including the death toll, were shrouded in secrecy. Estimates in the local press varied from ten to twenty-one fatalities.

Within the cluster of graves mentioned above are also the resting places of five victims of the 1939 disaster. These include John Houston (aged 40), Archibald Wright (aged 34), Dugald Baird (aged 21), Joseph Gibson (aged 28), and John Maxwell (aged 60). The last-named employee lived in Hayocks Road. This sombre concentration of victims related to deadly accidents at Ardeer is completed by the interment of Alexander Smith (aged 43) who was killed on 9 December 1943.

Most of the larger stones are in the earlier sections of the cemetery, but memorable gravestones are not always the largest. The design, inscription and epitaph makes every memorial special. There are several grey granite Celtic crosses; a small, dark granite headstone with an etching of a ship on the face; another granite memorial with a shield of a boar's head with the inscription 'nunquam obliviscar.' Another memorable headstone is a small, simple stone with the words 'treasured memories of Big John, from his friends.'

A number of local personalities and dignitaries are also buried at Hawkhill. These include Provosts Elizabeth Murdoch (nee Ward) J.P., Joseph Clark J.P., and James Forde J.P. Awarded the C.B.E. was Adam Wilson, and M.B.E. James Forde.

Finally, two diverse but inspiring inscriptions are worthy of mention. One stone states that Arthur Clarke and his wife Nellie were missionaries in China and Bermuda. The other reveals that Leading Aircraftman James Barlow Murray, 18, drowned on 9 June 1960 at Westerland, Sylt, Germany, whilst trying to save the lives of two German girls.

One surprising feature of the cemetery is the stark lack of scripture on the gravestones. One of the very few biblical inscriptions is from Isaiah 53, Verse 5:

> He was wounded for our transgressions
> He was bruised for our iniquities
> The chastisement of our peace was upon Him
> And with His stripes we are healed.

The preferred epitaphs seem to be 'Thy will be done', 'Sadly missed' and the ubiquitous 'R.I.P..' Some of the more distinguished verses include 'Tis only those who lived and lost/can understand the bitter cost', 'Home is the sailor home from the sea/And the hunter home from the hill', 'Fairest among thousands', 'Only that life is rich/which is kind', 'Dearly loved/happily remembered', 'Until the day breaks.'

Today the cemetery has doubled in size to four hectares compared with its area in 1926, and although burials continue at Hawkhill, the cemetery is no longer open for the purchase of new lairs.

WATER SUPPLY
GREENHEAD MOUNT FILTER STATION

The history and development of the Greenhead Mount filter station can be traced back to 1875. In this year the Irvine and District Water Board was initiated by the town council of the Royal Burgh of Irvine. The new board immediately instructed Messrs Leslie & Reid, Consulting Engineers, Edinburgh, to submit a scheme for the provision of a gravity water supply for the burgh and district. An order was obtained under the Public Health (Scotland) Act 1876 for the construction of a water supply for the area. The confirmation act was passed on 24 July 1876, and the construction of the original water works commenced in 1877. The scheme comprised an impounding reservoir on the Munnoch Burn, four kilometres from Dalry; a filter station at Greenhead Mount, with two slow sand filters capable of filtering 1 MI/d, a service reservoir for storing the filtered water and the construction of mains for conveying the raw water from the Munnoch to Greenhead and the filtered water from Greenhead to Irvine. These works were inaugurated on 8 August 1878.

The first thirty years of the scheme included the construction of eleven slow sand filters at Greenhead. Table 15 provides some relevant detail:

Table 15. Early Greenhead Filter Detail[1]

Filter No.s	Construction Date	Filter Area (Sq.Ft)	Capacity (G.p.D.)
1 and 2	1877	4,800	240,000
3 and 4	1882	4,800	240,000
5 and 6	1889	6,000	300,000
7	1893	3,000	150,000
8 and 9	1896	6,000	300,000
10 and 11	1907	9,000	450,000
		Total - 33,000	Total - 1,680,000

It should be noted that the proposal to secure a supply of gravitation water

1 Guild, W.G. Inspection of Works, Historical Notes on Water Supply and Extent of Undertaking. 1955.

for Irvine had been seriously discussed as far back as 1873 when trade was brisk and the population rapidly increasing.

The official opening of the scheme occurred on 8 August 1878. After the members of the local authorities of Irvine and Halfway returned from their visit to the reservoir and filters, a procession formed at the Townhouse and proceeded along High Street to Williamfield where the water was turned on by Provost Paterson's wife. On returning to the Townhouse, Mrs Paterson was presented with a silver key on which was inscribed the following message: 'Presented by James McLauchlan, contractor, Irvine, to Mrs Paterson, as a memento of the ceremony performed by her at the opening of the Irvine Water Works, 8th August 1878.'

The reservoir at the Munnoch had a capacity of 80 million gallons of water; at its deepest part being 11 metres deep; and covered an area of 14 hectares. The filters at Greenhead were expected to run 480,000 gallons per day; possessing a clear water tank capacity of 210,000 gallons. The total expenditure required to complete the scheme was approximately £40,000.

The Irvine Burgh Act of 1881 incorporated the Halfway District into the Burgh of Irvine and transferred the Water Undertaking to the Corporation of Irvine. It also authorised the construction of additional works, and powers were granted to enlarge the existing reservoir at the Munnoch. The Special Water District of Kilwinning received a water supply in 1878.

The next major development occurred in 1881 when Nobel's Ardeer Explosives Factory received a much-needed supply of gravitational water.

At Nobel's Ardeer site, the steady production of dynamite from around 1873, was punctuated by minor interruptions some of which arose due to the difficulty in connection with the water supply for the factory. In these early years water came from two sources. The Prince of Wales coal pit near Merry & Cunninghame's blast furnaces, contained a natural spring of good quality water, which was the only water available for drinking and cooking purposes. A bogie was sent each day along the ironworks company's line with four empty barrels to be filled and returned to the factory. For manufacturing purposes water pumped from the Lucknow pit just outside the factory periphery was used, and it was delivered into a large settling tank inside the factory. After settling, this water was used in the nitro-glycerine plant in the nitrating and separating, and also for the washing of the nitro-glycerine.

In the course of a few years much more satisfactory arrangements were made in connection with the water supply. A meeting of the local authority of Irvine, and Halfway Committee, was held in the council chambers on 30 August 1881, for the purpose of signing an agreement with Nobels for a supply of water from the Irvine Water Works. Provost Brown signed the contract on behalf of Irvine Council. The terms of the agreement included the sale of water to Nobel's Ardeer at the rate of 6½d per 1,000 gallons, and if 8,000,000 gallons per annum, or more, was taken, the rate would be 5½d per 1,000 gallons. Other aspects of the contract included the fact that the domestic and manufacturing supply of the Water District of Irvine and Fullarton would take precedence over that granted to the factory, and Nobels would have to pay all the costs of making connections, laying pipes, and other infrastructure requirements. The supply of water was obtained from the Irvine Waterworks by means of a four-inch supply pipe.

At the same meeting, Nobels made enquiries about securing a water supply for Ardeer House and other houses or farms in the district at the same rate as charged to the factory. The commissioners quashed this suggestion stating that the water rates for any private house or farm would be the same as those which applied in the neighbourhood of Irvine.

Nobel's Explosives Company Ltd desperately needed a reliable supply of clean, piped water at Ardeer to permit the continuing expansion of the site. A huge number of activities and processes depended on the availability of water to maintain safety. One example arose in the 'houses' where the nitro-glycerine and nitro-cellulose were being mixed. In such an environment the sandy floor had to be kept continually wet to obviate any danger from nitro-cellulose dust.

Also in 1881, discussions had been instigated between Irvine Water Authority and Stevenston Local Authority as to the possibility of the former supplying water to the latter. Such an arrangement would reduce the rates burden to Irvine residents. While these negotiations were being conducted both Irvine and Stevenston agreed to maintain as many of the public wells in the streets as possible. This decision was made as it had been discovered that the residents of Irvine and Kilwinning had, largely through wastage, increased their usage of water by 33%. The concern was that under these circumstances the supply of water could be interrupted.

In tandem with these discussions, Stevenston Local Authority had instructed Mr Gale C.E., Glasgow, to investigate other possible sources of water for the town. He concluded that four potential sources were available. These were: 1. Ashgrove Loch; 2. Diddup and Glen Burns; 3. Ardrossan Water-Works; and 4. Irvine. After examining a number of factors, including quality of water; the head of water from each of the sites to Stevenston; the reservoir capacities; the possibilities for future expansion; the cost of the necessary infrastructure; and the estimated cost of each project, Mr Gale recommended the adoption of the Glen Burn scheme. Its total cost being in the region of £14,000.

At a special meeting of Saltcoats Local Authority held on 4 August 1881 in Saltcoats Town Hall, the chairman read a copy of the resolution which had been sent from Stevenston Local Authority agreeing to adopt the Glen scheme jointly with Saltcoats. In the chairman's protracted statement he excluded an offer from the Irvine Water Authority, stating 'the authorities in Irvine have resiled from their former offer of partnership, and have included a clause in their bill empowering them to shut off all supplies when they see fit to from all other parties, this entirely precludes us from going there.' He also added that he considered the Glen scheme to be superior to all the others. At this stage in late 1881, the issue of a gravitational water supply in Stevenston and Saltcoats was heading towards the acceptance of the Glen scheme.

Divisive, and at times, rancorous discussions continued. This situation was caused by the fact that the Ardrossan Water Company already supplied the town with its water, and because the parish of Ardrossan included the western part of Saltcoats, this section of Saltcoats was also provided with water from this company. The eastern part of the town was part of Stevenston parish and had no access to piped water. The arguments centred around the possible solutions to keeping Saltcoats together without splitting Stevenston parish.

This intractable and increasingly polarised debate continued to rage for the next three years. During this period, many prominent and well-respected local figures raised their concern over the cost of implementing the Glen Scheme, and emphasised that Stevenston, like Kilwinning, could obtain a cheaper supply from Irvine. This acrimonious debate raged throughout 1884 and as late as 21 August, Mr William Gemmell chaired a meeting of Stevenston ratepayers. The gathering was called with the sole intention of terminating any possible arrangement between Stevenston Local Authority and Irvine Town Council in relation to Stevenston's water supply until a final financial statement became available.

The formation of a Water Committee for Stevenston was established on 8 December 1884 to agree on a final outcome. At long last a consensus was reached which resulted in Stevenston acquiring a piped water supply from the Corporation of Irvine. On 17 March 1885, Mr Adam Wilson of the Broom farm, on behalf of Stevenston Local Authority, signed the final agreement for a supply of water from Irvine. On the Saturday prior to this date this agreement was signed by Provost Wright on behalf of Irvine Town Council. The business of laying the pipes to link Stevenston to the network was started immediately. Therefore, four long years after Nobel's Ardeer reached an accord and signed a contract to accept a water supply from Irvine, Stevenston finally secured this vital commodity with all its associated benefits to public health.

After the agreement between the Corporation of Irvine and Stevenston Local Authority had been finalised, Saltcoats entered into a similar agreement to accept a supply of water on the same terms as Stevenston.

One of the few positive aspects to emerge from this prolonged fiasco was the removal of any opposition there might have been to the introduction of gravitational water as a supply.

By 1891, it was becoming increasingly apparent that the existing works at the Munnoch would soon be unable to meet the growing demand of the area and steps were taken to secure the Caaf watershed (See Map 6). In 1902, an order was obtained by Irvine Corporation authorising the construction of two impounding reservoirs on the Caaf Water but only one was constructed. It was inaugurated on 31 October 1906. By 1903, the demand for water - both industrial and domestic – continued to steadily increase. Additional mains for the conveyance of filtered and unfiltered water were laid, and the filter station at Greenhead greatly enlarged. This involved the original slow sand filters being augmented. During the First World War, demand for water increased dramatically, and between 1916 and 1918, the board installed a Paterson Rapid Gravity Filtration Plant. Later, a Bell Pressure Filtration Plant was also added. Also, a new pipe was laid between the Munnoch Reservoir and Greenhead Filters and came on stream in June 1915. The work was carried out by Messrs Shanks & McEwan at a cost of £1,200. The Water Quality Regulations - which the Greenhead plant was incapable of meeting - were introduced in 1990, and consequently Strathclyde Regional Council awarded a contract in 1995 for a new treatment works at Ashgrove, near the Diddup farm, designed to treat 30 MI/d. The plant was completed in 1997, but was never fully operational, subsequently being mothballed c. 2009. Today some of the buildings within the works are being utilised by other business units for equipment storage and office use.

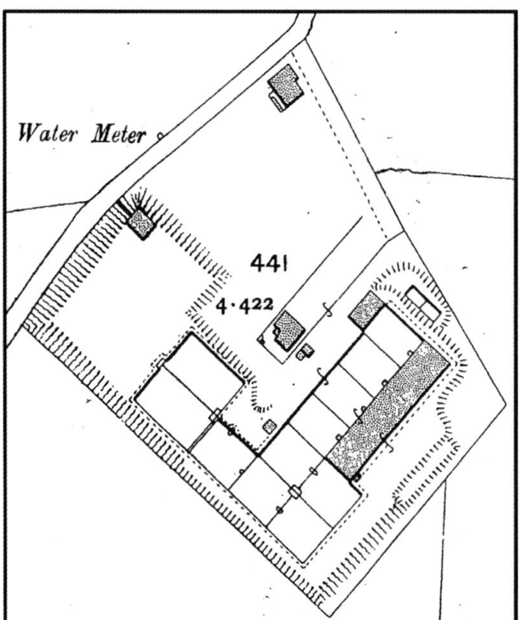

Plan 1. Greenhead Filters c. 1910.

Throughout the period from 1878 to 1995, Greenhead Filtration Plant was an integral component in supplying piped water to the immediate area (See Map 6). During this time, it was regularly upgraded and modernised, fulfilling an expanding remit (See Plans 1 & 2). One example was the laying of a pipeline from the Garnock Pumping Station to the filters between November 1963 and July 1964. This 15-inch diameter spun iron pipe was 3.2 kilometres in length. Another example concerned supplying the I.C.I. Nylon Plant at Ardeer. To this end, a meeting was convened at Nobel House on 3 August 1966. Mr Gilchrist from the Irvine and District Water Board indicated that the Nylon Plant requirements would increase the demand for water from Greenhead beyond the dependable yield of the reservoirs. However, he stated that Greenhead had filtering capacity

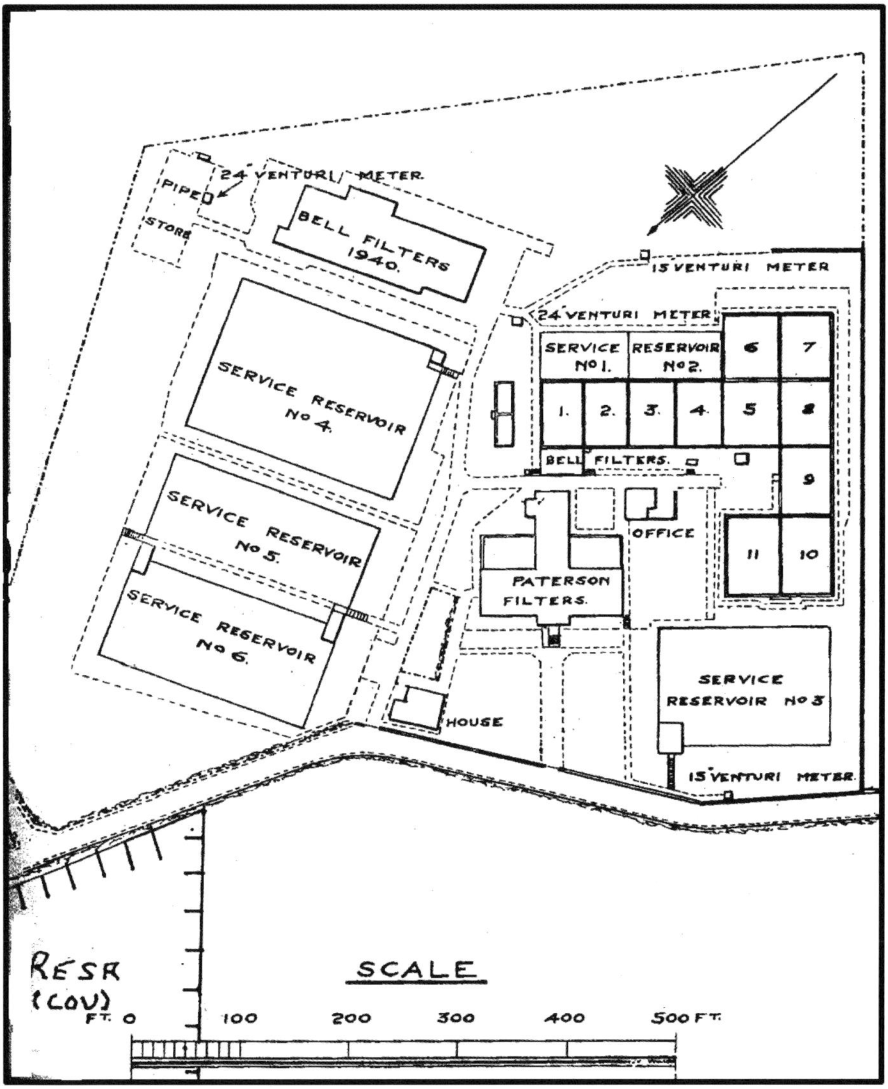

Plan 2. Greenhead Filters c. 1952.
NOTE – The 'Resr (cov)' – covered reservoir - on Plan 2 above was added sometime between 1968 and 2002.

in hand (up to 12,000,000 gallons per day), and it would be the raw water supply that might become critical. Mr Dawson (Babtie, Shaw and Morton) confirmed that this problem had already been considered and an arrangement for Ayr County Council to boost the Water Board's system through the 15-inch diameter Shewalton branch-main would be the most suitable method of maintaining supplies if a shortage arose at Greenhead.

The house which was built at Greenhead Mount was occupied over the years by a small number of men who maintained the filters. These included John McCulloch in 1904; Alexander Boyle between 1915 and 1929; Gilbert Christie up to 1960, and James Paterson in 1969.

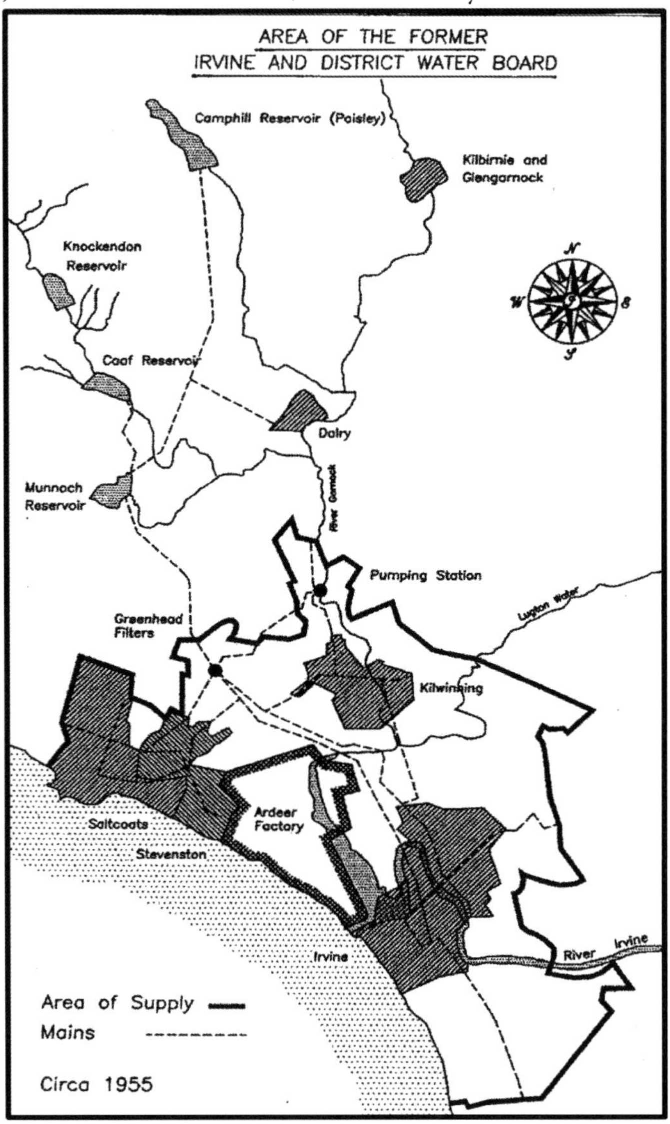

Map 6. Area of the Former Irvine and District Water Board, 1955.

10
Hayocks Community Hall

Hayocks Community Hall was opened in May 1984, and by the end of the month was being utilised by various local clubs. Community events were also being accommodated, for example, on 23 May it staged a Folk Concert starring Gaberlunzie and Danny Kyle as part of the Three Towns Festival.

Many of these 'clubs' were housed in the Ardchoille Pavilion before relocating to the newly provided premises. The community use of the hall expanded to include other sporting activities such as karate and football. A community café and 'drop-in' facility soon followed.

The project demanding a Community Centre in the scheme started as early as February 1974 when the first meeting of local women took place in Cambuskeith Road, resulting in the formation of a steering group. Approximately thirty women gathered in the home of Ann Jones to establish a strategy leading to the creation of this badly needed community hub. These local activists and determined individuals quickly secured the involvement of local councillor Theresa Beattie and Mike Kirby, the local Community Worker. During the late 1970s, the Hayocks Playgroup was meeting in Ardeer Halls and one of the initial tasks for the volunteers was to relocate this service to a more convenient site. The most sensible solution was to utilise the Ardchoille Pavilion. However, the building needed renovation, this being eventually carried out by Cunninghame District Council. The furniture and ancillary objects required for the pavilion were supplied by the committee of street women through their extensive fund-raising activities. Eventually, the pavilion provided space for various local groups including playgroups, young mothers, pensioners, Brownies, and several sports clubs. Unfortunately, the pavilion was too small to safely accommodate certain groups, for example, the Ardchoille Girls' Club had between 90 and 100 members and was forced to relocate to Hayocks Primary School before utilising the newly operational hall. Representatives from these groups, prior to the building of the hall, formed a Hayocks Hall Advisory Group which came under the auspices of Stevenston North Community Association. Stevenston Community Council under the guidance of Dorothy (Dot) Moore also became actively involved in the project.

Ann Clark from the Leisure & Recreation Department of C.D.C. was an important intermediary between the council and the Hayocks Hall Advisory Group, but early in the negotiations it became apparent that the available funding would be insufficient to provide this much-needed amenity. Cunninghame District Council agreed to finance the project for a smaller, less ambitious Community Hall, and included identical premises in the Woodwynd in Kilwinning in their overall plans.

The construction of the hall started in 1982 and lasted for two years, finally opening for business in mid-1984. The official opening occurred later in the year and was attended by many of the women who had worked tirelessly to achieve their ambition. Among this band of community activists were Ann Jones (who became the first caretaker), Mary Frew, Elinor Wilton, and many others. They were accompanied by a number of District Councillors, including Mrs Beattie, Community Councillors, including Dot Moore, and Community Workers. The venue has a main hall, 411m2 in size, which can accommodate 120 people for a seated function. There is also a spacious lounge/meeting area, foyer, administrative office space and utility rooms.

For a period of three years, the hall was under the control and maintained by a Management Committee representing the various groups using the facility. Although the committee was advised by Cunninghame District Council on financial matters, the group had autonomy and independence over the day-to-day running of the hall. This arrangement was terminated when C.D.C. restored its right to oversee all the organisational aspects of the enterprise.

Over the years since its creation, the resource has expanded its commitment to the local community. Today its operations include a community larder, café, emergency foodbank distribution, and practical advice on a whole range of financial and welfare issues. Access to computers for the public has also been expanded. Organisation and day-to-day management of the hall is undertaken by a committee of ten volunteers who are joined by a number of other helpers and participants. A further assignment for the committee is the task of organising events, in some cases to assist with fund raising. These have included race nights, football fan-zones, and fetes. Liaison with the council is the responsibility of a Three Towns Locality Partnership Officer.

It should be remembered that although C.D.C. was responsible for building the Hall and maintaining its fabric, its establishment and longevity were solely due to the indomitable spirit and organisational skill of a large group of volunteers and activists who had a good understanding of their community's needs and aspirations. This grass-roots movement consisted almost entirely of women, many of whom were already actively involved in youth programmes in the Hayocks. They were determined to increase their input into the design and delivery of services for their community, as well as providing active, positive responses to local difficulties. As time passed the vision of a Community Centre intensified and came to fruition in 1984. This monumental achievement remains a relevant and invaluable resource which continues to strengthen community bonds within the Scheme.

11
21st Century Developments

THE THREE TOWNS BY-PASS

In the recent past, the most noticeable disruption to the physical fabric of Hullerhirst Estate was the 'Three Towns Bypass.'

Several possible bypass alignments were examined, including the original route proposed in 1989 (see Map 7). In 1996 a more northerly route was adopted by the Scottish Office as its preferred route, and further development of this design resulted in the 2000 proposal. This attempted to minimise the environmental impacts on the bypass on agricultural interests and existing housing, and at the same time avoided inhibiting any possible future development at the edge of the Three Towns.

In the 1990s, the existing A78 Truck Road within the Three Towns carried a large volume of traffic which was particularly troublesome at peak hours, and which resulted in congestion and increased journey times for both local and trunk road users. The level of traffic also gave rise to concerns about road safety and adverse environmental impacts such as noise and air pollution.

The section of the 6.4 km long bypass relevant to this study, stretches from the roundabout just north of Sharphill Cottage, running eastwards towards the Hayocks area, passing beneath the extension of Hayocks road

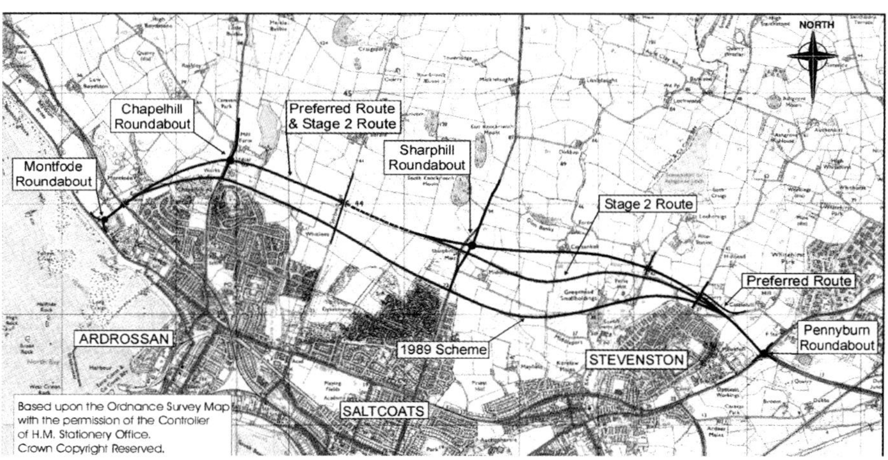

Map 7. Showing the Three Possible Routes for the Three Towns Bypass.

29. Corsankell Farm, mid 1980s.

(known locally as the 'Middle Road.') before connecting to the Pennyburn roundabout.

The main benefits accruing from the construction of the road were very high economic advantages; high accident reduction rate; large reduction in journey times; reduced noise and air pollution along the existing A78; general amenity improvements to the urban areas of Ardrossan, Saltcoats and Stevenston, and the possibility of further development of the Three Towns in the area between the urban fringe and the new road.

The land-use through which the bypass proceeded was largely agricultural and two farms, Lochwood and Sorbie, experienced severance. However, within the boundaries of Kerelaw and Hullerhirst estates the two main casualties were Corsankell farm and the Hullerhirst lime kilns.

The land in the bypass corridor was not designated as being of high landscape value, but the sites of both Corsankell and the lime kilns were carefully surveyed and recorded. In respect of the lime kilns, Headland Archaeology was commissioned by Historic Scotland (on behalf of the then Scottish Executive Development Department, Transport and Planning Division) to undertake a series of works. These excavations took place in 2002 and 2003. Headland Archaeology Ltd also undertook an archaeological excavation at Corsankell during January and February 2003. The farm had been demolished shortly before this date. The loss of these two well-known features was considered by many individuals and community groups to be wasteful and unnecessary. It is necessary to state however, that the two draw kilns were in a ruinous condition, and the examination of the

30. Aerial photograph of the Eastern Section of the A78 By-Pass

remains revealed a surprising wealth of detail concerning their construction and sequential phasing. The largest and earliest kiln was inscribed 'VK 1776' on the keystone above the main arch; it was built into a substantial artificial bank incorporating an inclined trackway to its top.

With reference to Corsankell farm, we find that although the farm was demolished, trenching in the vicinity of the building revealed the remains of structures and surfaces thought to be late mediaeval/Early Modern, and a probable precursor to the modern farm. Immediately to the north of the farm the archaeological work discovered the remains of an enclosed yard and buildings, possibly ancillary to a larger farm complex.

The landholdings which were impacted by the road in the early 2000s were Lochwood farm (arable/livestock rearing/suckler cows) – 131 hectares in size; Corsankell farm (paddock) – 4.1 hectares; Greenhead smallholding (paddock) – 2.5 hectares; Kerelaw Mains farm (all grass, suckler cows/beef cattle rearing) – 22 hectares; Lochcraigs (suckler cows/ livestock rearing/cropping) – 46 hectares; Hillhead farm – 43.5 hectares; Hawkhill – 10.7 hectares; Granada Hospitality – 3.1 hectares; Corsankell farm house – 1.6 hectares; Hullerhirst (dairy/livestock rearing/all grass) – 6.5 hectares.

The bypass opened almost six months ahead of schedule on 21 December 2004 (construction began in August 2003), and unusually, within its £26 million budget. It was officially opened by Cunninghame North MSP Mr

Allan Wilson at a ceremony held between the Sorbie Road Bridge and Sharphill Roundabout. In fact, Mr Wilson was deputising for Transport Minister Nicol Stephen who had been called away suddenly to make an announcement concerning the abolition of tolls on the Skye Bridge.

The large number of dignitaries present included North Ayrshire Provost Drew Duncan, Cunninghame South MP Brian Donohoe, Cunninghame South MSP Irene Oldfather, North Ayrshire Council leader David O'Neill, and councillors Sam Taylor and Margaret Munn.

Also in attendance at the opening ceremony were representatives of the Morrison Mowlem Joint Venture, including Morrison Construction's chief operating officer David Tydeman and Mowlem Construction Ltd infrastructure north managing director Peter Clay.

The luminaries present heard Rev Johnston McKay bless the road before Mr Wilson cut the ceremonial ribbon. As part of his brief speech, the MSP for Cunninghame North stated his hope that the road would improve access to the Three Towns as well as relieve congestion, improve the environment, and open-up the area to economic development.

Major technical input was provided by Scott Wilson, Scotland Ltd (engineering consultants), and the ASH Consulting Group (environmental consultants).

LOCHCRAIGS SOLAR FARM

The most recent addition to the rural landscape is the Lochcraigs Solar Farm dating from 2017. In March of that year this scheme involving the use of solar photovoltaics began generating clean energy.

The Thomson family of Lochcraigs farm have no involvement in the ownership, operation or maintenance of the solar farm. They simply leased 12.27 hectares of land, comprising three fields, to SBC Renewables Ltd for a period of 25 years. This area had previously been planted with barley, but is now rough pasture supporting sixty sheep and lambs in the summer. The site ranges in altitude from 45 to 55 metres above sea level.

The site satisfied the conditions required for such an enterprise:

1) An area of relatively flat land.
2) Proximity to an electricity sub-station.
3) Removed from main roads due to the potential effects of glare on drivers.
4) An open aspect, with few, if any, obstacles.
5) Visually unobtrusive.
6) Initially, lack of potential objectors.

The location also provided some additional advantages to the developer.

31. Lochcraigs Solar Farm, Looking North-West

These included the presence of existing screening around the periphery of the site. These trees and bushes which included birch, would be augmented by the planting of fast maturing tree species like willow. A spin-off of this plant barrier would be the provision of valuable and diverse habitats for local wildlife.

The planning application was submitted to North Ayrshire Council on 1 May 2015 by an agent, AE Associates from Auchtermuchty, Fife, acting on behalf of SBC Renewables Ltd, Monmouth. Construction commenced in October 2016. The generator became live on 31 March 2017. The scheme has a capacity of marginally less than 5MW of electricity which is sufficient to power 1,100 households per year.

There are 15,600 photovoltaic panels on site, each with dimensions of 1956 x 992 x 40 millimetres. The panels, which are ground mounted, have an adjustment of 2 rows 'portrait', and are tilted at an angle of 24O. Further specifications include an overall height rack of 2.5 metres; a row-to-row distance of 6.12 metres; a gap of 0.9 metres between the bottom of the

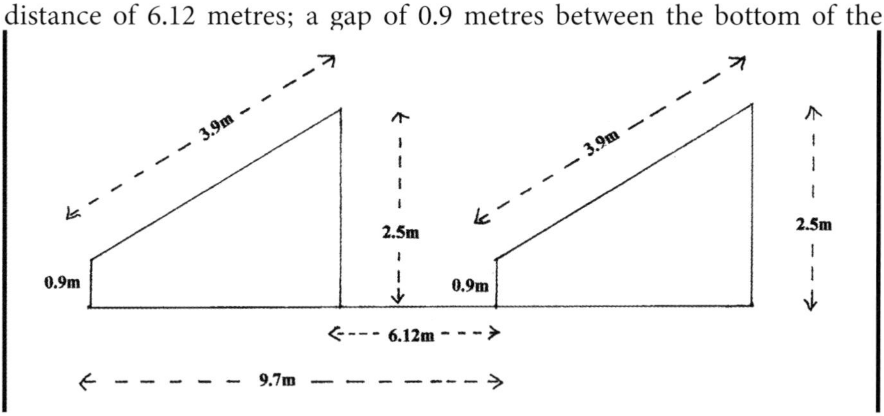

Sketch 1. Size and Spacing of Solar Panels.

panels and the ground surface (permits grazing sheep); and ramming post foundations. Within the labyrinth of panels there are two Inverter stations and one Transfer station, while the entire site is enclosed by a 1,500-metre-long fence (See Sketch 1 over).

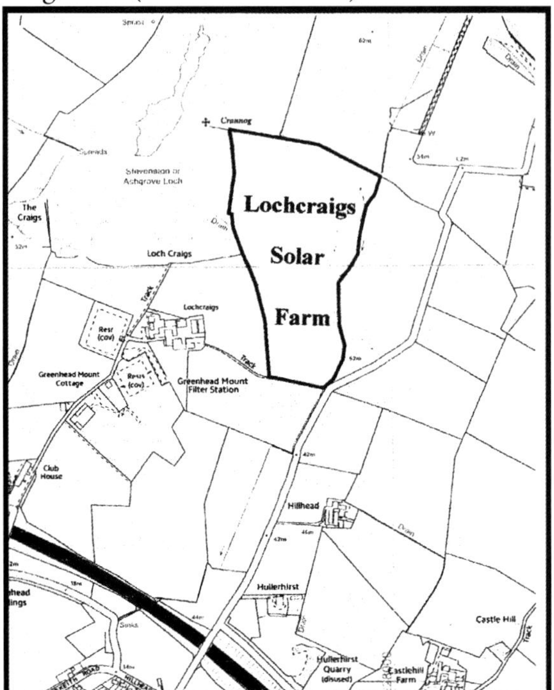

Map 8. Location of Lochcraigs Solar Farm.

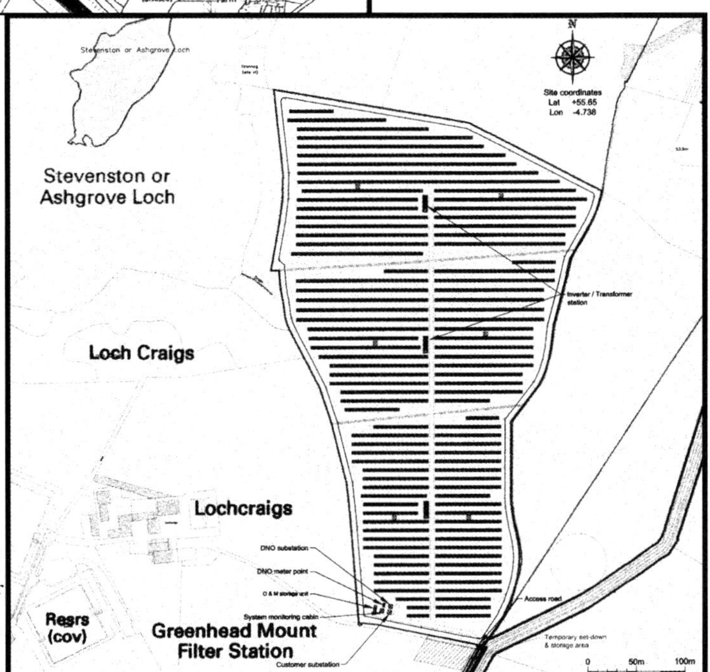

Map 9. Internal Details of Lochcraigs Solar Farm.

12
What Might Have Been

THE GLASGOW, PAISLEY & JOHNSTONE CANAL

In 1791, the twelfth Earl of Eglinton formed a committee with the object of improving Saltcoats harbour and connecting it with Glasgow by canal. The possibility of such a development was warmly received by the Kelso family in Hullerhirst, as it would facilitate a more cost-efficient method of transporting the estate's coal and limestone to the harbour for export to Ireland, and receiving a supply of the more refined imported Irish lime. Unfortunately, Patrick Kelso died in December 1791.

The Kelsos were desperate to maximise their mining business having built a new house at Hullerhirst in 1777.

The proposed route of the canal between Glasgow and Saltcoats was surveyed by John Ainslie and John Rennie and a report submitted in

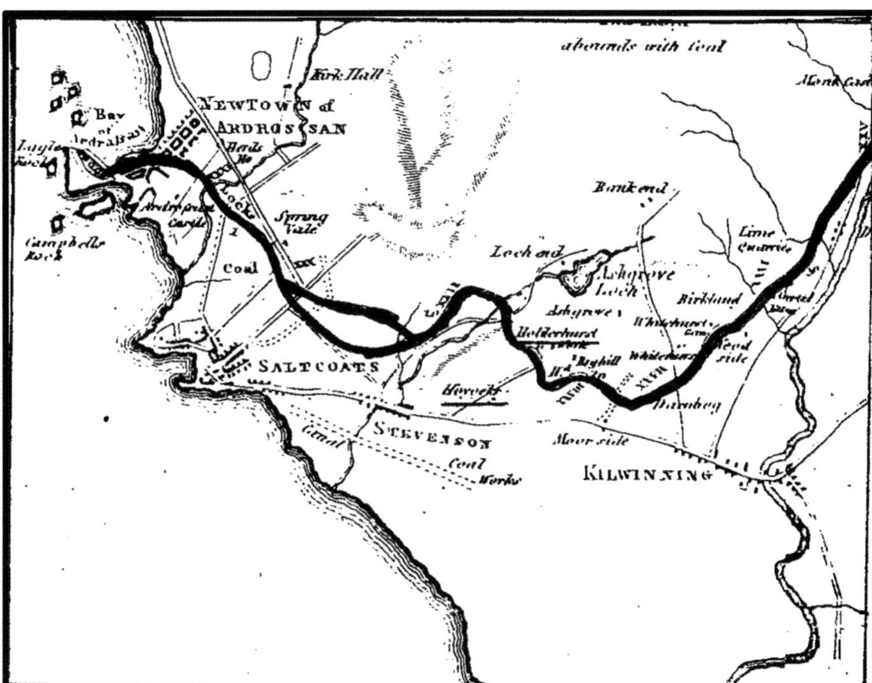

Map 10. Route of the Proposed Glasgow, Paisley and Johnstone Canal (The Dalry to Ardrossan Section).

October 1804. It was at this time that the proposed terminus of the canal was altered from Saltcoats to Ardrossan (Saltcoats being linked to the canal by a branch line). John Rennie's map of the canal route shows the lime works at Hullerhirst as the only existing ones in Stevenston parish and close enough to be able to profit from the canal.

The south-west section of the proposed canal terminated on the Ayrshire coast at Ardrossan. South of Dalry it skirted Monkcastle and Dalgarven before turning westwards at Kilwinning and by-passing Byrehill. It virtually touched the boundary of Hullerhirst estate before turning north-west via Springvale to the New Town of Ardrossan (See Map 10). Feeders were planned to tap Ashgrove Loch and the rivers Garnock and Calf.

The entire length of the canal between Tradeston and Ardrossan was fifty-one kilometres, with the cost estimated at around £135,000. Travel time from Ardrossan to Glasgow along its course amounted to eight hours.

The eighteen-kilometre section of the canal between Tradeston and Johnstone was started in 1807 and completed in 1811, but financial constraints and wranglings resulted in the project ending at Johnstone. Tenuous plans to complete the canal were finally dropped in 1820.

Had the canal reached its original destination at Ardrossan, its impact on the local area and Hullerhirst would have been economically profound, and its failure to reach the coast undoubtedly had a negative effect on the potential profitability of the estate.

HULLERHIRST QUARRY AND ASHGROVE LOCH

For many years, the disposal of refuse in the towns of Ardrossan, Saltcoats and Stevenston utilised the facilities at Brewery Park, between Saltcoats and Stevenston. By early 1975, the site had been exhausted, requiring a search to be made to find an alternative dumping space.

At a meeting of the Public Health and Roads Committees of the three councils held on December 1974 in Saltcoats, the problem was discussed. It was stated that the situation was so acute that a new coup would be required within four months. The burgh surveyors of the three towns reported on three suggested sites where dumping might be possible.

Hullerhirst Quarry was initially considered to be a feasible option. Although located in close proximity to the Hayocks housing scheme with the attendant problems of noise, smell and dust, the site was screened from view by trees, with blinding material available nearby. The biggest impediment to the project was the provision of appropriate vehicular access. The Stevenston representatives at the meeting were apprehensive about utilising the Hullerhirst site due to it being only 180 metres behind Castlehill Road and Hillhead Road.

Ashgrove Loch was considered briefly as a potential location for couping, but councillor, Dr David White, commented on the difficulties of securing this site due to the prominent conservation issues attached to the loch.

The loch was first notified as a Site of Special Scientific Interest (SSSI) in 1975. Although the feature has an area of 22.65 hectares, only around 10% of its surface remains as open water, the remainder being covered by a floating raft of vegetation. The body of water is mesotrophic meaning it possesses a moderate level of nutrients which results in the existence of a balanced ecosystem with a diverse range of plant and animal life. Two of the many plant species found in situ in this botanically rich environment are tufted loosestrife and cowbane. Many insects attracted by the fen and swamp conditions are also present. Breeding birds such as sedge warbler, snipe, and reed bunting, attract bird watchers to the site.

When the various freshwater habitats are considered collectively, it is not surprising that Ashgrove Loch is regarded as one of North Ayrshire's most treasured wildlife locations.

Its prominent reputation among conservationists and its notification as a SSSI, made its consideration as a potential land-fill site rather strange, if not incomprehensible.

In 1974, a general agreement had been reached between Stevenston and Kilwinning Town Councils and Irvine District Council on proposals to make the area of Ashgrove Loch into a countryside park. Ayr County Council was requested to undertake a feasibility study of the plan. The three local authorities involved were made aware of the archaeological and botanical attributes associated with the loch, along with the leisure and recreational potential of the area. The enthusiasm to get the project underway was fortified by the looming spectre of local government re-organisation.

Bailie James Forde from Stevenston, who presided, summed up the feelings of the meeting commenting that there was complete agreement from the representatives of the three authorities to develop the venture. The meeting was reminded by Mr James Campbell, town clerk of Stevenston, that the county council was the planning authority, and the question of land ownership may be problematic. The end result of this suggestion was 'leave well alone.'

A comprehensive investigation of the crannog on the east side of the loch is covered in a later section of the book.

13
Back to the Beginning

EARLY HISTORY

An abridged account of Stevenston parish was incorporated into chapter one. This exposition is a more comprehensive explanation of the early history of the Stevenston area which not only focuses on the origin of the parish but also considers the importance of baronies.

According to George Chalmers,[1] Stevenston derives its name from Stephen, son of Richard Loccard who had acquired a grant of lands, about 1170, from Richard de Morville, the Lord of Cunninghame and High Constable of Scotland (died 1189).

Cunninghame, which was feudalised during the reign of David 1 (1124-1153), was the area in Ayrshire which lay north of the River Irvine. The parish of Stevenston was granted to Stephen Loccard in the twelfth century, but it is unclear whether a hamlet, having another name, existed on the site that became Stevenston. However, the nucleus of Stevenston was mentioned in a charter of the Loudoun family into whose possession it had passed – as early as 1240.

In Cunninghame the most powerful retainer of King David I was Hugh de Morville. This soldier was a Northamptonshire baron and in 1131 his name appears in the Pipe Rolls as a proprietor in the counties of Rutland, Northampton, and Huntingdon. Although an English landholder, he was of Norman type, and his name may be taken from the castle of Morville in the Costentin, Normandy. In the absence of any dominant local figure in the area after the extinction of the de Morvilles, a number of Cunninghame vassals rose to fill the vacuum.

As these vassals spread over the shire into their centres of authority, they had of necessity to set up residence. All dwellings were called 'vills.' These vills were residences surrounded by a defined area of jurisdiction. Once a vill had been established there was around it a specified area of land which came under the authority of the lord who held the vill. Such vills play a dominant part in the erection of parishes. Not only did each vill have a church, but provision had been made for its maintenance by the setting aside of lands, pasturage and teinds. Where a vill was already

1 Chalmers, George. *Caledonia or Historical and Topographical Account of North Briton.* Alexander Gardner. Paisley. 1902.

established its boundaries became the limits of the parish. It is to be noted that parishes evolved in a process of time and not in one grand multiple genesis. The shire did not in one movement develop all its parishes. When the need arose a parish was created.

A parish was an area under the jurisdiction of a church and usually used for administrative purposes. On the other hand, baronies were territorial as opposed to personal titles, which meant that they were attached to an area of land erected into a barony by the king. In the early medieval period, a man was not personally granted a title of nobility, he became a baron by being granted a barony which generally meant that if he disposed of the lands he ceased to hold the title, which passed to the new holder of the lands; this was normally his heir, but could be a 'stranger in blood,' including a purchaser. Scottish feudal baronies could therefore be acquired by purchase as well as inheritance, and they survived as territorial titles until the abolition of the feudal system in Scotland in November 2004.

One half of the Barony of Stevenston was called Stevenstoun-Campbell, from having been held by the Campbell family, a cadet of the Campbells of Wester-Loudoun. It consisted of four properties, viz: Ducathall, Saltcoats-Campbell, Bogend and Ardeer, and Hullerhirst. The other half was named Stevenstoun-Cunninghame having been acquired by the Cunninghames of Kilmaurs.

For some time before the Reformation, circa 1517, the Barony of Stevenston and Stevenston Parish were not identical. The barony incorporated the Stevenston Parish boundary, plus the lands of Crosbie in West Kilbride, and the lands of Gill and Munnoch in Dalry which belonged to the Earl of Glencairn.

THE ASHGROVE LOCH CRANNOG

A crannog is a form of ancient loch-dwelling. The earliest example so far located in Scotland is from the Neolithic period, approximately 5,000 years old, but recycled crannogs were used up until the seventeenth century AD. The general academic consensus is that most Scottish crannogs were built, used, and re-used over a period of 2,500 years, from the Iron Age (began c. 2,800 years ago; ending c. 1,600 years ago) to the post-medieval period, c. 800 BC to AD 1700. Throughout their history, crannogs performed a number of functions, from farmers' homesteads, refuges in turbulent times, fishing and hunting stations, holiday residences, or simply status symbols.

The term crannog translates from Gaelic as 'son of tree' or 'young tree'. Their foundations were built by driving long timber piles into the bed of a loch before filling in the interior with stones or other natural materials to create a solid foundation.

The landscape in the area which includes Ashgrove Loch was fashioned by the actions of glacial erosion which occurred during the Quaternary Period, when the region was covered by ice on several separate occasions. The landscape was also modified by the deposition of materials directly from the ice sheets or via the meltwaters as the ice retreated.

Ashgrove Loch itself (NGR NS 275443) is located in a shallow hollow or basin, almost certainly glacial in origin. The north-east to south-west orientation of the ice flow contributed towards the creation of a drift-filled buried meltwater channel where the loch now lies. In the period since the last glaciers retreated from this area, about 10,000 years ago, the landscape has changed relatively little by natural processes. After the departure of the ice, the loch would have formed in this low-lying hollow which due to the nature of the underlying rock would already have been poorly drained. Throughout its existence, water levels within the loch fluctuated on a seasonal basis. Map evidence from the late nineteenth century and early twentieth century show no apparent changes to the outline of the loch. However, it is clear that the margins are becoming increasingly clogged through vegetation growth. Photograph 32 shows the level of the loch during the winter of 2024-25, and clearly indicates its original dimensions.

The loch is underlain by the Carboniferous Limestone Series, mainly consisting of shales and sandstones, and from this bedrock has developed a deep, clay till. This soil is part of the Ashgrove Association and when combined with the gently undulating topography created the perfect conditions for the establishment of the Loch.

Cartographic evidence indicates that the loch's water level was higher before the 1850s, but its level by 1911 had become significantly reduced due to attempts at drainage. This would suggest that land improvements had

32. Ashgrove Loch looking south-east from Lochwood farm.

33. Ashgrove Loch Looking north-west from the Loch Craigs.

started in the area in the middle of the nineteenth century. It is therefore plausible that the land near the loch had been ploughed.

The crannog in Ashgrove Loch (there may be another five, although this is unlikely) which is sited on the east side, was inadvertently discovered by the farmer of nearby High Smithstone farm, Mr William Stevenson, while in the process of erecting a fence. He uncovered a bed of shells, fragments of deer's horns and a variety of bones.

John Smith, the well-known and respected local natural historian, antiquarian, and geologist, was informed of the finding, and on 9 August 1886, he dug an exploratory trench close to the spot where the fence-post had been inserted.[2] The trench section is described below:

1) Rotted bits of yellowish sandstone and lumps of sandstone	0.4 metres
2) Dark sandy clay with pieces of sandstone, whinstone, and large Quantities of Common Periwinkle, complete bones, split bones, jaws, Horns of red deer, etc.	0.6 metres
3) Brown peat.	0.3 metres
4). Fine bluish clay (only the top part was dug into).	

In number 2 bed above, were discovered two fine bone chisels (Fig 1), and a bone needle (Fig 2) sharpened at both ends, and with a hole in the middle – the relics from the crannog are housed in the National Museum of Antiquities of Scotland.

2 Smith, John. *Archaeological & Historical Collections relating to Ayrshire & Galloway.* Vol VII. 1894.

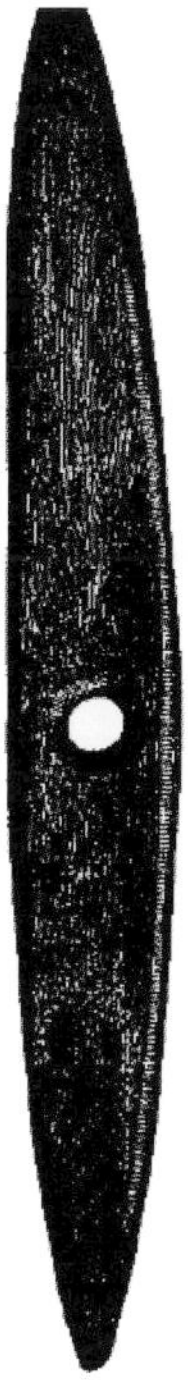

FIG. 1.—Bone Chisel. Scale ⅔. FIG. 2.—Bone Needle. Scale full size.
Both from Crannog in Ashgrove Loch.

Sketch 2. Stone chisel and needle found at Ashgrove crannog.

From the detail given in the section above, Mr Smith produced the following explanation: 'On top of a bluish clay-bed there had accumulated a bed of brown moss, possibly entirely from the decay of water-plants, one foot in thickness on the land side of the crannog, and four feet thick on the loch side. Then the position was occupied by man, who laid on top of the moss a layer of branches, and built a stone crannog, forty-three feet in largest outside diameter, with a built water-tank under the floor, the interior of the dwelling being possibly divided into compartments, roughly paved, and carpeted with heather.' The model and section provided by Mr Smith (See Sketch Map 2) provides a visual representation of his findings. The drain had been excavated in the moss, with its sides built with rough sandstone blocks. Mr Smith conjectured that this feature was a primitive water tank, and its zigzag pattern possibly indicating that the area within the circular wall was divided into compartments inhabited by different families, each having an independent water supply.

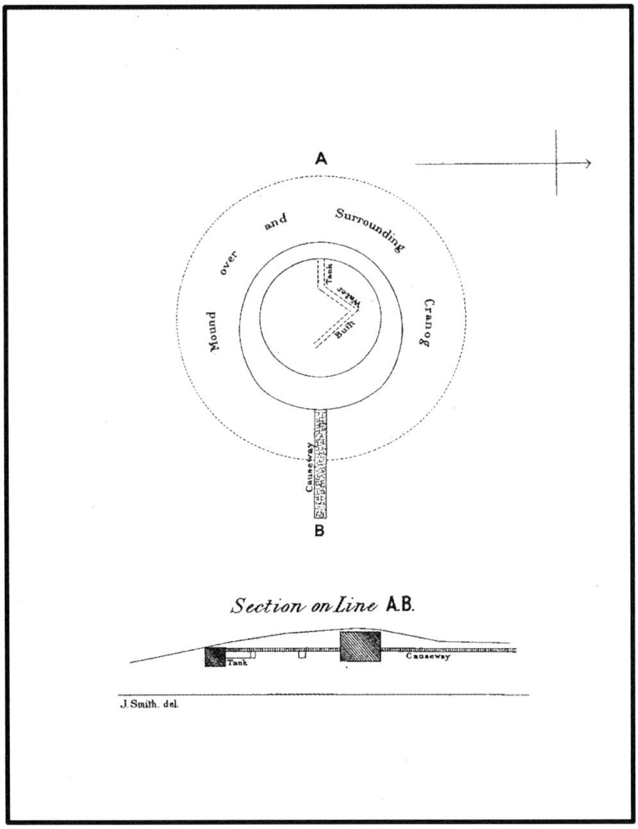

Sketch Map 3. The Model and Section Prepared by John Smith.

The kitchen midden was located on the south-east side of the building and disclosed the following relics:

1. A large number of bones, both entire and split, of red deer, ox, pig, sheep, and goat.
2. Several bone chisels and a bone knife, a bone wedge, a large bone needle, perforated in the centre, a well-made bone spoon, and a narrow bone needle.
3. Several hammer-stones, and a few smooth stones.
4. A bit of gas coal with a hole bored through it.
5. A pair of 'steel' sheep-shears.
6. Numerous specimens of Littorina Littorea (common periwinkle).

From the bones found in the kitchen midden, it is highly likely that the inhabitants of the structure must have had extensive hunting privileges in the neighbourhood.

Although this excavation was only partially completed, Mr Smith discovered a circular stone wall enclosing a space of about nine metres in diameter. Before this circular wall was unearthed, it presented the appearance of a mound near the edge of the loch. However, in former times the mound would, due to the higher water level, have been sited further out from the land. Falling water levels associated with the extraction of water from the loch may have facilitated the discovery of the crannog. It should be noted that a supply of water was available for Stevenston Mill from Ashgrove Loch. This water was removed from the south-west corner of the loch using a wooden slide valve which transferred the water into a stream which flowed through Lochcraig's farmland into Stevenston Burn.

The incomplete investigation of the crannog by Mr Smith may account for the absence of ash deposits and the remains of cereals, although the inhabitants were probably hunter/gatherers.

John Smith made a number of assumptions based on his remarkable but limited excavation. These included that the Ashgrove example was the only lake-dwelling that had been originally constructed of stone; that the inhabitants were in all likelihood 'lords of the manor'; that there may well be another five unexplored crannogs in the loch; that the area within the wall had been a place of human habitation as well as a fortress.

Due to its antiquity and the basic nature of its excavation in 1886, it is impossible to accurately date its construction and longevity. While the majority of finds were consistent with the Iron Age – contemporary with or post-dating the Roman occupation of Scotland – the iron shears has been dated to much later, the twelfth to thirteenth century AD.

It must be remembered that this excavation along with a number of associated conclusions occurred 139 years ago, and although an outstanding piece of scientific investigative work, its context should be taken into consideration.

The possibility that the crannog was constructed with stone is strengthened by the fact that in the 1950s a sandstone quarry was situated on a bluff at the south-west end of the loch, north of Lochcraigs farm and near the source of the Stevenston Burn. This deposit may have been known to earlier settlers who used the sandstone for building purposes.

Finally, the Ashgrove Loch site was revisited in 1956, 1965, and 1982 by representatives of the Royal Commission on the Ancient and Historical Monuments of Scotland who made several additional observations. The 1965 investigation stated that the two metre wide 'dry approach' between NS 27604431 and NS 27644430 is more likely to be the base of an old stone dyke rather than a causeway. The 1982 input was simply some aerial photography carried out by the RAF.

There have been repeated visits by Ordnance Survey field teams throughout the twentieth century, which have failed to confirm any additional crannogs. Aerial photographs of the loch – while clearly showing the Ashgrove Loch crannog as a grassy mound surrounded by marshland – shows nothing which may be interpreted as a similar feature.

Due to the fact that only one detailed examination of the crannog site was carried out, and that occurred in 1886, it is understandable that many questions concerning all aspects of the discovery remain unanswered. As time passes, the possibility of a fully-funded, technologically advanced research project becomes more remote. The nature of marine archaeology with its associated expense and lack of urgency means our understanding of the crannog at Ashgrove Loch will remain very limited. Historic Environment Scotland is fully aware of the historical background relating to the existence of the crannog, but show no inclination to further explore the feature.

--oOo--

In the historical context of Stevenston, the Hayocks in relatively recent, having been planned and developed in the mid to late 1930s as a residential extension to the town. As with many other aspects in the evolution of Stevenston the driving-force behind the expansion of housing north of Glencairn Street was Nobel's Explosive Co. Ltd. However, due to the demise of Nobel's/I.C.I. at Ardeer, the close association of the working population of the Hayocks with the factory has disappeared.

As time and generations have passed, the Hayocks is no longer considered an 'outlier' of the town, and although it retains its identity as a close-knit community, its integration into the town is now complete.

Finally, my sincere wish is that the publication of this book will act as an incentive to others to record the developments that transpire in the Hayocks over the next ninety years.

Alex McLatchie

Selected Bibliography

Ayrshire Archives. Ayr County Council Housing Committee Minutes: CO3/8/2/41, CO3/8/2/43.

Ayrshire Archives. Ayr County Council Education Committee Minutes 1964 – CO3/10/5/24.

Ayrshire Archives. Ayr County Council Education Committee Minutes 1973 – CO3/10/5/33.

Ayrshire Archives. Stevenston Burgh Minutes 1955/56. Gk1/1/2.

Ayrshire Archives. Stevenston Burgh Minutes 1953: GK1/1/1.

Ayrshire Archives. Stevenston Burgh Minutes 1972-1975. Gk1/1/11.

Ayrshire Archives. Stevenston Burgh Minutes 1963-1964. Gk1/1/6.

Ayrshire Archives. Irvine and District Water Works. CO3/14/31, CO3/14/70, CO3/14/43, CO3/14/48.

Chalmers, George. *Caledonia*. Alexander Gardner, Paisley. 1902.

Clements, James. *Stevenston:The Kernel of Cunninghame*. Gilmour & Lawrence Ltd, Glasgow. 1974.

Close, R. and Riches, A. *The Buildings of Scotland. Ayrshire and Arran*. Yale University Press. 2012.

Davis, Michael. C. *The Castles and Mansions of Ayrshire*. Spindrift, Ardrishaig, Argyll. 1991.

Dobie, James D. *Cunninghame, Topographized by Timothy Pont 1604 – 1608*. John Tweed, Glasgow. 1876.

Glasgow Advertiser 1789. Mitchell Library, Glasgow.

Glasgow Mercury 1778 & 1779. Mitchell Library, Glasgow.

Graham, Eric. J. T*he Shipping Trade of Ayrshire 1689-1791*. AANHS, September 1991 Ayrshire Monograph No 8.

Heaney, George. *Sixty Years of A.1. Service*. 1991.

Kelso, Clarence. *E. Kelso of Kelsoland*.

Landsborough, Rev. David. *The New Statistical Account of Scotland. Parish of Stevenston*. Vol V. 1842.

Millar, A.H. *Castles and Mansions of Ayrshire*. Edinburgh: William Paterson. 1885.

Mills, A.D. *A Dictionary of British Place-Names*. Oxford University Press. 2011.

Munro, R. *Prehistoric Scotland and its Place in European Civilisation*. Wm Blackwood & Sons. Edinburgh & London. 1899. Pages 420-421.

McClure, David (Ed). *Ayrshire in the Age of Improvement*. AANHS,

Monograph 27. 2002.
McLatchie, A. *Kerelaw House; A History of the Ayrshire Mansion, Families, and the American Connection.* 2017.
McLatchie, A. *Last Orders; The History of Pubs and Clubs in Stevenston.* 2019.
National Records of Scotland. CS96/639.
North Ayrshire Directory – 1935-36-37. County of Directories – Ayr. Hassell Street Press. 2021.
Parker, William. *Reflections on a Century, St Cuthbert's Church, Saltcoats 1908 – 2008.*
Robertson, William. *Ayrshire its History and Historic Families.* Vol 2. 1908.
Scott, N.M. *The Scottish Historical Review.* Vol 19. Maclehose, Jackson & Co, Glasgow. 1922.
Smith, J. *Archaeological & Historical Collections of Ayr & Wigton.* Vol VII. Pages 56-61.
Wilson, Stuart. *The Ancient Society of Kilwinning Archers: A History of the Society from 1483 to the Present Day.* 2020.
Wodrow, Rev. J. *Old Statistical Account of Scotland – Vol XII. Parish of Stevenston*, 1793.

Acknowledgments

The writing of this book was made possible by the assistance and encouragement of many people, and I owe a particular gratitude to the individuals listed below.

Alex Reid; Daniel Reid; Tom Millar; Robert Murray; Tom McCutcheon and Graham McCutcheon (Whitehirst Park Farm); Hall Thomson (Lochcraigs Farm); Stuart Wilson (Historian of the Ancient Society of Kilwinning Archers); William Parker (Elder of St Cuthbert's Church, Saltcoats); Dinah McDonald and Janice Hampson (Kilmun Visitor's Centre); Gerry Pollock; Mary Frew and Elinor Wilton (Committee members of the Hayocks Community Hall); Canon Martin Poland (St John's Church, Stevenston); Karen McAllister, Deborah Reid, and Karen McGuire (Staff at St John's Primary School, Stevenston); Tom Grayston; Matt Smith; Ann Jones (Local Community Activist); Jim Campbell; John McMillan; Alan Gallacher (Ardeer Mains Farm); Katie Morrison (Scottish Crannog Centre, Kenmore); Kirsty Gilchrist (Assistant Curator), and Mike Scott (Research Volunteer), at the Scottish Maritime Museum, Irvine); Iain Davies (Senior Development Management Officer, Planning Department, North Ayrshire Council); Melanie McBlain, and Ann Wilson (Staff at Stevenston Library); Sheena Harling; Iain Hamlin; Hazel Menzies (Research Assistant, North Ayrshire Council); Councillor John Sweeney, Ward 5, Saltcoats and Stevenston, and Depute Provost; Claire Keane and Nicolle Crawford (Ayrshire Archives, Ayr); Leanna Lennox (Visitor Services Assistant, North Ayrshire Heritage Centre, Saltcoats), and Jill McColl (Cultural & Heritage Officer at North Ayrshire Council).

Much of the detail contained within the cover of this volume was researched from the written word, but a significant portion of the book was shaped by conversations and interviews I had with a number of the individuals listed above. Many shared their views and reflections, answering my questions with enthusiasm, understanding, and patience. I appreciated their empathy, humour, and at times, analysis.

Photograph Credits

Photograph 1. Lauchlan, R. *Back in Time. The Parishes of Ardrossan and Stevenston.* 1997.
Photograph 2. McSherry, R & M. *Old Stevenston.* Stenlake Publishing. 1998.
Photograph 3. Author's Collection.
Photograph 4. Author's Collection.
Photograph 5. McLatchie, A. *Last Orders: The History of Pubs and Clubs in Stevenston.* 2019.
Photograph 6. Unknown.
Photograph 7. Janice Hampson and Dinah McDonald. Historians at Historic Kilmun Visitors Centre.
Photograph 8. Janice Hampson and Dinah McDonald. Historians at Historic Kilmun Visitor's Centre.
Photograph 9. Author's Collection.
Photograph 10. Unknown.
Photograph 11. Robertson's Fine Foods Pamphlet.
Photograph 12. Parker, W. *Reflections on a Century, St Cuthbert's Church, Saltcoats 1908-2008.*
Photograph 13. Maxwell, W.
Photograph 14. Author's Collection.
Photograph 15. Unknown.
Photograph 16. Alex Reid.
Photograph 17. Laura Alexis Bailey. Paper entitled Hullerhirst Quarry and Lime Kilns, North Ayrshire.
Photograph 18. Unknown.
Photograph 19. Heaney, George. *Sixty Years of A.1. Service.* 1991.
Photograph 20. Souvenir Brochure of the Solemn Opening of St John's Church.
Photograph 21. Souvenir Brochure of the Solemn Opening of St John's Church.
Photograph 22. Grayston, Tom.
Photograph 23. Wilson, Stuart. *The Ancient Society of Kilwinning Archers: A History of the Society from 1483 to the Present Day.* 2020.
Photograph 24. As Photo 23 above.
Photograph 25. Unknown.
Photograph 26. McSherry, R & M. *Old Stevenston.* Stenlake Publishing.

1998.
Photograph 27. *Ardrossan & Saltcoats Herald.* 22nd April 2005.
Photograph 28. John McMillan.
Photograph 29. Ann Wilson.
Photograph 30. Scottish Office Development Department.
Photograph 31. Author's Collection.
Photograph 32. Author's Collection.
Photograph 33. Author's Collection.

Index

Kilwinning Co-operative Society, 105-6